Lovecraft: An American Allegory

Hippocampus Press Library of Criticism

S. T. Joshi, *Primal Sources: Essays on H. P. Lovecraft* (2003)

———, *The Evolution of the Weird Tale* (2004)

———, *Lovecraft and a World in Transition: Collected Essays on H. P. Lovecraft* (2014)

Robert W. Waugh, *The Monster in the Mirror: Looking for H. P. Lovecraft* (2006)

———, *A Monster of Voices: Speaking for H. P. Lovecraft* (2011)

Scott Connors, ed., *The Freedom of Fantastic Things: Selected Criticism on Clark Ashton Smith* (2006)

Ben Szumskyj, ed., *Two-Gun Bob: A Centennial Study of Robert E. Howard* (2006)

S. T. Joshi and Rosemary Pardoe, ed., *Warnings to the Curious: A Sheaf of Criticism on M. R. James* (2007)

Massimo Berruti, *Dim-Remembered Stories: A Critical Study of R. H. Barlow* (2011)

Gary William Crawford, Jim Rockhill, and Brian J. Showers, ed., *Reflections in a Glass Darkly: Essays on J. Sheridan Le Fanu* (2011)

Massimo Berruti, S. T. Joshi, and Sam Gafford, ed., *William Hope Hodgson: Voices from the Borderland: Seven Decades of Criticism on the Master of Cosmic Horror* (2014)

John Michael Sefel and Niels-Viggo S. Hobbs, ed., *Lovecraftian Proceedings: Papers from NecronomiCon—Providence: 2013* (2015)

Lovecraft Annual

Dead Reckonings

Lovecraft: An American Allegory

Selected Essays on H. P. Lovecraft

Donald R. Burleson

Hippocampus Press

New York

See p. 243 for initial appearances.

The publisher would like to express gratitude to Phillip A. Ellis for his assistance in the preparation of this volume.

Published by Hippocampus Press
P.O. Box 641, New York, NY 10156.
http://www.hippocampuspress.com

Cover design by Barbara Briggs Silbert. Photograph of H. P. Lovecraft courtesy of Donovan K. Loucks. The photograph is tentatively dated to 2 March 1935. Robert Ellis Moe, son of Maurice Winter Moe, visited Lovecraft 2–3 March 1935, and may have been behind the shutter.

Hippocampus Press logo designed by Anastasia Damianakos.

First Edition
1 3 5 7 9 8 6 4 2
ISBN 978-1-61498-138-1

Contents

For my wonderful wife Mollie,
with all my love forever.

Abbreviations

AT	Lovecraft, *The Ancient Track: The Complete Poetical Works of H. P. Lovecraft,* ed. S. T. Joshi, 2nd ed. (Hippocampus Press, 2013)
CE	Lovecraft, *Collected Essays,* ed. S. T. Joshi (Hippocampus Press, 2004–06; 5 vols.)
CF	Lovecraft, *Collected Fiction: A Variorum Edition,* ed. S. T. Joshi (Hippocampus Press, 2015–16; 4 vols.)
CoC	*Crypt of Cthulhu*
HPL	H. P. Lovecraft
LS	*Lovecraft Studies*
SL	Lovecraft, *Selected Letters* (Arkham House, 1965–76; 5 vols.)

Darkness and Light: Lovecraft's Impact on My Life

In 1954, when I was twelve years old, my parents gave me a copy of the Modern Library volume *The Complete Tales and Poems of Edgar Allan Poe.* They cannot have realized what they were starting; I doubt that they really intended to give me a lifelong obsession with dark literature, but that was the effect. Always an avid reader, I devoured the Poe book and loved it.

Not long after this time, during the summer of 1955 when I was thirteen, I joined the Science Fiction Book Club, and one of the books in the introductory offer that I chose was Groff Conklin's *Omnibus of Science Fiction,* which contained a story called "The Colour out of Space." (Well, they edited the spelling to "Color.") This tale hit me like a brick. I read the whole tome and rather liked most of the stories, but "Colour" was stunning, unlike anything I had ever read before. It haunted me, and to this day it is my favorite of the author's stories, much as it was (I would later learn) his own favorite of his stories.

That was my introduction to H. P. Lovecraft. About a year later I encountered an Avon Books paperback called *Cry Horror!*—a short story collection that was all Lovecraft this time. And I was hooked for life. At that young and inexperienced age I scarcely knew why, but even then I sensed that there was something strangely enchanting and unique about Lovecraft's fiction.

Over the years that followed, I not only sought out other books—e.g., Arkham House's *The Dunwich Horror and Others* and companion volumes—but came to refine my reasons for finding Lovecraft's writing uncommonly intriguing. And, significantly, I found that my fascination with Lovecraft had imparted to me an abiding interest in literature more generally, motivating me to read not only the likes of

Arthur Machen and Algernon Blackwood, but everyone from Henry James to Herman Melville to James Joyce to Shelley to Shakespeare.

And all this in contradistinction to the fact that my chief intellectual interest has always been mathematics! Professionally I have spent my career as a mathematician and educator, but literature and literary criticism have come to loom large in my life as well. Some people make difficult decisions by just ordering everything on the menu, and I guess I'm one of those folks, having gone through graduate school both in mathematics (master's program plus some coursework beyond) and in English literature (master's and doctoral programs). If one buys the dubious notion that literature is right-brain and mathematics is left-brain, I'm probably not the best poster child for cerebral lateralization. At any rate, even though I have spent the great majority of my academic life teaching college mathematics, occasionally I have taught English too, now and then wedging a class in horror fiction writing in between trigonometry and calculus.

I was invited to teach those writing courses because, besides studying literature, I have also pursued a modest career of my own in horror fiction writing, though (considering my interest in Lovecraft) oddly little of that has been in the Lovecraftian manner. I cheerfully acknowledge a considerable influence from Ramsey Campbell, whom I have long especially admired; it was a high point for me when he wrote the introduction to *Beyond the Lamplight,* one of my short story collections. Aside from influences, I have of course sought to maintain my own fictional voice, my own manner and style, though what that precisely is, readers can tell better than I; like most writers, I am not a superb judge of my own work. I will say that as far as that work is concerned, I must admit I have written some short stories that I would probably not want to take with me to a sanity hearing.

But back to Lovecraft. For a long time I entertained my ongoing interest in him *in vacuo,* at first seldom meeting anyone who had even heard of him. Around 1970 I visited Providence, Rhode Island, for the first time and delighted in searching out such real-life Lovecraft story settings as Benefit Street and the Shunned House (I was once shown into its basement), finding, however, relatively little popular awareness of Lovecraft in his hometown at that time. I still felt as if I were pursuing Lovecraft somewhat in a vacuum. But in the early 1970s I went out of my way to establish a correspondence friendship with Lovecraft's old friend Frank Belknap Long, and we exchanged letters for years. I would meet him face to face (taking him out to dinner at an Italian restaurant) in October 1975 at the First World Fantasy Convention in Providence. Frank soon got me in touch by correspondence with Lovecraft scholar Dirk W. Mosig, whom I would meet in Phoenix in 1978, sharing a panel discussion with him as well as with J. Vernon Shea, Fritz Leiber, and the incomparable S. T. Joshi. Through S. T., back in New England, I was soon to meet publisher Marc Michaud, artist Jason Eckhardt, and other Lovecraft enthusiasts. I was no longer alone in indulging my interests. When S. T. started the journal *Lovecraft Studies* I soon became a fairly regular contributor, and would in time contribute articles as well to Robert M. Price's celebrated *Crypt of Cthulhu* and other publications.

At first my articles of Lovecraft criticism were fairly conventional, sometimes dealing in studies I had been conducting with regard to Lovecraft's story settings and sources in Vermont and western Massachusetts. But my essay writing soon evolved into formalist criticism on various tales and poems, and I published the book *H. P. Lovecraft: A Critical Study* with Greenwood Press in 1983. At length when my critical interests turned to the realm of poststructuralism, I began writing deconstructionist treatments of Lovecraft's works, bringing him into that critical arena in which language itself is shown to be playfully self-subverting in ways that extend the interpretability of literary texts. My book *Lovecraft: Disturbing the Universe* (University Press of Kentucky, 1990) was a full-blown deconstructionist study. I fear I have rather annoyed some people in the field of Lovecraft studies by subjecting Lovecraft texts to such seemingly *outré* readings, but I felt (and still do) that this has been necessary in order to lay the Lovecraft oeuvre open to a broad range of critical response, as it should be. In fact, it is my view that deconstruction, like other approaches to literary criticism, sheds new light on the nature of Lovecraft's fiction and poetry.

All this has made for an interesting time, and without Lovecraft, needless to say, none of this activity might ever have been a part of my life. But I would be gravely remiss not to mention the even more profound way in which H. P. Lovecraft changed the world for me. To wit: I met my wonderful wife Mollie because of Lovecraft.

It was at the Fifth World Fantasy Convention, in 1979 in Providence, that I found myself standing in the lobby of the Biltmore Hotel with Lovecraft's erstwhile correspondence friend J. Vernon Shea introducing me to a lovely lady from the Chicago area. I had come to that convention to be on a Lovecraft panel discussion, and Mollie was there because of her longtime interest in Lovecraft. When I went home to Nashua, New Hampshire, and she went home to Carpentersville, Illinois, we stayed in touch by mail, and after Mollie became Official Editor of the Esoteric Order of Dagon (EOD) amateur press association, she recruited me as a member. Our relationship, albeit at a distance of a thousand miles, ripened over time, and we got together in September 1981 and were married in April 1982. (The first person we told when we got engaged was Peter Straub, and after we tied the knot we received congratulatory notes from Robert Bloch and Donald Wandrei. Definitely a marriage made in R'lyeh!) Mollie—my love, my best friend, my constant companion, and herself a fine writer of fiction, literary criticism, and poetry—has enriched my life in ways I cannot even begin to enumerate. And had it not been for Lovecraft and our common interest in him, we most likely never would have met. Lovecraft has brought me not only the restless darkness of a haunting literary vision, but the light of a life I could scarcely have hoped to lead without him.

How does one hope to repay the Gentleman from Providence for all this? Well, probably one cannot. But I will mention that from the beginning, from the early days of my interest in his work, I always lamented the fact that Lovecraft was little known in mainstream literary circles— I always wanted to see him become a respected presence in the realm of American literature. This of course has indeed come to pass, over the intervening years, and unquestionably the person primarily responsible for that phenomenon is my friend and colleague S. T. Joshi. But if my own critical essays have contributed in any small way to Lovecraft's growing recognition, then they have been time well spent. In any event, I have always assuredly enjoyed writing them.

DONALD R. BURLESON, PH.D.

Roswell, New Mexico

THEMATIC STUDIES

Zen and the Art of Lovecraft

The thinking and general Weltanschauung of Howard Phillips Lovecraft interact with Zen philosophy in various ways—decidedly in consonance with it in some respects, decidedly at variance with it in others, but sufficiently in consonance with it to allow definite streaks of Zen thought to be discerned in Lovecraft's fiction.

Any treatment of such a topic—the manner in which a given author's works reflect patterns of thought consistent with the Zen outlook—should logically encompass a statement answering the basic question: what is Zen, anyway? And therein lies a fundamental problem: Zen by its very fundamental nature does not lend itself to sharp definition or clear-cut explication. Any "definitive" encapsulation of the meaning of Zen is sure to fall short of the mark; just as Taoist sage Lao Tzu states, in the opening line of the *Tao Te Ching,* that the Tao which can be spoken of is not the real Tao, any Zen master will be likely to tell us that what is verbally "explained" or "defined" as Zen is not Zen in its most central essence.

Thus one may only "talk around" the nature of Zen. It must be sufficient to point to a few general attitudes commonly found in the thinking of Zen Buddhists, in order to see to what extent this sort of thinking is found in Lovecraft's writing.

Primarily, much of the flavor of Zen is to be found in natural spontaneity—in the attitude that the real "meaning" in reality is ultimately to be found in the non-verbal or preter-verbal understanding that the effortless experience of the present moment is what is real, and that such understanding comes only in a way unfettered by self-consciousness and linguistic and intellectualizing analysis. Hence the stories of Buddhist monks who struggle long and unavailingly with intellectual efforts to understand the teachings of their masters, only to awaken one day to what has eluded them, by a slap in the face or by the sound of a gong. Just as a Bach fugue finally must simply be heard rather than plumbed for some sort of discursive "content," life to a Zennist must simply be lived rather than pondered; one should no more strain or struggle to cope with life than an organist should hurry through a piece by Bach just to get it played and over with, thus missing the point entirely. To a follower of Zen, the present moment and place and activity and perception must form the center of all existence—one's hearing the stroke of a gong is simply oneself, all that there is, experiencing the sound, all that there is, without comment and perceived in an awareness of cosmic unity, an awareness that the ego-separate-from-environment is misconception, that in looking at the stars one is simply a nerve-ending through which the entire universe is experiencing itself. Beyond such rather peripheral observations, one must simply admit that Zen cannot absolutely be defined; as Wittgenstein says, "Whereof one cannot speak, thereof one must be silent" (189). (The interested reader may peruse, nonetheless, some capable "talking around" of Zen in the books of Alan Watts and D. T. Suzuki.)

Certainly there are some important ways in which the personal philosophical stance of H. P. Lovecraft differs widely from the views of Zen, with its Taoism-derived attitude that ultimate understanding transcends ratiocination. Lovecraft made it clear that he most admired, among contemporary philosophers, those (like Bertrand Russell) to whom logical analysis and the power of the intellect are supreme. Further, his own letters are crowded with meticulous intellectual argument, and he was known by friends and correspondents to be given to closely reasoned contention as a consistent matter of habit; so that it is difficult to imagine Lovecraft's directly embracing a philosophical view in which intellectualization is relegated to a secondary post, or is even held responsible for impeding a "higher" understanding. Still, there are attitudes in Lovecraft that are consistent with the Zen outlook.

Lovecraft, as is well known, had no use for religion in any form, Western or Eastern. "Half," he says, "of what Buddha or Christus or Mahomet said is either simple idiocy or downright destructiveness, as applied to the western world of the twentieth century; whilst virtually all the emotional-imaginative background of assumptions from which they spoke, is now proved to be sheer childish primitiveness" (*SL* 3.47–48). Yet the Zen school, an outgrowth of Mahayana Buddhism as influenced by Chinese Taoism, is so bereft of dogma, of articles of faith in the usual sense of the term, of reliance upon "revealed" textual sources, of the conventional trappings of religion, that some philosophers of religion, Alan Watts among them, doubt whether it can be called a religion at all without encouraging misunderstanding of its nature and function. Certainly Lovecraft would not have disapproved of its lack of an absentee-landlord-style biblical god; many Buddhists incline toward a kind of pantheism—an organic view of the cosmos decidedly different from Lovecraft's view of the universe as a blind and dead mechanism—but the notion of a separate, supernatural creator-god has nothing to do with the practice of Zen, which maintains about such matters a silence insufficiently committal of interest even to be called agnosticism; and had Zen been widely enough known in the West for Lovecraft to have read of it in his day, it is doubtful that on this score he would have had any essential quarrel with the Zennists, though one supposes he might still have seen their attitudes as unduly mystical because unsupported by intellectual analysis. (Even so, he might well have been interested to read modern accounts of the apparent consistency between science and oriental "mysticism" currently perceived by some researchers in particle physics; see Fritjof Capra, *The Tao of Physics*.)

Zen is a complex of preter-reflective "attitudes," of spontaneous responses to the world, transcending the necrotic confines of dogmatic religion, and whatever Lovecraft might or might not have thought of it as a philosophy, had he been familiar with it, we may ask the question: in what ways is a Zen worldview suggested, at least at times, in Lovecraft's fiction? It would probably be oblique and Procrustean in the extreme to try to argue that such a view is expressed in anything like a pervasive or consistent way in Lovecraft's fictional works—yet these works do reveal clear instances of what may only be called Zen thought.

On a general level one may look to Lovecraft's personal credo of fantastic fiction. It is well known that he held plot and character development to be secondary artistic concerns, at least in his own work, and that in his writing he attempted primarily to capture and preserve certain oneiric images, impressions, atmospheric feelings that resided in his fancy, or in some cases in his sense-experience. In this respect he comes close to a Zen outlook, for Zennists maintain the flashes of feeling or impression or non-intellectual "understanding" are valuable in themselves, defying any attempt at analysis or verbalization but amounting to true insight or enlightenment for the individual. Lovecraft's constant use of such words as "ineffable" and "unspeakable" and "unutterable" suggests (apart from the idea that some things are too horrible to be described) that his visions are ultimately not to be fully communicated or understood, but rather remain a species of private, non-verbal experience. Whether Lovecraft would have elevated these experiences to the Zennist level of *satori*—of enlightenment as to ultimate "meaning" to existence—is of course doubtful; but that he had inexpressible flashes of vision, vision in some central way important to him, is scarcely to be denied. To the follower of Zen, these private experiences—the clack of a gourd, the sight of a tree against the sky somehow transverbally suggestive—are the very "meaning" of reality, reality that is in the philosophy of non-duality essentially meaningless. Lovecraft would naturally have warmed to the notion that the cosmos is without meaning—but an important difference is that while in Lovecraft's case there is a sort of spirit of resignation to this meaninglessness (Lovecraft having held that in a senseless cosmos one might as well make the best of it, enjoying aesthetic stimuli and the camaraderie of like-minded friends), Zennists express no such sense of resignation, holding, rather, that the universe is not supposed to "mean" anything in particular, that *satori* or *kenshō* experiences are not supposed to be expressible or intellectually ponderable. (Lovecraft, of course, had to try to express his; not to do so is not to be a writer, at least a writer of Lovecraft's kind.)

But there are some specific things to be found in Lovecraft's fiction expressive of views consistent with Zen. One of his most self-revealing fictional pieces is "The Silver Key," of which, interestingly enough, he once said, "It was not only non-intellectual but *anti-intellectual*" (*SL* 4.177). Lovecraft's introspective and disillusioned Randolph Carter here seems to function as a sounding-board for some of Lovecraft's own ennui. Carter, upon finally failing to find edification in the prosaic pronouncements of science, is told that he is "immature because he preferred dream-illusions to the illusions of our physical creation" (*CF* 2.74). The tale's narrator is clearly sympathetic in tone to Carter's plight, and at least as a fictional narrative stance this statement of the illusory nature of physical reality is quite in keeping with Hindu-Buddhist-Zen attitudes. Carter goes on to bewail "how shallow, fickle, and meaningless all human aspirations are" (*CF* 2.74), in consonance with the Zen-Buddhistic notion that grasping, conventional aspiration is a chief source of human misery and is a misconstruance of the nature of reality. Interestingly, Carter has tried to find solace in the "gentle churchly faith" of his fathers, being repelled finally not because that faith is untrue, but because its proponents insist on taking it as meaningful *only* if literally true: he is put off by "the stale and prosy triteness, and the owlish gravity and grotesque claims of solid truth" attached as "earthly reality" to myths for which "misplaced seriousness killed the attachment he might have kept for the ancient creeds" had their advocates been "content to offer the sonorous rites and emotional outlets in their true guise of ethereal fantasy" (*CF* 2.75). These statements would be well received by many followers of Zen, who learn from their masters that a "misplaced seriousness" can indeed be a dead hand on one's throat. Consistent with Zen thinking, too, are Carter's references to "the delusion that life has a meaning apart from that which men dream into it" and to "the secrets of childhood and innocence" (*CF* 3.76)—there being a perception among Zen followers that, like animals and trees, children are Buddhistically natural and un-self-conscious, until the superfluous claptrap of life deadens their spontaneous reactions.

Lovecraft similarly refers, in "Celephaïs," to "that world of wonder which was ours before we were wise and unhappy" (*CF* 1.185); this work thematically and philosophically adumbrates Lovecraft's novel *The Dream-Quest of Unknown Kadath,* and indeed this complex work—a confluence of many of Lovecraft's most cherished ideas, attitudes, and enthusiasms—provides a decidedly Zen-like statement in its ending. Randolph Carter, a Lovecraftian Ulysses who survives numerous episodic horrors in mythic quest of the "sunset city" of his dreams, finally learns from Nyarlathotep the truth that has eluded him like the answer to an unfathomable Zen koan, when the Crawling Chaos tells him: "Your gold and marble city of wonder is only the sum of what you have seen and loved in youth" (*CF* 2.206). It is the simple beauty of Carter's (Lovecraft's) native New England with its cobbled lanes and antique gables. "These, Randolph Carter, are your city; for they are yourself" (*CF* 2.207). Thus Carter learns, like many a Buddhist monk, that he has looked too sedulously and too far afield for enlightenment—that he has carried it within him all along. Biographically, one may speculate that Lovecraft, recently returned from his "exile" in New York when he wrote this experimental novel, may well have perceived (and recorded Randolph Carter as perceiving much the same, metaphorically) that his pursuit of external goals—a marriage, a life in New York, a career as a writer away from Providence—has simply obscured his vision of the potential happiness that was there, in his native city, waiting for him all along to embrace it. However this may be, the ending of this novel cannot but put us in mind of the incident in which the Zen master Po-Chang is said to have been asked, by one of his monks, how one went about seeking one's Buddha-nature; he replied, as legend has it, that to do so at all would be like riding out on an ox in search of the ox (Capra 111). Randolph Carter receives much the same enlightenment from, surely, the strangest Zen master of all.

One might search at length through Lovecraft's fiction to identify other specific Zen-like elements, and no doubt would find some—many are the private visions that peek through, suggestive of things ultimately as ineffable as *satori*. Suffice it to say that although Lovecraft's professed philosophy is not entirely in consonance with Zen views, his works at times suggest something of the spirit of Zen. It is a pity that we cannot know exactly what Lovecraft would have thought of modern Zen literature. A conversation between Lovecraft and Alan Watts would be highly interesting, but alas—such an exchange is not to be, this side of Kadath.

A Note on Lovecraft, Mathematics, and the Outer Spheres

It is well known to anyone who has perused Lovecraft's letters that he did not get on too well with mathematics. He abandoned his youthful obsession with chemistry at the point where that science began to grow ineluctably mathematical, remarking that the very sight of a page of equations from organic chemistry would suffice to give him a pounding headache. In the same way he found it necessary to remain a dilettante at astronomy, whose concern with differential equations and tensor analysis could ultimately have spelled untold grief for him. The kindest thing that he ever found it possible to say about mathematics was that it filled him with melancholy; at other moments he spoke of the subject using words like "abhor" and "detest."

But Lovecraft's disinclination toward mathematics was more one of temperament than intellectual ability. If he lacked the patience and the particular species of endurance requisite to becoming a mathematician, he decidedly did not lack intuitive insight, or aesthetic or intellectual appreciation of the nature and importance of mathematics. His stories and his letters show him to be possessed of deep intuitive understanding.

In his essay "H. P. Lovecraft and Pseudomathematics," Robert Weinberg, focusing upon the protagonist Walter Gilman in "The Dreams in the Witch House," remarks that when Lovecraft has Gilman studying "non-Euclidean calculus" (*CF* 3.232) at Miskatonic University, he reveals his ignorance of the fact that there is no such thing. L. Sprague de Camp, on the other hand, in his *Lovecraft: A Biography,* remarks that Lovecraft knew that there is no such thing as non-Euclidean calculus but resolved to use the term anyway because it sounded good for fictional purposes.

I must respectfully disagree with both these assertions. As a literary critic specializing in Lovecraft's works, I agree at least that a fantasy writer sometimes assumes a narrative stance (persona) such that it is convenient to pretend to believe in something in which the flesh-and-blood writer does not literally believe. Lovecraft, for instance, made it quite clear in his letters that he did not believe in hereditary memory, yet he obviously found it to be an irresistible fictional device. But as a mathematician I must give assurance that the term "non-Euclidean calculus" is decidedly *not* nonsensical.

The problem is: what did Lovecraft *mean* by "non-Euclidean"? Possibly he may have used the term in the sense that "Euclidean space" is associated with familiar three-dimensional space. But this would not be the most strictly correct usage, for mathematicians and scientists routinely make use of four- and higher-dimensional mathematical systems—even infinite-dimensional spaces as in the case of Hilbert space. These are still thought of as Euclidean, and in them formulae for distance between two points can be defined by analogy to lower-dimensional spaces, so that calculus can be done in these higher realms. More strictly, non-Euclidean geometry generally involves eschewing the Euclidean Parallel Postulate—which is independent of the other postulates of Euclid and which states that given a line and a point not on the line, there is exactly one line through the given point parallel to the given line—in favor of some other axiomatic assumption; e.g., that there are *two* such lines, or none at all, giving rise to such alternative geometries as the Lobachevskian or the Riemannian. In fact, Walter Gilman is said to be adept at "Riemannian equations" (*CF* 3.240), so that it is possibly this sense of the term "non-Euclidean" which Lovecraft had in mind when he wrote of Gilman and Keziah Mason, and when (in "The Call of Cthulhu") he said that the geometry of R'lyeh was "abnormal, non-Euclidean," (*CF* 2.51) *"all wrong"* (*CF* 2.43).

However, it is possible that Lovecraft dreamed of realms far more abstract and indescribable. It is possible in higher mathematics to define "spaces" or realms of the imagination in which such common geometric notions as distance have no ready meaning. For example, a mathematician may work with the abstract structure called a "locally compact topological group," and in that context define an abstract "measure" and what is called the Haar integral—so that even in this wholly abstract setting one may do a kind of "calculus." Who is to say to what nebulous and unthinkable realms Lovecraft's imagination may have carried him, or what ineffable and soul-annihilating entities he may have found dwelling there? Who is to explain the *real* reasons why he may have "abhorred" mathematics?

Indeed, why is it that when I cast a glance at the volume on topological group theory on the bookshelf near this desk, I feel a tantalizing sensation of wonder pulling and tugging at my mind, a sensation redolent of something that I should remember, of the elusive strata of being that must lie *beyond* . . . ?

I must interrupt this writing to open that book. When I have peered into it and satisfied my soul, I shall return to the typewriter to add several paragraphs more on Lovecraft and mathematics, On the other hand, if I do not return, I pray that my dear Mollie may put caution before audacity and see that this manuscript meets no other eye.

[The above manuscript, in its incomplete state, was brought to us by Ms. Mollie Werba, accompanied by her pet squirrel Brown Jenkin. Mr. Burleson seemingly cannot be reached.—*Editor*.]

Lovecraft and Chiasmus, Chiasmus and Lovecraft

Central to the craft of any fine writer is the ability to create the requisite tensions and rhythmic flow of a piece of writing through a healthy combination of rhetorical and syntactic forms. H. P. Lovecraft evidently learned much of this art by reading his admired neoclassical authors of eighteenth-century England, who in turn derived their own sense of linguistic integrity and propriety from Augustan models for whom the notion of efficacious and well-balanced language was paramount.

The primary rhetorical form around which a writer may creatively design his syntax is that of parallelism, by which different prose or prosodical utterances reflect each other by having comparable items in comparable positions, as when Lovecraft's narrative voice in *The Case of Charles Dexter Ward* describes College Hill in Providence as being "crowned by the vast new Christian Science dome as London is crowned by St. Paul's" (*CF* 2.224), or when the narrator in "The Statement of Randolph Carter" says, "Vision or nightmare it may have been—vision or nightmare I fervently hope it was" (*CF* 1.133).

Clearly, however, a story or novel or poem would be structurally and tonally monotonous if its syntax consisted of an unrelieved use of parallelism, and, aside from such other devices as the periodic sentence, perhaps the chief alternative rhetorical form to which a writer may appeal for an effective variety is that of *chiasmus,* a device that not only modulates the flow of prose or poetry when judiciously interspersed with parallelistic forms (parallelism being the dominant, chiasmus being the minor form), but does so in a manner conducing to poetic balance of linguistic elements, setting up pleasing tensions (often unconscious relations) in the mind of the reader. Chiasmus derives its name from the form of the Greek letter *chi* (χ), suggesting a crossing-over of sentence elements by which the second half of what would otherwise be a parallelism is inverted to produce the form *abba.*

Neoclassical writers sometimes employed chiasmus in prose; see, for instance, Joseph Addison (in *The Spectator* No. 10, Monday, 12 March 1711): "I shall endeavour to enliven morality with wit, and to temper wit with morality." But the device chiefly occurs in the heroic couplets of their poetry. (They had, of course, been anticipated in this in earlier poets, particularly John Milton, and even that Elizabethan master of form Edmund Spenser.) See, for one among numerous examples, Lovecraft's revered Alexander Pope, in *The Rape of the Lock:*

> The hungry judges soon the sentence sign,
> And wretches hang that jurymen may dine. (III.21–22)

Here the elements of the chiasmus operate at the imagistic level rather than the strict verbal level of the Addison example; the image of "hungry judges" is echoed at the end by "dine," while in the middle the image of "sentence" is followed by that suggested in the words "wretches hang." Pope, of course, was also known to employ chiasmus in its stricter form, as in this line from *Eloisa to Abelard:* "Rise in the grove, before the altar rise" (*Satires* l. 276) Even here the form is flexible in application, in that "in the grove" and "before the altar" reflect each other merely by being prepositional phrases similarly employed. The writers of this period clearly recognized the power of this device, applicable in many variations and at various linguistic levels, to enhance their effusions by gently varying the otherwise largely parallelistic flow of their sentences and by charming the reader's mind with a sense of verbal balance.

And Lovecraft recognized this as well. Like William Faulkner, Lovecraft began his writing career as a poet, later carrying forward an abundance of poetic principles that would profoundly color the prose writing to which he had turned. While much of Lovecraft's poetry, particularly the early efforts, may be of little enduring artistic value, the experience of writing it did leave him with a lasting sense of linguistic control, and even among the poems themselves one finds worthy accomplishments here and there.

The poetry, while in the vast majority of instances exhibiting parallel structure, does afford some examples of variegation by the device of chiasmus. One sees, for instance, in "The Nightmare Lake," the lines

> In nightmares only it is told
> What scenes beneath those beams unfold;
> What scenes, too old for human sight,
> Lie sunken there in endless night . . . (*AT* 50)

Here the repetition "night(mares)," "scenes," "scenes," "night" reveals the pattern. It seems, though, to be in his poems structured around the true heroic couplet that Lovecraft is most inclined to make use of this device, reflecting the influence of such of his idols as Pope and Dryden. See, for such an example, his "To Templeton and Mount Monadnock," in which we find:

> Silent, pine-girt hill
> Whose majesty could move a Whittier's quill;
> Whose distant brow the humbler pen excites;
> Whose purpled slope the raptur'd gaze invites . . . (*AT* 279)

("Move," "quill," "pen," "excites" for an imagistic chiasmus rather reminiscent of those of Pope.) The last two lines, of course, also show a parallelism, illustrating how well the two forms work in concert; and Lovecraft here also employs the device of anaphora, in the repetition of "whose." But even in poems of far different structure, the *abba* pattern may be discerned, as in this example, on the phonemic level, from "Nemesis":

> Where they roll in their horror unheeded, without *kn*ow*l*edge or *l*ustre or *n*ame. (*AT* 27)

While chiasmus is usually understood to operate by way of larger syntactic elements or images, its characteristic pattern may emerge in linguistic units as small as phonemes, where it produces an effect more subtly pleasing than ordinary alliteration or consonance.

But we find by far the more notable Lovecraftian use of chiasmus in his prose, particularly in those tales of a genuinely poetic cast. Even in works of lesser poetic inclination the device is noticeable. The novel

The Case of Charles Dexter Ward, for instance, is a work narrated (for all its other scarcely deniable kinds of appeal) in a rather reportorial manner not attaining to the beauty of the more colorful tales, but it does yield up some examples of Lovecraft's use of chiasmus to vary and enhance the general flow of his syntax, as when (concerning Charles Ward's activities at the Pawtuxet bungalow) the narrator says, "Before long queer tales began to circulate regarding the all-night burning of lights; and somewhat later, after this burning had suddenly ceased, there rose still queerer tales" (*CF* 2.302); or when he describes Ward's (actually Curwen's) typewritten communications: "Those notes are not in Ward's normal style; not even in the style of that last frantic letter to Willett" (*CF* 2.311). These examples, however, are sparse and relatively unimpressive, and to see, in the novel, a more typical usage, one must look to Orne's letter to Curwen—"Ask of the Lesser, lest the Greater shall not wish to Answer" (*CF* 2.252)—where Lovecraft abandons the more general prosaic style of the novel to imitate seventeenth-century prose, the immediate forerunner of his admired neoclassicism. Overall, in any case, one must appeal to less dryly narrated tales, where effective examples abound.

Many of these are obvious and structurally simple, as when the famous subject of Richard Pickman's painting (reflecting Goya's Saturn) "glared and gnawed and gnawed and glared" (*CF* 2.69); as, similarly, certain entities "pawed and groped and groped and pawed" in *The Dream-Quest of Unknown Kadath* (*CF* 2.210); or when the narrator of "The Colour out of Space" remarks, of the blasted heath, that "no other name could fit such a thing, or any other thing fit such a name" (*CF* 2.369); or when Johansen in "The Call of Cthulhu" experiences "hysterical plunges from the pit to the moon and from the moon back again to the pit" (*CF* 2.55); or when the narrator of that same tale remarks, in the final apocalyptic paragraph, "What has risen may sink, and what has sunk may rise" (*CF* 2.55); or when the narrator of "The Shadow out of Time" says, "The particular structure I was in was known to me. Known, too, was its place in that terrible elder city of dream" (*CF* 3.428); or when the narrator of "The Dreams in the Witch House" opens the tale with "Whether the dreams brought on the fever or the fever brought on the dreams Walter Gilman did not know" (*CF* 3.231); or when the autobiographically philosophical narrative voice of

"The Silver Key" remarks that "the blind cosmos grinds aimlessly on from nothing to something and from something back to nothing again" (*CF* 2.74).

And of course there is that resounding double chiasmus from the *Necronomicon* in "The Dunwich Horror": "Man rules now where They ruled once; They shall soon rule where man rules now. After summer is winter, and after winter summer" (*CF* 2.434). Lovecraft had much earlier employed a two-chiasmus structure in the opening lines of "The Doom That Came to Sarnath": "There is in the land of Mnar a vast still lake that is fed by no stream and out of which no stream flows. Ten thousand years ago there stood by its shore the mighty city of Sarnath, but Sarnath stands there no more" (*CF* 1.122). Interestingly, the pattern of the second sentence is actually *abccba,* a level-topped pyramidal form, where "there" is in one instance an expletive and, in the other, an adverb of place; the pattern generates three instances of chiasmus folded together; *abba, bccb,* and *acca,* the first two being more solid in sense and rhythm than the third. This sentence also suggests, in a wedding of sense to form, the coming and going of the mighty city.

The simplicity of most of these examples notwithstanding, Lovecraft is by no means limited to such straightforward employment of the device of chiasmus. One could hardly find a more pleasing example than that reflection of the outsider: "it were better to glimpse the sky and perish, than to live without ever beholding day" (*CF* 1.267). Here the pattern involves verbs of like meaning ("glimpse," "beholding") on the outside, with opposites ("perish," "live") on the inside, and the effect is highly poetic. Clearly, when Lovecraft later disparaged "The Outsider" as an overwritten tale, he was being unduly harsh as a self-critic. In this and the preceding examples, he employs chiasmus as an effective playoff against other forms for a very effective prose style.

Lovecraft's conscious or unconscious inclination toward the *abba* pattern can on occasion even be discerned on as subtle a level as that of narrative point of view. In particular, "The Terrible Old Man" (*CF* 1.140) opens with an editorializing narrator (ironic in tone to the point of sarcasm) whose stance is essentially omniscient; the point of view narrows to that of Messrs. Ricci, Czanek, and Silva, planning to rob the old man; the point of view narrows a little further to the consciousness of Czanek, waiting in the auto and encountering the old man; the story ends with a return of the ironic-toned and editorializing narrator, to complete the pattern. While the term chiasmus generally does not refer to such considerations as narrative point of view, its characterizing pattern may here be observed on that level, so that as a habit of mind in Lovecraft the pattern seems to range from the phonemic level through the level of syntax all the way up to the most global level that a story may encompass. Clearly chiasmus and kindred phenomena are a substantial facet of that body of poetic instinct that Lovecraft, the poet-turned-fiction-writer, brought to his work from early literary encounters with his classical and neoclassical mentors.

Lovecraft and the World as Cryptogram

It is evident even to casual readers of H. P. Lovecraft's fiction that the motif of cryptography—ciphers or secret writing—is one that recurs throughout his writing career. Evidently having imbibed at least a layman's interest in the subject in early childhood upon reading Poe's "The Gold Bug," Lovecraft returns to the fictional use of the motif again and again. In *The Case of Charles Dexter Ward* Charles Ward encounters the cipher manuscripts of Hutchinson and Curwen. In "The Dunwich Horror" Henry Armitage struggles to decipher Wilbur Whateley's cryptographic diary. "In The Whisperer in Darkness" Henry Akeley seeks Albert Wilmarth's aid in deciphering the inscription on a stone. (This would be more an act of translation than of decipherment, though the puzzling out of a message in an unknown language or script is very similar to decipherment in the usual sense—the Rosetta Stone being, in effect, a cryptographic "key" to ancient Egyptian hieroglyphs, for example. The difference, of course, is that such scripts were not deliberate concealments of meaning, but merely had their meanings lost. Lovecraft's use of cryptography on the level of metaphor actually operates close to this sense of the term "decipherment.") In "The Haunter of the Dark" Robert Blake (whose name itself is a thin "cryptographic" rendering of Robert Bloch) labors over the cryptogram found in the church in Federal Hill. Clearly Lovecraft was as fascinated with the motif of secret writing as he was with the recurrent motif of masks; indeed, a cryptogram is a linguistic mask.[1]

---

1. The cipher-breaking activities to which a number of HPL's protagonists apply themselves is properly termed *cryptanalysis,* the science of deciphering messages to which one is not supposed to be privy. *Cryptography* is simply the art of writing messages in cipher or code to begin with, while *cryptology* is the mathematical theory of

Lovecraft's most elaborate textual play with the cryptography motif occurs in "The Dunwich Horror," where Henry Armitage fortifies himself with the writings of numerous authorities on the subject. The amusing thing about this literary episode is that Lovecraft copied the necessary cryptographic arcana, in some spots almost verbatim, from the *Encyclopaedia Britannica*.[2] In "The Dunwich Horror" he mentions "Trithemius' 'Poligraphia', Giambattista Porta's 'De Furtivis Literarum Notis', De Vigenère's 'Traité des Chiffres', Falconer's 'Cryptomenysis Patefacta', Davys' and Thicknesse's eighteenth-century treatises, and such fairly modern authorities as Blair, Von Marten, and Klüber's 'Kryptographik'" (*CF* 2.449) in the exact order in which they are mentioned in the encyclopedia article. The Whateley cipher in Lovecraft's tale is said to be "one of those subtlest and most ingenious of cryptograms, in which many separate lists of corresponding letters are arranged like the multiplication table, and the message built up with arbitrary key-words known only to the initiated" (*CF* 2.494), reflecting the encyclopedia reference: "The greatest security against the decipherer has been found in the use of elaborate tables of letters, arranged in the form of the multiplication table, the message being constructed by the aid of preconcerted key-words. The deciphering of them is one of the most difficult of tasks."

Thus we see that Lovecraft's actual depth of involvement in cryptanalysis was apparently that of the uncommonly well-informed layman. Given his disposition, we may say that he probably would have found the real job of deciphering cryptograms as excruciatingly tedious as he found mathematics and organic chemistry to be; but, laudably enough, he took the trouble to read up on the subject to lend verisimilitude to his writing.

The overt references to cryptography in his tales, however, do not by any means exhaust the ways in which the notion of secret writing

---

cipher systems. For an excellent text on elementary decipherment of cryptosystems, see Gaines, *Cryptanalysis*.

2. I am indebted to David E. Schultz for providing me with the text of the article "Cryptography" in an edition of the *Encyclopaedia Britannica* printed in 1900, a text no doubt virtually identical with that (in the 9th edition, 1896) to which HPL had access. My own ready access at Rivier College was to the eleventh edition, 1910; the articles in question, however, are essentially the same, suggesting that little if any updating occurred between fin-de-siècle editions.

pervades his work on all levels. One notes, significantly, the scene in "The Whisperer in Darkness," where Wilmarth, the narrator, is being driven through the wild Vermont countryside by Akeley's supposed messenger Noyes; Wilmarth feels that "the very outline of the hills themselves held some strange and aeon-forgotten meaning, as if they were vast hieroglyphs left by a rumoured titan race whose glories live only in rare, deep dreams" (*CF* 2.511). The notion that there are hidden layers of meaning beneath the surface-level impressions of the world is a notion that runs through much of Lovecraft's fictive thinking, and the expression of this notion amounts to the use of the cryptography motif on the level of extended metaphor. To Wilmarth, the Vermont hills are a cryptogram, a "ciphertext" beneath which is hidden some "plaintext" message whose meaning has been obscured or lost.

The same sort of thing happens with many Lovecraftian characters themselves; they are often living cryptograms. For example, the Terrible Old Man, to the robbers and the townspeople, is a ciphertext whose true underlying plaintext (or real nature) is only problematically readable at best. This metaphorical usage often operates with Lovecraftian settings as well; the town of Innsmouth appears one way (an integument of encipherment) to the narrator, but has a hidden "textuality" underneath. The thing that makes the Lovecraftian ciphertext-versus-plaintext duality (the bipolar tension between seeming and being) truly unique is that unlike the common cryptanalyst, we, when we confront the Lovecraftian "cryptogram"—whether it be in the form of such characters as Dr. Muñoz or Erich Zann or Wilbur Whateley, or in the form of such settings as Kingsport or Arkham or Antarctica—we, as cryptanalysts, reading ourselves into the minds of Lovecraftian characters, often do not know that the common surface appearances are cryptographic in nature, and when we do "solve the cryptogram," we find the plaintext message invariably disturbing.

Lovecraftian characters may at times even misread the plaintext. In "The Dunwich Horror," when Henry Armitage literally solves the Whateley cryptogram (the written one—Wilbur himself is a cryptotext), he fails to solve the greater, more philosophical cryptogram that lies yawning where his "solution" leaves off. Armitage, using incantations, and aided by his colleagues Morgan and Rice (themselves metacryptograms on the in-joke level, since their names are derived from details of Lovecraft's experiences in western Massachusetts), does battle with the monstrous twin atop the mountain and finally delivers a foolishly homiletic speech, to the Dunwich farmers, that makes it clear that he supposes humankind to have emerged victorious, when in fact it is equally clear that the problem for humankind is one eternally irremediable. Armitage is like a man who finds a cryptogram, solves it, sees that the plaintext reads YOUR GOOSE IS COOKED, and concludes, with a sigh of satisfaction, that he has just been invited to dinner.

The existence of further levels of hidden meaning in such cryptographic scenarios is indicative of the fact that the cryptography motif in Lovecraft metaphorically extends even to the broadest thematic levels. The suggestion is that the universe itself is a cryptogram, whose surface-level ciphertext is, in effect, a comforting patina of apparently anthropocentric "meaning" concealing the real meaning—the plaintext of an underlying universe indifferent to the presence of humankind. (This situation, where the ciphertext itself looks like, but really conceals, a plaintext, is analogous to the so-called null cipher, in which, e.g., the text "Sound echoes near Dover giving us nice sensations" conceals the message "Send guns" seen in the words' initial letters.) Many a Lovecraftian protagonist "deciphers the cryptogram" to find annihilation of soul in the text of the solution.

This notion of *world as text*—the world as a ciphertext obscuring a plaintext—relates interestingly to poststructuralist theories of literary criticism, in which literature is not so much about "the world" as about literature itself, in a web of intertextuality. For Lovecraft, even if literary texts are about the world, the world that they are about is still itself a text, a text that yields up its nether meanings only to destroy the self-assessment of the cryptanalyzing intelligence, which prior to "solving the cryptogram" has moved about in a ciphertext thought to be the real world, a world in which humankind seems to have "meaning." But humankind, after descending to plaintext, finds itself (like "null" letters in a cryptogram) to have amounted to superfluous text, in light of the larger and deeper message of the cosmos. In Lovecraft's universe, to resolve the ciphertext into plaintext is, paradoxically, to lose meaning rather than to gain it—more exactly, it is to lose the illusion of meaning. If the world is a cryptogram, the meaning of its solution is that there is no meaning.

Lovecraft and the Death of Tragedy

H. P. Lovecraft in his letters made abundantly clear his admiration of Joseph Wood Krutch, and specifically of a provocative 1929 work of that writer. In 1930 Lovecraft discussed the phenomenon that the advance of human thought had placed humankind in a position in which comforting myths had been pushed back to the brink of extinction, leaving humankind only the prospects of a starkly materialistic world to contemplate. Lovecraft advises, "Read Joseph Wood Krutch's *The Modern Temper* if you want the authentick, expert low-down on all this" (*SL* 3.139–40). He goes on to pose the question "whether man can or cannot adequately nourish himself with absolute reality alone," and concludes that he cannot; while myths that deny known reality are of no use, one must have imaginative expansions beyond that reality to live life with anything akin to satisfaction.

Krutch's book contains a brilliant chapter titled "The Tragic Fallacy" (79–97), an essay exploring the reasons why modern literature does not reflect the true olden spirit of tragedy. The real tragic vision, Krutch argues, as seen in the literature of Periclean Greece and Elizabethan England, depends upon a lofty assessment of human worth; true tragedy can only function with the premise, profoundly felt, that in the midst of calamity humankind has the greatness to endure and prevail—that we have it in us to triumph ultimately over despair and assume a role of central importance in the universe. Shakespeare—particularly the Jacobean Bard whose dramatic vision had shaded off from Elizabethan comedy to an increasingly somber artistic reaction to his world—wrote of kings and their courts because he believed that human beings possessed a spirit and an intrinsic worth that could be regal; in the Ptolemaic worldview of the times, humankind, though fraught with misery, could stand with pride at the center of all creation and play a kingly role. But we modern writers "do not write about kings," Krutch says, "because we do not believe that any man is worthy to be one and we do not write about courts because hovels seem to us to be dwellings more appropriate to the creatures who inhabit them." Tragedy, he says, can thrive only in the soil of what would now logically be called (if we possessed it) the "tragic fallacy," a sort of extended "pathetic fallacy" amounting to the *illusion,* at least, that each of man's acts "reverberates through the universe," in the absence of which postulation man "is never strong enough in his own insignificant self to stand alone in a universe which snubs him with its indifference." In the modern Weltanschauung, Krutch concludes, "the best that we can achieve is pathos and the most that we can do is feel sorry for ourselves." The irony is that "our need for the consolations of tragedy has not passed with the passing of our ability to conceive it."

The worldview reflected in the fiction of the Lovecraft Mythos rings clearly in consonance with this modern view. (By the time Lovecraft read *The Modern Temper,* his own basic viewpoint along these lines was already well established, but we may suppose that Krutch's incisive comments must have been instrumental in clarifying and strengthening that viewpoint.) Lovecraft's central and recurrent fictive thesis is that upon encountering the realities of his place in the cosmos, man can only discover his mote-like evanescence in a universe wholly indifferent to his presence. It is through the conduit of the emotional and intellectual responses of Lovecraft's characters that we as readers experience this debasing revelation, and it is this "ironic impressionism" (as I have elsewhere termed it) that characterizes the Lovecraft Mythos—the cosmically absurd but (to the protagonist) poignant circumstance by which man is just sufficiently sensitive and well-developed a creature to be made to know and feel his own insignificance, an insignificance that mocks the very intelligence that perceives it. When (e.g.) Nathaniel Wingate Peaslee in "The Shadow out of Time" (perhaps Lovecraft's most penetrating exploration of this central notion) finally does flick his flashlight on and look upon his own handwriting in that unthinkable crypt in Australia, we profoundly feel for him and with him, and we realize that our very sympathy for him and (by implication) for ourselves is but a facet of that human emotional and mental organization that has just collapsed into a dust-heap of insignificance in some nameless corner of an uncaring universe.

Here as elsewhere in the Lovecraft canon, one finds the very antithesis of that departed tragic vision, described by Krutch, by which one might have hoped to believe "that however much things in the outward world go awry, man has, nevertheless, splendors of his own." If a Lovecraft protagonist were to think of his revelatory experience as "tragic" the term would apply in only a degenerate sense, because true tragedy presumes a human capacity to stand great and tall above despair—and in Lovecraft's world, such greatness does not emerge; humankind is simply alone, his despair not to be mitigated, his pain not to impart to him any such aura of importance as would be imparted to a Lear or an Oedipus.

Krutch understandably bemoans the fact that "we read but do not write tragedies"—the fact that something of dignity has passed out of the human race's view of itself. And surely the Lovecraft Mythos reflects a conviction that Periclean tragedy has indeed declined to the vanishing point. It is as if Lovecraft drives the last and most reverberant nail into the coffin of the tragic vision of old. The act of doing so is no act of betrayal, but is rather a realization on Lovecraft's part that if the human self-view of classical tragedy has perished, it was bound to do so with the coming of a clearer perception, a perception capable only of an accuracy that must banish mendacious self-comfort. The passing of the tragic vision is no more to be denied than is the kindred process of entropy in all nature, one may say, and if one accepts this premise (unattractive though it may be), then it is highly worthy and characteristic of Lovecraft that he simply saw things as they were: he saw that far from the world of Ptolemy, in which humankind was center-stage, the modern world itself denies the tragic vision in placing humankind nearly offstage altogether. Lovecraft did not, after all, deal any death-blow to tragedy, but rather, perceiving the demise, gave it a memorable funeral and a decent burial, as it were. That he admired the classical tragic tradition is clear, but wishing it still alive would not have made it so. Whether it can ever live again is open to debate, but doubtful at least in any future most people would care to foretell. Like Lovecraft's Outsider, we cannot very well sneak back down the ancestral tower and recover our old innocence and ignorance.

The irony that when we read Lovecraft we may marvel at that cosmic revelation that mocks our very capacity to marvel, is but another level of the supreme Lovecraftian irony, and our sense of the "tragic" in our situation is but a shadow of the classical sense. If our reactions to the irony of Lovecraft's indifferent universe are to stand as any sort of ersatz reflection of the position of the tragic hero of old, then they are a pale reflection indeed—we perceive our position in the cosmic fabric, but we have no remedy for the implications of the perception, no overriding greatness to fling back at the gods, no cry of "Some among us may have fallen, but it is the great who fall, and we endure in spirit." In the Lovecraft Mythos, the gods that prevail are not those classical gods fashioned to reflect a human centrality of concern in an orderly universe; rather, they symbolize ultimate chaos, they are metonymy for a world in which the true tragic vision is but a construction out of unfounded hopes. When chaos rules, true anthropocentric tragedy is without meaning; it seemed noble while it lasted, but it rested upon illusion of a kind ultimately not to be maintained.

Yet this philosophical stance of Krutch and of Lovecraft, like any meaningful philosophical position, is not one to which we may ascribe metaphysical closure, finality, simple completeness. Like any well-conceived worldview, any philosophy of substance, it turns in upon itself to produce paradoxical complexities of self-subversion.

Krutch posits a binary opposition, a supplementarity consisting of the classical capacity for tragic vision on the one hand as the primary term, and, on the other hand, as the secondary term, the modern failure to sustain this vision without what he calls a "tragic fallacy" to fall back upon. Lovecraft follows (or even anticipates) him in this structural postulation, cleaving our mental world into a bipolarity between meaningful existence (due, for Lovecraft, to a merciful ignorance of our true circumstances) and ironically self-understood insignificance. In these bipolar schemes, one may discern that each extreme end of the axis contains, as an enabling condition, the other end.

Looking at Krutch's secondary term first, the loss of the tragic vision, we may observe that there could be no such loss felt, without an innate sense of what that tragic vision once was; lacking such an innate sense, we could in no meaningful way comment upon the loss, for we could not comprehend *what* had been lost. Krutch's position thus turns upon itself on the point that to feel the loss of tragedy is in some sense still to know what it is, or in principle could be. Conversely, looking at

Krutch's primary term, the classical capacity for true tragedy, we may observe that in the days when that tragic view was really humankind's, it could not have been so without the peripheral realization that it could be lost; indeed, it is a commonplace even in early Shakespearean comedic drama that the characters fear a loss of the balance and harmony of their world, in effect a loss of anthropocentric being. If humankind in Elizabethan and Jacobean times had possessed an absolutely unshakable capacity for entertaining the tragic vision, then the vision would have been trivialized, in a sense; it would have been a structural feature of their lives not possible to lose: something to take for granted. And in any case, their descendants *did* lose the vision. Thus Krutch's classical tragic vision and its modern loss are mutually implicative; each contains the differential trace of the other.

Lovecraft's bipolarity dismantles itself in a like manner, reinscribing itself as a similarly undecidable oscillation. For humankind to have (through merciful ignorance) a self-view of meaningful existence and worth, and for such a view not to be logically trivial, the view must be capable of being lost through inroads of destructive revelation; such a self-view defines itself through its potential absence. Conversely, the loss of the vision is logically meaningful only if there is still a residual but clear sense of what was lost. Imagined human significance and revealed human insignificance are traces of each other, defining each other; they set up an irresolvable oscillation that grows more complex with each new level of contemplation. While it is clear that Lovecraft writes in high consonance with Krutch's view of the status of tragedy, it is equally clear that, with reference to both writers, there is no logical closure to escape the aporetic reversals and alternations inherent in seeing each bipolar opposite as the trace of the other. Tragedy and the assumption of human significance were meaningful only because they were impermanent and could be lost, and their loss is meaningful only because we retain an essential understanding of the nature of what was lost, and retain something of the capacity not to suffer those qualities that have been lost to have been, after all, unquestionably impermanent or lost beyond all *imaginable* recall. Reading Lovecraft, we will continue to dwell upon the nature of the tragic vision in one way or another; the oscillations will continue to resound, and there can be no final word on the matter.

Lovecraft and Romanticism

Probably the most dramatic rift in the flow of the theory and practice of literature from ancient times to the present resides in the transition from the Neoclassical school of the early and middle eighteenth century to the Romantic movement of the late eighteenth and early nineteenth centuries, a transition involving a fundamental shift in attitudes and concerns. How does H. P. Lovecraft fit into this picture? Although the question would seem to be an easy one to answer, given Lovecraft's avowed preference for the Neoclassical period over the Romantic, a quick response is apt to be somewhat facile, for the question is problematized not only by the fact that the defining boundaries of Neoclassicism and Romanticism are ultimately not so clearly drawn as one might assume, but also by the fact that in Lovecraft's own theory of literature one may discern the sorts of indeterminacies that ineluctably invade all attempts at codifying human thought into a rigid and structure-bound system.

Lovecraft's closest approach to an overt statement of assessment regarding Romanticism perhaps lies in his oft-quoted remark about the crafting of weird fiction:

> Now all my tales are based on the fundamental premise that common human laws and interests and emotions have no validity or significance in the vast cosmos-at-large. . . . Only the human scenes and characters must have human qualities. *These* must be handled with unsparing *realism,* (not catch-penny *romanticism*) but when we cross the line to the boundless and hideous unknown—the shadow-haunted *Outside*—we must remember to leave our humanity and terrestrialism at the threshold. (*SL* 2.150)

While admittedly Lovecraft's use of the term *romanticism* here seems to refer more to matters of stylistics and technique than to a formal school of literary theory, there is clearly a strong suggestion of a stance antithetical to some of the basic tenets of Romanticism, and particularly to the Romantic notion of elevating human feelings to a position of central importance in the scheme of things. Yet this statement is not without its implicative difficulties, in the context of differences between Romanticism and Neoclassicism; in suggesting that human laws "have no validity," Lovecraft in a certain sense sounds more like a Romantic than a Neoclassicist. In the Neoclassical world, laws and rules and underlying structures—order as understood by humans—were of primary concern and respect; while in the Romantic movement, freedom from the rigidity of mundane law was a central notion. The Neoclassical mind conformed to the propriety of law and structure as a *donnée;* the Romantic mind sought spontaneity and liberation. Lovecraft again addresses these notions when he states: "Time, space, and natural law hold for me suggestions of intolerable bondage, and I can form no picture of emotional satisfaction which does not involve their defeat" (*SL* 3.220). Here again the suggestion is one of yearning for liberation from the constraints of law and structure, even if the implication is that in fiction one only *seems* to espy a promise of bringing about that liberation.

What are the fundamental distinguishing characteristics of Romanticism as commonly understood? Although no thoroughly satisfying definition of this protean and shifting term can be agreed upon, one may say in historico-literary terms that, primarily, the Romantic movement marked a shift in basic literary concern, from the earlier mimetic and didactic concerns (the notion that literature should reflect that which is worthy of reflection in the world, and the notion that, in mirroring reality, literature should teach us something about how to live—notions going back to Horace and Aristotle) to the *expressive* concern. In the Romantic milieu, the concern was not that the artist should mimic and teach, but that the act of writing should be a cathartic activity of the writer's mind. Today, in terms of modern theories of literature (poststructuralism in particular), both the Neoclassical and the Romantic configurations of concern are problematical, in that the whole notion of *purpose* is something quite beside the point with regard to the uncontainable activities of textuality itself; texts are public documents that perpetuate and expand themselves, that continue to write themselves, as it were, by being read and creatively misread. But we are interested here in periods of literary-theoretical development that nonetheless centered about concerns of purpose, however peripheral or problematized those concerns may be from the point of view of more recent thinking.

Wordsworth, in his critical preface to the second edition of the *Lyrical Ballads,* made what is often regarded as a key statement of the emerging spirit of Romanticism, when he wrote that a poem is "the spontaneous overflow of powerful feelings." Enter the expressive concern. But it is not possible to regard this concern as one of cathartic expression alone, in terms of actual literary activity. Wordsworth himself did not just utter his poetry as a primal cry that had to be cried; he published his work, after all. There are relatively few documentable instances of *pure* catharsis in literary work. One thinks of stories of the Chinese T'ang Dynasty poet Li Po's sitting drunk beside a river and writing poems on slips of paper and dropping them into the water to watch them swirl away to oblivion, but one scarcely imagines Wordsworth's entertaining himself similarly in the Lake District; nor can one readily imagine Lovecraft's dropping the pencilled manuscript of "The Shadow over Innsmouth" into the Seekonk, having satisfied himself in the mere *in vacuo* catharsis of writing it. In the "expressive" concern there generally lurks also a *preservative* concern, a desire to *record* what is imagined. (Lovecraft often remarked that he did not care whether anyone read what he wrote or not, because he wrote stories simply to please himself, but in fact he usually sought their publication, and was often extremely distressed at editorial rejections, as in the case of *At the Mountains of Madness.* And when he says, "if I could find tales or books or poems expressing everything I wish to say, I would not write at all" [*SL* 2.111], he is clearly suggesting that the act of expression alone is not all that is at stake; there is a preservative concern, a concern not only that writing take place but that reading take place.) But even with this somewhat modified view of Wordsworth's definitive statement, we may note that much of what Lovecraft says about his own philosophy of writing is markedly in consonance with the expressive concern. He writes that an author has

> . . . his one legitimate goal of emotional catharsis & harmonious expression. . . . Art is not the devising of artificial things to say, but the mere saying of something already formulated inside the artist's imagination & automatically clamouring to be said. . . . The proper function of a short story is to reflect powerfully a single mood, emotion, or authentic situation in life. (*SL* 4.263–67)

While there is a suggestion here of the old mimetic concern (in the reference to reflecting an "authentic situation in life"), and while the word "harmonious" certainly echoes Lovecraft's admiration for the proprieties of Neoclassical writing, the primary thrust of the statement is clearly one of expressive concern much in keeping with Wordsworth's "spontaneous overflow." Lovecraft says:

> There can be no real authorship without a genuine and imperative urge for expression—I have not that urge except in connexion with the haunting conception of impinging cosmic mystery & the liberation implied in the suspension or circumvention of the tyranny of time, space, & natural law. (*SL* 4.94)

And here we are come back around again to the theme of liberation. With regard to the reference to the "tyranny" of law, one readily thinks how naturally those figures central to the Romantic movement of the early nineteenth century were drawn to the spirit of the French Revolution. They and the revolutionaries were kindred spirits, and Lovecraft's is, thematically, a kindred spirit as well, his Toryist objections to America's own revolutionary unsettling of established law notwithstanding.

The passage just cited also treats of Lovecraft's sense of *wonder,* a notion very much present in Romantic thought and very expressly discouraged by some of the Neoclassicists. One recalls Samuel Johnson's remarks that "wonder is a pause of reason" and that "all wonder is the effect of novelty upon ignorance." Lovecraft on this score could scarcely be farther away from Samuel Johnson when he says: "Somehow I cannot be truly interested in anything which does not suggest incredible marvels just around the corner" (*SL* 2.160).

As much as Lovecraft expressed admiration for Dr. Johnson, it is remarkable how different Johnson's attitudes were from Lovecraft's. The well-known Johnsonian dictum that "no man but a blockhead ever wrote except for money" is alone enough to drive a substantial wedge between them, given Lovecraft's attitudes about "hawking his wares," and Lovecraft is starkly at odds with Johnsonian/Neoclassical didacticism when, e.g., in "Supernatural Horror in Literature" he chafes even at what he perceives as didactic overtones in Hawthorne. Even when Lovecraft is extolling the virtues of his Neoclassicist favorites—"There has never been any prose as good as that of the early eighteenth century, and anyone who thinks he can improve upon Swift, Steele, and Addison is a blockhead" (*SL* 4.33)—he remarks, in the very same letter, that the "best prose is vigorous, direct, unadorn'd, and closely related (as in the best verse) to the language of actual discourse." Upon reading this, one can scarcely avoid thinking of Wordsworth's remark that a poet is a man using "language really spoken by men." In many respects, one feels that contrary to his statements about Dr. Johnson, Lovecraft might have found a readier colleague in Wordsworth than in the eminent Doctor, in that in Wordsworth's view, free and spontaneous and natural expression was paramount.

The expressive concern is evident in numerous other Lovecraftian statements about the philosophy of writing. He remarks: "What [a *really serious* weird story] sets out to be is simply *a picture of a mood*. . . . I'm simply casting about for better ways to crystallise and capture certain strong impressions . . . which persist in clamouring for expression" (*SL* 5.198–99). For Lovecraft, "[w]ords and images well up & demand to be set down" (*SL* 5.136). And he says:

> Emotion makes itself felt in the unconscious choice of words, management of rhythms, & disposal of stresses in the flow of narration; whilst an image or idea of natural or spontaneous occurrence is a thousandfold more vivid than any which can be arbitrarily invented. (*SL* 3.213)

Here we have direct reference to emotion and spontaneity in creative activity, conceptually echoic of Wordsworth's "spontaneous overflow of powerful feelings."

But Lovecraft recognized that "schools" and facets of literary creativeness have to blend:

> In my own humble and careless effusions, one sees the convergence of two separate tendencies—a liking for well-modelled expression in the traditional manner for its own sake, and a wish to get on paper some of the images and impressions constantly running through my mind. (*SL* 2.107)

Here he has melded together the Neoclassicist concern for "well-modelled expression" with the Romantic concern for expression and preservation of mental images and feelings. And indeed, the traditional boundaries between the two periods are in some respects more of the nature of stresses which stand as spatial metaphors *for* boundaries (metaphors whose metaphoricity may be forgotten) than of the nature of boundaries that are in any more substantial way "real," permanent, or unassailable.

While any ultimately defensible definition of Romanticism remains impossible, one of the best-known characterizations of the difference between the Neoclassical and the Romantic spirit resides in the formulation given by M. H. Abrams in *The Mirror and the Lamp,* where the imagery of the title refers to the notion that in Neoclassical thought, the mind (as it enters into literary creativity) is like a mirror that faithfully reflects that which it finds, or at least reflects that which is worthy of being reflected, in the world-showing the mimetic concern—while in Romantic thought the creative mind is more like a lamp that does not merely reflect nature, but rather shines upon it, adds to it, helps create it. While it is true that Lovecraft, in this formulation, comes across decidedly pre-Romantic (in that the thematics of his fiction involve humankind's acceptance of a cosmic situation in which humans are debased, a situation which humankind is no position to modify), one may observe that there are problems with the formulation itself, in that it draws its energies from a bipolarity that, as we are coming to find common of bipolarities, cannot avoid dismantling the very spacing of the poles of which it consists.

With the Neoclassical notion of the mind as mirror as opposed to lamp (where one realizes that historically a Neoclassicist would scarcely have thought of the "lamp" metaphor), we must note that the creative mind still creates; in "mirroring" nature, it must still add something to that nature that it mirrors in the very act of expression. A purely mirroring mind would simply *contemplate* what was paraded before it, and this is not what even a Neoclassical artistic mind did—obviously, writers are writers only by virtue of writing, of making a lamp of their minds. It may be that the lamp, from the point of view of Neoclassical thought, sheds but a puny light upon the grandeur of the surrounding reality that it is supposed to reflect, but it sheds a light nevertheless; to reflect or describe is to iterate, and to iterate is to change what is iterated, to modify its texture in the very act of reflection. Conversely, a mind as conceived by the Romantics, the mind as lamp, does not manufacture its light out of nothing; it fashions what it radiates from perceptions of the world around it—in short, it radiates by reflecting. Neither pole of the bipolarity is so distinct from the other pole as it pretends to be; in each pole resides a covert kinship with the other pole. A mirror, here, is a shining mirror; and a lamp is a reflecting lamp. In fictionally portraying humankind, in story after story, as discovering its own ironically self-understood insignificance in the universe, Lovecraft in the schema of Abrams is painting mind as mirror—characterizing the human condition as one of submission to the inevitabilities of the cosmos—but mirrors give back light as well as absorbing it, and there remains an interplay between humankind and the cosmos, even if, as Lovecraft once remarked, "the joke is on mankind" (*CE* 5.54). It is not that one cannot place Lovecraft at one pole of the binary opposition that Abrams posits; it is, rather, that the poles tend to collapse together.

Thus, despite the fact that in some respects Lovecraft's thought owes much to the Neoclassical spirit, and seems opposed to Romanticism—Lovecraft's humankind is debased, Wordsworth's and Shelley's humankind is uplifted—one finds that the categoricality of this thinking leaves something to be desired. Perhaps in a perverse kind of way Lovecraft is a sort of Romantic, though doubtless he would have cringed at the epithet. He may be viewed, paradoxically, as a Romantic in whom the Romantic quest is one led ever on by ultimate futility, led on to a dark acquisition of vision that mocks the very notion and spirit of an acquisition of vision. He would seem to be a Neoclassically bred Romantic in whom the quest of Romanticism, the quest to find expression and human meaning, leads to expressing the pointlessness of expression, and leads to a discovery of the impossibility of assigning any ultimate meaning to the quest itself. Lovecraft in practice embraces a certain kind of Romantic spirit, yet his is a Romanticism *manqué,* in which the yearning for liberation from the delimitations of law is colored by a realization at such liberation is ultimately not to be—but in which also the very recognition of the inevitability of cosmic law entails a basic yearning for freedom from that law, a yearning rendered all the more intense by the unreachability of liberation.

Yet in this paradox, this aporia of unresolved oscillation between the quest and the futility of the quest, there is a reinscription of that mass of complex textuality that synecdochically we call Lovecraft, a reinscription of Lovecraft on the texture of literature in terms forever resisting facile reduction to "truth." What is reducible to univocal truth amounts to textual death; what resists this reduction is textual perpetuity. The deepest and best texts are unreadable: intrinsically incapable of reduction to "settled" readings. We must continue to read what is most unreadable. A text is unreadable to the extent that it leads one ever onward into the eerie pleasures of uncertainty. In this regard, the unsettled and unsettling Lovecraftian profile has its contours pressed deeply into the fabric of textuality and language, for that profile is open and undecidable, and invites endless speculation. Lovecraft the avowed Neoclassicist may well be the ultimate Romantic, because the ultimate Romantic quest leads (with a paradoxical Lovecraftian "adventurous expectancy") into the undying ecstasies of the Abyss.

Lovecraft: An American Allegory

Philip Shreffler once characterized Lovecraft as a writer whose work is especially American in theme and flavor. With Lovecraft, he says, "vast sweeps of space and time are the rule rather than the exception. And this is what gives Lovecraft such a peculiarly American character." From Jamestown onward, Shreffler continues, "American writers have responded one way or another to the sheer immensity of their natural landscape . . . a kind of huge blank canvas on which grandiose philosophical ideas can be painted on a cosmic scale." (4) Here of course Shreffler is arguing, with particular reference to Lovecraft, what has often been argued with reference to American literature generally: that the immensity and dark mystery of the New World gave American writers, from the beginning, both the opportunity to write and think expansively and the psychological necessity of doing so—the opportunity and the need to think in terms not only of seemingly limitless vistas of physical landscape, but of truly limitless depths of psyche-landscape: the depths of the human mind or soul as illumined, however tentatively and incompletely, by humankind's pondering of new lands—depths subsequently explored by Hawthorne, Poe, and others. In this respect, of course—in terms of immensity, limitlessness—nothing comes to mind more readily than the works of H. P. Lovecraft, as a fleshing-out in literature of the wonderful and frightening prospect of what was once called the New World.

However much Lovecraft (with all his Toryism and his impassioned cries of "God save the King!") might have cringed at being called a quintessentially *American* writer, I believe that this view is basically correct—not, however, for only the reasons heretofore given.

One notes that Shreffler's characterization is positioned primarily around *spatial* imagery: the notion, for American writers, of the "sheer immensity of their natural landscape." Lovecraft himself suggests much the same when he points out that aside from European literary inheritances, the formative stirrings of American literature had much to do with "the keen spiritual and theological interests of the first colonists, plus the strange and forbidding nature of the scene into which they were plunged. The vast and gloomy virgin forests in whose perpetual twilight all terrors might well lurk; the hordes of coppery Indians whose strange, saturnine visages and violent customs hinted strongly at traces of infernal origin" ("Supernatural Horror in Literature" 60–61). Here, however, with talk of aboriginal races, we have a hint of something more than overwhelming spatial vistas. In colonial America, the problem right away was that Shreffler's "huge blank canvas" was not really blank. The new lands in which the colonists settled had people already there, and those people had a *past*—their *own* past, in which the come-lately colonists had no part—a past rendering the term "New World," from a more synoptic viewpoint, ludicrously ironic.

And here of course we begin to see an especially strong suggestion of thematic bonds between Lovecraft's fiction and the circumstances implicit in the settlement of the so-called New World. What matters here is not just space, but *time:* the depthless yawnings of time suggested by pre-existing races. Shreffler's remarks, quoted above, though mentioning both time and space, come to dwell primarily upon spatial considerations. But Lovecraft's own well-chronicled literary theory expressly evinces an equal or greater concern with time. He says, in a letter: "Time, space, and natural law hold for me suggestions of intolerable bondage, and I can form no picture of emotional satisfaction which does not involve their defeat—especially the defeat of time, so that one may merge oneself with the whole historic stream" (letter to August Derleth, 21 November 1930; *Essential Solitude* 1.288). Elsewhere he remarks: "The reason why *time* plays a great part in so many of my tales is that this element looms up in my mind as the most profoundly dramatic and grimly terrible thing in the universe. *Conflict with time* seems to me the most potent and fruitful theme in all human expression" ("Notes on Writing Weird Fiction," *CE* 2.176).

It is in application of this principle to the situation of settlers in the New World that Lovecraft's fiction most clearly allegorizes something of essence in American literature: in Lovecraft story after story, humankind finds itself facing its terrifying *other:* races of alien creatures with a past of their own, *an abyssal past that excludes the observer* (or threatens to exclude the observer, yet at the same time threatens *not* to).

In fact, it is from a Lovecraft-ghostwritten narrator that we first hear directly of this connection between denizens of the New World and the Lovecraftian concern with time. In "The Mound" we read: "It is only within the last few years that most people have stopped thinking of the West as a *new* land. . . . We think nothing of a Pueblo village 2,500 years old, and it hardly jolts us when archaeologists put the sub-pedigral culture of Mexico back to 17,000 or 18,000 B.C." Arizona is described as "an ancient, lonely land," and the narrator has a sense of "the stupefying—almost horrible—ancientness of the West"[1] (*CF* 4.208). Here it is curious how self-subverting the text is as to what is to be our preponderant response to the West's ancientness; first we hear that "it hardly jolts us" to learn of uncommonly ancient archaeological sites in Mexico, but then we hear that such ancientness is "stupefying—almost horrible." It is as if, in the first quote, "hardly" meant not "scarcely" but rather "in a hard manner," or "harshly," in keeping with the second quote but out of keeping with the fact that "we think nothing" of 2,500-year-old Pueblo villages. The text self-deconstructively opens up a problematised space of relations between antiquity and humankind's response to it, and such enigmatic relations are of course a peculiar thread running through much of Lovecraft's fiction.

But in any case the passage in question serves to underscore the role of aboriginal races, in the New World to which colonial American settlers came—a role connected allegorically to elder races throughout Lovecraft's fictional canon, and a role helping to define the relation between early settlers and the Indians (a people with their own past) as

---

1. In these remarks one could read the term "West" as meaning "New World" generally, i.e., the Western Hemisphere, though in context it would seem more simply to refer to the American West and contiguous lands (northern Mexico), as opposed to the eastern seaboard. And in this sense, the narrator makes a good point; New Englanders, for example, often tend to suppose that early American history is more or less the account of the settlement of New England and the other Colonies, when in fact Francisco Vasquez de Coronado came through New Mexico in 1540—twenty-four years before Shakespeare was born, and eighty years before the landing at Plymouth Rock—laying the groundwork for vast spans of historical development in the American Southwest.

being allegorically connected to the relation, in Lovecraft's fictional world, between humankind and those timeless elder beings with whom they inadvertently cross paths. In both cases, what is at stake is the question of *pasts* and the question of whether one belongs, oneself, to a particular past. The examples, throughout Lovecraft's work, are many and obvious. For example, when Wilmarth and, before him, the hapless Akeley, in "The Whisperer in Darkness," come upon the Winged Ones of the deep woods in Vermont—an immemorial race whose immense past is one in which humankind has no part—the encounter seems to allegorize the historical encounter of the early colonial settlers with the Indians, a people (it gradually came to be known) with an extremely long past stretching back through centuries of cultural development excluding the European newcomers.

But does "The Whisperer in Darkness" allegorize the settlers' meeting the Indians, or does this historical encounter allegorize the Akeley-Wilmarth experience, of coming upon the Winged Ones? After all, the latter encounter, though fictional, is conceptually the larger, the more implicative of the two (in that humankind's discovery of its own non-primacy as a *species* on the planet would dwarf the impact of the colonial settlers' discovery that a red-skinned race of people was already living in North America)—problems abound: questions of directionality, of primariness versus secondariness, of centrality versus marginality. What allegorizes what? It might be suggested that in raising such a question, even in passing, one seems to threaten to allow the tail to wag the proverbial dog; but—given that poststructuralist thought routinely interrogates taken-for-granted relations between the central and the marginal, or subject and object, or cause and effect, or the highly significant and the less significant—who is to say that tails do not in fact wag dogs? Is not the history of European settlement in the New World also "fictional" in the sense of being *narrative,* so that with that history on the one hand and Lovecraft's fictive world on the other, an allegorizing relation of *mutual textual commentary* arises? In a situation where something allegorizes something else, I would claim that there can be no clear-cut, definitive, or settled understanding of direction; if X "allegorizes" Y, or Y "is allegorized by" X, then we may ask: which relation is (in a mathematician's terms) the primary relation and which the inverse relation? Is there not a flow of allegorical connectivity back and forth across such bondings, and is there not a confounding of subject and object, product and source?

So, does the fundamental setting (as we have described it: a terrifying new landscape and, more importantly, timescape) of American literature provide a birthplace for the fiction of H. P. Lovecraft, or does the fiction of H. P. Lovecraft *create*—define, inform—the fundamental setting of American literature? We can scarcely answer such questions by referring to such matters as temporal priority, which, e.g., does not model the traditional notion of literary influence entirely satisfactorily, at least not from the poststructuralist point of view—readers help to create texts by reading, and if a reader perusing Ovid's *Metamorphoses* brings to that text the mental coloring derived from a recent experience reading Kafka, is there not a radicalized sense of the term "influence" in which Kafka "influences" Ovid? (It was Nietzsche—in those aphoristic notebook-jottings that we now call *The Will to Power*—who first deconstructed the temporal-priority notion of cause and effect.)

In any event, it would seem that Shreffler's characterization of Lovecraft as an especially "American" writer may be a plausible characterization for reasons other than the ones ordinarily advanced. The thing, it seems to me, that most dramatically epitomizes the scene of American literature, is the circumstance of encounter between "elder" races (equipped with their *own* long pasts or histories or tradition-streams) and newcomers seeming to have no part in the past of the "elder" races they meet. It is true that in some Lovecraft stories, the past of humankind per se *is* involved, intertwined with the grander prehuman history being unfolded; e.g., in *At the Mountains of Madness* it is suggested, as is well known, that in the heyday of the barrel-shaped Old Ones of Antarctica, certain of their protoplasmic experiments with life forms produced not only the slave-creature shoggoths, but also (as "a jest or mistake") the earliest humans; and a connection is made explicit in "The Mound" as well: the primordial dwellers beneath the mound were our ancestors.

But this connection serves only to weave more complexity into the allegorical image of colonial American settlers and Indians; while the settlers from Europe tried very hard to avoid it, they ultimately had to admit that the copper-skinned denizens of the woods were *human,* and thus that their (the settlers') history was, in some remote and indirect way at least, a thread in the largely unshared history and prehistory of the aborigines. (One notes the efforts of the settlers to Christianize the Indians, an amusing spectacle that persists to this day. The Spanish *conquistadores,* in subduing the Aztecs, are reported to have baptized Indian babies before bashing their brains out—thus postulating, however crassly, a common humanity.)

In the early history of New World exploration as in the fictional world of Lovecraft, the pattern seems to have been one of encountering elder races, finding oneself excluded from the past of those races, yet coming to fear, paradoxically, that perhaps the exclusion is not total as one might have thought. The relation is thus one of ambiguity and ambivalence; in Lovecraft's world, the "newcomers" (i.e., humankind) are both shocked to find that the newly discovered time-vistas (stretching backward, theretofore unexpected) are a culture-stream that does not seem to include them, and yet shocked also to find that such vistas *may* in some sardonic fashion include them after all. It galled the *conquistadores* that the Indians (present on the land since time out of mind) were human; it horrifies Lovecraft's humanity that it has commonalities with the elder races; and in both cases, while the elder races' past in effect swallows up that of the newcomers, a certain principle of exclusion still operates—the elder races were here first, the land is not really ours.

This bristling bundle of allegorical connections—though problematized, complex, contradictory, indeterminate even as to direction—would seem to suggest more than just that Lovecraft is a writer having, as Shreffler has said, "a peculiarly American character." Thematically, the Lovecraftian fictional world and the "text" of European settlement in America would seem to be pre-inscriptions of each other; each is the trace of the other, always already being written. H. P. Lovecraft's fiction in its own way may just have done as much as that of Poe or Hawthorne or Melville to begin to suggest a thematic shape for that sprawling web of tenebrous matter that we call American literature: a literature notoriously dark, a literature of orphans, a literature forever driven by anxiety about the past.

Lovecraft and Adjectivitis: A Deconstructionist View

One of the most oft-repeated negative criticisms of H. P. Lovecraft's fiction is that his prose style suffers from "adjectivitis," which presumably—but, as we shall see, not unproblematically—means a tendency to sprout adjectives needlessly. This notion raises a number of difficult questions.

With his well-known diatribe against Lovecraft's stylistics, Edmund Wilson raises the issue of adjectivitis early on, arguing that one of Lovecraft's "worst faults" is the tendency toward "sprinkling his stories with such adjectives as 'horrible,' 'terrible,' 'frightful,' 'awesome,' 'eerie,' 'weird,' 'forbidden,' 'unhallowed,' 'unholy,' 'blasphemous,' 'hellish,' and 'infernal.' Surely one of the primary rules for writing an effective tale of horror is never to use any of these words—especially if you are going, at the end, to produce an invisible whistling octopus" ("Tales of the Marvellous and the Ridiculous" [1945], in Joshi, *H. P. Lovecraft: Four Decades of Criticism* 48). This last clause, presumably designed to poke fun at Lovecraft's fictional horrors (which Wilson characterizes as unconvincing), weakens what otherwise would be an argument with a certain trace of validity to it; in the end Wilson seems merely to suggest that if one's fictional horrors were more convincing than Lovecraft's, one might after all be justified in employing the adjectives cited, whereas the argument might have been that whatever the ultimate horror of a story, adjectives like "horrible" and "frightful" break the old rule that a writer should show rather than tell—that the writer's job is to *make* the story scary without telling the reader than it's supposed to be.

This much Lin Carter reiterates: "Rather than creating in the reader a mood of terror, Lovecraft *describes* a mood of terror; the emotion is applied in the adjectives" (*Lovecraft: A Look Behind the Cthulhu Mythos*

21). Referring to Lovecraft's story "The Nameless City," Carter cites as an example the description of the ruins' antiquity, in that tale, as "unwholesome," and adds: "Of course, if you stop to think about it, such terms are meaningless. A stone is a stone, a valley is a valley, and ruins are merely ruins" (*Lovecraft: A Look Behind the Cthulhu Mythos* 21). While again there is a certain residuum of truth in this argument, there are also serious problems with it. Even from traditional critical standpoints one could respond, with reference to Carter's example, that (1) the adjective "unwholesome" is not merely a descriptor but an eloquent indicator of perception and feeling on the part of the first-person narrator, and (2) that "unwholesome" is a literarily effective and significant modifier of "antiquity" precisely *because* antiquity as such is not normally regarded as unwholesome. Here the characteristic reversals of deconstructive thinking begin to emerge, and, as it turns out, there is a great deal more to the matter than one might suppose.

In the first place, there is something peculiar in the way adjectives work—something paradoxical, in fact, in the whole notion of grammatical "modifying." In terms of the production of meaning by linguistic signifiers, what really happens when an adjective modifies a noun? Presumably, when the adjective arrives on the scene as a signifier, it brings with it the potential for producing meaning *beyond* that which the noun alone could produce, whatever its own plurisignificational possibilities (and these are generally considerable). But, in a way, the very opposite is true: in modifying a noun, an adjective narrows rather than broadens the semantic field at hand.

The signifier "cat" points (in one of its many directionalities) to a certain class of signifieds, indicators of a certain class of referents. With the addition of, say, the adjective "black," the phrase "black cat" now refers to a substantially diminished subclass of referents. (Indeed, with the right adjective, while still having some signifieds—ideas to which the signifiers point—one may end up with no referents at all; see, e.g., what happens with "Milton-quoting cat" or "twenty-ton cat.") In one sense, the effect of introducing an adjective is to narrow the field of signification that the noun alone would have commanded. Yet one also regards the production of meaning as enlarged by the adjective's effect; if one is asked to be on the lookout for a lost cat and subsequently is told, "By the way, the cat we're looking for is black," one's response is: "Ah, now I know more about the matter than I did before" (i.e., "Now I know more about what is meant by this signifier 'cat' that refers to the lost animal"). In the strange realm of production of meaning by signifiers, more is not *simply* more, and less is not simply less. Does "black cat" mean more or less than "cat" does? Or, in the case of Lovecraft's prose, does "unwholesome antiquity"[1] mean more or less than "antiquity"?

The question comes down to one of specificity versus generality, a bipolarity over which the notion of meaning is self-deconstructing. An unmodified noun has a broad field of signification characterized by generality; when this same noun (but is it really still the "same" noun?) is joined by a modifying adjective, the resulting phrase has a narrowed field of signification characterized by specificity. Yet, as we have noted, in some respects specificity has the effect of extending meaning, while generality has the effect of restricting meaning. On the one hand "cat" means much while "black cat" means less; on the other hand, "cat" is vague enough to have little meaning (to someone asked to search for a lost cat), while "black cat" is specific enough to mean more. Classical binary logic will not suffice here; a noun modified by an adjective means both more *and* less than an unmodified noun. In an uncanny way, when Lin Carter remarks that "unwholesome" in "unwholesome antiquity" is meaningless, the remark has an oblique sort of validity—such an adjective is meaning-loose: indeterminate as to the extent and the manner of its enhancement of, or other effects upon, textual meaning.

The very etymology of the word *adjective* prefigures this meaning-looseness. The word's Indo-European root (for *-ject-*) is *ie-* or *ye-*, "to throw," "to cast down"; this root produces the Latin *jacere*, "to throw," and its frequentative *jactare*, "to toss to and fro," "to waver" (of opinions)—an etymological adumbration of the oscillations to which we have alluded. Further, the root *ie-* is responsible for both the word *gist*

---

1. For convenience, we use the expression here as a simple noun phrase; the passage in question actually employs a predicate adjective: "The antiquity of the spot was unwholesome." See HPL, "The Nameless City" (*CF* 1.233). Note that the expression "noun phrase" privileges nouns over other grammatical entities that may belong to such a phrase; as we have been in the process of seeing, this privilege is specious.

(suggesting central essence) and the word *adjacent* (suggesting peripherality), and this mutually antithetical pair of derivatives allegorizes another indeterminacy—that of centrality versus marginality. Are adjectives grammatically and syntactically central or marginal? The word *adjective* itself is, directly, an elliptical reflection of the phrase *adjectivum verbum,* "added word," a characterization which positions the adjective as something supplementary or extra, something added to a noun; by this schema, while a noun is central and essential, an adjective is peripheral and auxiliary. But is it? In the supposedly adjectivitis-ridden prose of H. P. Lovecraft one finds reason to wonder.[2]

With regard to such Lovecraftian configurations as "unwholesome antiquity," one notices that with critical charges of adjectivitis, the very criticism that brings these charges also works to focus attention on adjectives—to centralize them and to marginalize the nouns that they modify. But such adjectives are quite capable of focusing central attention on themselves. In "unwholesome antiquity," there is nothing remarkable about antiquity—the whole universe is, after all, old—but there *is* something remarkable about its (antiquity's) being described as unwholesome, precisely because (in the prosaic backdrop of common understanding, at least) antiquity *cannot* be unwholesome. The very narrative and literary force of the adjective resides in its defying the impossibility of its own application in the context where the Lovecraft text applies it. Much the same is true of such phrases as "horrible shadows," "unfriendly sky," "diseased abysses," "monstrous overnour-

---

2. It is curious that in the derivation of *adjective* from the Latin *adjectivum verbum,* the noun *adjective,* though a noun, actually derives from an adjective. The same etymological roots (Indo-European *ie-*, Latin *jacere*) give rise to such other words as the nouns *subject* and *object,* and one would think the similarly derived noun in question here should have been *adject,* with the form *adjective* reserved for being an adjective in the same way that *subjective* and *objective* are; instead, to get an adjective from *adjective* we have to go to the form *adjectival.* This strange circumstance further allegorizes the problematical relation between the status of nouns and the status of adjectives in literary language. It is interesting to note, further, with regard to the pejorative "adjectivitis," that the ending *-itis,* meaning "inflammation," is commonly attached to nouns standing for things regarded (in the absence of inflammation) as healthy, as in the case of *laryngitis;* a larynx is ordinarily a normal presence, and so, one may say, is an adjective. On the other hand, if "adjectivitis" means "proliferation of adjectives," one wonders what "laryngitis" means.

ished oaks," "mad spaces between the stars," "trees of unholy size," "vegetation unnaturally thick and feverish," and numerous other examples in Lovecraft's fiction.[3] These adjectives are powerfully effective *because* they do not literally apply to the nouns that they modify. They are striking because they are creatively misapplied; because they are "wrong," they are eminently right.

In many cases, in fact, they bespeak mental states, on the part of fictional characters, that represent thematic concerns in the fiction. A character *feels* that vegetation is "feverish" or that the size of trees is "unholy" or—especially—that antiquity is "unwholesome" and interstellar space "mad," and this narrative impressionism reveals not only the literary propriety of such adjectives' use but also the broad thematic concerns that prompt such character reactions. To feel that certain signs of antiquity are "unwholesome" is to face that old Lovecraftian thematic trauma that mocks humankind: the realization of one's vanishingly small and insignificant place in the cosmos. Simply to reject "unwholesome antiquity" as overwrought prose is to fail to read Lovecraft in the light of such thematic concerns.

In any case the whole question of the stylistic propriety of such adjective-heavy prose style is perturbed and problematized by the difficulties we have noted: that one cannot simply characterize adjectives as either peripheral or central, because they are both; that one cannot simply decide whether adjectives enlarge or restrict meaning, because they do both simultaneously. It is perhaps significant that the Indo-European root *ie-* responsible for *adjective* also gives rise to the word *jest*—which is not to say that Lovecraft's adjectives reflect any tongue-in-cheek agenda in terms of some authorial intent (which intent would be, after all, irretrievable), but rather that language is always inherently and irrepressibly ludic, and that in Lovecraft's colorful and sometimes seemingly outrageous adjectives, language has found a particularly striking way of scintillating with this uncontainable verve.

---

3. In any case, as S. T. Joshi has pointed out, such prose styles come and go on the stage of reader popularity and are not "good" or "bad" in any intrinsic or permanent way; see Joshi, "Lovecraft Criticism: A Study," in *H. P. Lovecraft: Four Decades of Criticism* 21.

Lovecraft and Chaos

One has to wonder what H. P. Lovecraft, whose fiction thematically celebrates chaos on a cosmic scale, would have thought of the modern mathematical theory of chaos. Lovecraft's disinclination toward mathematics is well known, and it is unlikely that he would have had a great appetite for delving into a textbook rigorously exploring the mathematical world of chaos theory. But in a number of ways its piquant paradoxes tend to parallel those self-deconstructive paradoxes that appear upon a careful look at Lovecraft's fictional worldview.

In mathematics, chaos theory emerges as a peculiar product of the study of nonlinear dynamical systems: mathematical systems in which we start with some functional definition, feed a starting-value into it, get an output, feed that result back into the function as input, and so on indefinitely, in such a way that peculiar suggestions of pattern eventually appear where there would have been no reason to suppose any existed. It is typical of such systems that small changes in the initial conditions may lead to spectacular changes farther along (Ray Bradbury explored this idea many years ago in the story "A Sound of Thunder"), and such systems can be wholly predictable (chaos-free) only if the initial conditions can be specified with infinite precision. (The applications of the theory are many, and include fluid dynamics, marketing, and genetics.) There are two "schools" of chaos: what one may call respectively the order-out-of-chaos school and the orderly-descent-into-chaos school; the first stresses chaos as characterized by subtle order in disorder, the second stresses chaos as disorder in apparent order. The two schools, though having common interests, use different language and different methods, and sometimes find it difficult to communicate with each other.

But the point here is that the term chaos is a highly problematized one, from whatever viewpoint one wishes. "Chaos" in its mathematical context(s) does not simply mean "disorder" or "randomness," but rather suggests, in the supposedly stable opposition between order and disorder, a third term which unsettles and displaces the original terms of the opposition. Chaos as a concept can be entirely absorbed neither into the notion of order nor into the notion of disorder, being both and/or neither, a sort of paradoxically predictable unpredictability.

Anyone familiar with deconstruction in philosophy and in the theory of criticism will quickly realize that deconstruction and dynamical-systemic chaos have a great deal in common. (The similarities between poststructuralism and mathematical chaos have been ably explored by N. Katherine Hayles, of the University of Iowa, in her book *Chaos Bound: Orderly Disorder in Contemporary Literature and Science.*) Indeed, the trace of which poststructuralist theory speaks is in essence mirrored in and by the mathematical notion of chaos.

The deconstructive trace operates in a way that can be illustrated by citing the Lovecraftian thematic opposition between a human-centered universe and a universe indifferent to the presence of humankind. As is well known, Lovecraft's fiction argues thematically for an indifferent universe, a cosmos utterly uncaring toward humankind; but one may point out that the gesture of postulating such a universe is self-deconstructing, in that one's language anthropomorphizes or personifies the universe anew when trying hardest to do the opposite: when attributing to the universe that supremely human quality, indifference.

The problem is not that Lovecraft's thematic concerns lack a consistency that they could have had; the problem, rather, is that classical binary logic itself collapses (or shows itself to have been language-dependent, a product of rhetoric, to begin with) when it tries to hold the poles of the caring-versus-indifferent opposition apart. "Indifference," one of the supposedly stable poles, contains—as its very condition of possibility—the trace of what is supposed to be its opposite, in that one cannot speak of an uncaring universe without positing the notion of caring; in the absence of the very idea of caring, there could be no notion of indifference. Conversely, the notion of a universe that in some sense "cares" about humankind can scarcely be meaningfully entertained without the lurking-about of the trace again, this time the trace, in the notion of caring, of the supposedly opposite possibility that a universe that "cared" might conceivably not have; without the possibility (or threat) of indifference—i.e., in a schema in which the cosmos must have cared—"caring" would be trivialized and rendered meaningless by its very necessity, its very lack of an opposite trace. Each half of the opposition differs internally from itself.

In mathematical chaos one sees the same sorts of concerns. Chaos has to do with order and disorder, operating, in effect, as a "trace" that collapses the imagined binary opposition between the two. Obviously, the notion of "order" is meaningless unless the term contains, covertly, the trace of disorder (otherwise, what distinction does "order" have?), and conversely one cannot understand the notion of "disorder" without at some point thinking of it as disarranging something that should have been "order," so that between the two terms floats the deconstructive trace, the third term irreducible either to "order" or "disorder" alone. (Mathematicians now speak of the "deep structure" of chaos, simultaneously crediting both notions, order and disorder, in characterizing it.)

Thus when Lovecraft, for example, in "The Whisperer in Darkness," lets his narrator reflect, "I started with loathing when told of the monstrous nuclear chaos beyond angled space which the 'Necronomicon' had mercifully cloaked under the name of Azathoth" (*CF* 2.521), the presence of the term chaos in the text raises a number of problems, problems that in fact permeate the canon of Lovecraft's fiction. What does "chaos" mean?

What, especially, is nuclear chaos? (One could transmute "nuclear" into "unclear" and not be unfaithful to the spirit of the thing.) "Nuclear" suggests focus, centrality, and symmetry—and these things bespeak a high order of structure. But given, in the text, that this "nuclear chaos" lies "beyond angled space," we may well think of this structure as the sort of deep structure to which chaoticians refer: a structure paradoxically unsettling any superficial notion of structure, a kind of deeper making-of-sense that denies the sense we would have liked to make of the cosmos. Lovecraft's "nuclear chaos" is, after all, "monstrous" from the human standpoint; it is system-making (our Nietzschean will to power, our rage to make sense of things) systematically desystematized, dismantled. It is a revocation of our license to practice law and order; or rather, it is the revelation that that license, like a prize in a cereal box, has never had any validity. This revelation, we read, is "mercifully cloaked" under a name: metonymically displaced, shifted, hidden.

Yet nothing is quite that simple—the matter of Lovecraft's thematic stance is still no more or less complex than the troubling notion of chaos itself. Just as chaos involves both order and disorder, Lovecraft's universe is describable only by reference both to caring and indifference, teleology and purposelessness, because of the trace which inhabits and perturbs the supposedly separable poles of such oppositions. And here we may bring in another connection.

Noël Carroll recently discussed (in *The Philosophy of Horror; or, Paradoxes of the Heart*) the notion that horror derives from "category mistakes," from the impossibility of consigning some things to hard-and-fast Aristotelian categories. Real horror dwells in the crevices between categories. (We could say that a splendid example is to be found in the partly human, partly aquatic creatures of Lovecraft's "The Shadow over Innsmouth," in that they are horrible precisely because they are hybrid, neither proper humans nor proper sea-denizens.) This notion of the "interstitial" or category-denying nature of horror immediately suggests that Lovecraft's universe itself is, as a big category mistake, an all-encompassing horror: neither capable of being indifferent to humankind unless human compassion is taken into account, nor capable of being compassionate without the unsettling deconstructive trace of indifference.

But in this respect Lovecraft's universe intriguingly mirrors the mathematical notion of chaos, which itself is describable only in such paradoxically deconstructive terms. Chaos inhabits a twilight-realm (a crevice) somewhere between order and disorder, and Lovecraft's universe, inhabiting such a twilight-crevice itself, is assuredly "chaotic" in the most modern and most delectably mysterious sense of the term.

Mathematical chaoticians speak of "strange attractors": unaccountable regions or "pockets" of locally ordered behavior appearing like uncanny islands of order in a sea of disorder. Perhaps human consciousness itself, in Lovecraft's world, is a kind of strange attractor that has formed in the cosmic swirl: a lonely isle of local coherence that both enlivens the need to see the cosmos as purposeful and yet characterizes it as uncaring once again. We must ask: which is more important, that the activity in a strange attractor is locally suggestive of order, or that this island of apparent order is exceptional, rendering the surrounding system all the more senseless? Are we a meaningful part of the cosmos or not? Given the nature of chaos, perhaps the answer must be: both and neither. If so, it may be an unsatisfying answer, but then such is life in a chaotic Lovecraftian universe, where even the logic of our desire to have questions answered "yes" or "no" may be order or the illusion of it. Or both, or neither.

Lovecraft and Interstitiality

In her study *Purity and Danger,* anthropologist Mary Douglas discusses the manner in which things perceived as "impure" or repulsive may be characterized as transgressions of culturally determined categories. She gives the interesting example of a primitive tribe that regards the flying squirrel with horror because it violates the culture's expected categorizations; the creature is not a proper flying animal because it does not have two feet like a bird, yet it is not a proper four-legged land-rover because it flies—consequently, it becomes, for these people, an object to be shunned. (To some extent, of course, what constitutes horror is a matter of reacting to specialized cultural constructs, such as the mental categories that one's culture sees as compelling; one starts from one's own particular cultural perspective.) In his study *The Philosophy of Horror; or, Paradoxes of the Heart* (31–35), Noël Carroll takes up this notion of impurity and applies it to the theory of horror, or at least to that aspect of horror fiction (and film) concerned with monsters. (It may be objected that not all horror deals in monsters, but one may say that in any case Carroll's discussion of what constitutes monstrousness does generally apply and will prove useful to pursue here.)

Carroll's analysis of horror argues that our fascination with horror involves at least two perceptions or responses: fear together with repugnance or loathing. He further argues that we neither fall under the illusion that fictional horrors are real, nor merely pretend to be frightened and disturbed—rather, even knowing that fictional horrors are not actual, we are—optimally, in response to a successful horror story—genuinely frightened and disturbed by the thought of the horror. And here perhaps we may observe that with this view of horror-response, Carroll finds the Mary Douglas notion of impurity readily and naturally applicable to his own theory of horror fiction—for if our reactions to horror reside in assessments of our own thoughts (rather than, e.g., reaction to some monster that we make ourselves really believe in, or rather than our merely pretending to be disturbed), and if our own thoughts are characteristically given to categorical thinking, then it is not an unnatural connection for Carroll to make when he suggests that in horror fiction, the monster (or, let us say, more inclusively, the monstrousness) to which we react is essentially and typically a sort of category mistake, something that is interstitial, something that falls into the crevices between the categories that we attempt to establish as cultural constructs. And in Western thought our proclivity for such categorizing is well known; exhibiting an inbred Nietzschean will to power, we possess and are possessed by—from our classical Greek philosophical forebears onward, for better or worse—a rage for categorization, for chopping the world up into neat little pigeonholes with which we can control it, or control our understanding of it. We do not escape from this metaphysical structuring even when we most criticize it. Also, though one might think, with respect to the whole problem of things' becoming interstitial and slipping into the crevices between categories, that one could sidestep the problem by becoming even more avid at categorization and making new categories out of the crevices, one quickly notices that such a ploy only exacerbates the problem; where there are categories A and B, if one makes a new category X out of the crevice—assuming there to be only one such—between A and B, now one has crevices between A and X and between X and B, at least. More categorization only multiplies the possibilities.

And in poststructuralist thought, which seeks to challenge and perturb such categorical thinking, we may well find a new fascination in the fact that while horror resides in the failure of categorizability, this failure or instability looms as a possibility at every turn—we have not only the difficulty that things sometimes resist being neatly tucked away into categories, but also the difficulty that categories themselves tend, with deconstructive thinking, to waver, to flicker in and out of existence, to blur their boundaries and problematize themselves, showing themselves to be more figural constructs of language than "real" metaphysical entities and thus showing themselves to partake of all the teasing indeterminacy of the web of language in which they find themselves woven. I propose this: that to the extent that one credits the Douglas notion of impurity as categorical violation, and the related

Carroll view of monstrousness as the production of category mistakes (and I must say I find these characterizations attractive), then—given, in the poststructuralist view, the problematical and shifting nature of categories to begin with—the result is that the world (the "real" world, any fictional world) is more redolent of the potential for horror than has previously been thought. Horror lurks in our inability to categorize fully and satisfactorily, and we find the world awash with elusive and shimmering linguistic images of categories that themselves further subvert our passion for forcing things into those categories—which is to say, the potential for horror is ever closer at hand than one might think, ready to blossom forth. In a fictional setting, of course, the manner in which (and intensity with which) this shifting and moiling potential may be worked out will vary from one context to another.

It is my purpose here to suggest that in H. P. Lovecraft's fictional universe, the interstitial potential for horror is particularly outstanding. A truly exhaustive search of the Lovecraft canon, identifying evidence of the interstitiality of Lovecraft's fictional creations in all his texts, would of course require many hundreds of pages and indeed could never really be finished. It will suffice here to explore some especially compelling examples, both in terms of specific fictional devices in some of the stories and in terms, more generally, of Lovecraft's major thematic concerns as they permeate his field of texts.

We may well start with "The Outsider," a tale in whose very title the specter of problematized and problematizing categories may be seen to emerge, in that we are immediately aware of a looming dispute between insideness and outsideness. These categories themselves present difficulties as to their very integrity, being matters of perspective; what is "outside" a given context from one viewpoint is "inside" that context from another viewpoint. (Draw a circle on a sheet of paper, lay the paper flat on the table, and suspend a coin on a string an inch above the center of the circle. Viewed from above, the coin is "in" the circle; viewed from an appropriate spot to the side, the coin is outside, and indeed the circle is no longer a circle but an ellipse.) These categories—species of spatial metaphor—make for eternally oscillating contexts for the Outsider as she attempts[1] to define her place in the scheme of things.

The Outsider of course has the crux of her problem from the outset in being inside—imprisoned within the ancestral chambers up whose frightful tower she resolves to climb to the outside. When she is outside, on her way to the brightly lighted castle, she is anticipatory, free, close to happiness; in conventional spatial terms it is only now that she is the Outsider, and only as (in this sense) outsider is she free, whereas we have been encouraged to think of her "outsideness" as a source of misery, which indeed it is, when we honor other senses of the notion "outside." Back inside, spatially, when she enters the gaily lighted ballroom, she again assumes a mantle of darkness and horror. (Here she is an insider, and the "merry company," who become a "herd of delirious fugitives," are now the outsiders in spatial terms.) It is clear that a "literal" view of insideness/outsideness (the question of being inside or outside physical enclosures) has its problems. Other notions of insideness/outsideness are of course spatial metaphor whose metaphoricity we run the risk of forgetting; but in any case such other notions have their problems, too.

The seemingly most natural sense in which the Outsider is an outsider is that in which we see her (and in which she sees herself) as outside the fold, as it were—outside the comfortable confines of proper humanity. Yet her form before the mirror is a "travesty on the human shape" (*CF* 1.271), and in her corruption we surely see, the fleeing revelers surely see, what we must all come to in the dissolution of the grave: she is a synecdochical figure—she is humankind, she is ourselves. But then she is within the defining borders of humankind; if she is an outsider, then (to the extent that we credit the notion that she is metonymy for ourselves) so are we all. This state of affairs of course problematizes our categories; how can we all be "outside"? Outside of what, then? Outside of some idealized notion of human existence in

1. My wife, Mollie L. Burleson, has argued (see "The Outsider: A Woman?") that the first-person Outsider, theretofore always assumed to be a man, is more likely a woman—that she is even a thematic allegory of woman as outsider. I find the argument cogent; certainly it is not possible to prove the Outsider to be male in any case. I shall employ the feminine pronoun.

which we might live shielded from the awareness of our carrion-tending mortality? Possibly; but then who or what is inside such a category? Or if we are all inside the category of humankind-as-potential-carrion, what does the outside of that category mean? Is an empty "category" still a category in any meaningful sense? We have difficulties so long as we see the Outsider as being simply inside or outside a category, especially when the available categories themselves shift and feint with us; we find no clear boundaries to such categories as "proper humankind" and "humankind as dead meat"—such categories are, as categories tend to be, linguistic constructs.

But the Outsider is a real horror to the extent that she refuses to be categorizable in any such facile manner even supposing the categories to be stable. She is, in effect, a sort of zombie—not a proper human being because of her "bone-revealing outlines" (*CF* 1.271), not a proper corpse because of her insisting on walking about and being conscious. What she sees of herself in the mirror is "not of this world" (*CF* 1.271), because even in her own mind to be "of this world" is to belong to one cultural category or another: living or dead, conscious or beyond consciousness. She is both, and neither; she is interstitial, a crevice-dwelling category mistake whom the mirror reflects in all her thus undefinable horror. (Again, we do not escape by trying to multiply categories. If, e.g., we think of such zombie-like beings as the Outsider as constituting a category unto themselves, we create new crevices, and the Outsider herself may even slip into these new abysms from time to time—in being as articulate of mind as the narration of the tale suggests, for example, she tends to slide into the crevice opening up between the zombie-category and the category of "normal" humanity. Indeed, it is her narrative articulateness, the flow of her thoughts, that makes her truly horrible; what more tragic property could a pile of rotting flesh have than the ability to be reflective and expressive?) And the whole problem of the Outsider heightens in complexity when one further recognizes that, aside from the difficulty of locating her in one or another supposedly stable category, one has the difficulty that the categories "inside" and "outside," as poles of an opposition, are unstable to begin with; each contains a trace of the other as an enabling condition, in that one cannot conceive of externality without internality, or conversely, so that each aspect of the bipolarity inside/outside differs with itself. The very quality of being an outsider smacks of a certain trace of internality; one cannot be "out" without, from some perspective, also being "in." The Outsider then becomes an aporetic figure, an eternally oscillatory being, a vagabond-wraith not only wandering the night, but also wandering a wavering labyrinth of failed aspirations to categorization.

Lovecraft's fiction thrives upon such horrifically uncategorizable entities, even at times pondering aloud the notion of horror-as-category-mistake. In "The Festival," when the narrator follows his townspeople in their descent into the bowels of the earth beneath the central church and sees the "horde of tame, trained, hybrid winged things that so sound eye could ever wholly grasp, or sound brain ever wholly remember," the key word is hybrid. He dwells upon the point: "They were not altogether crows, nor moles, nor buzzards, nor ants, nor vampire bats, nor decomposed human beings; but something I cannot and must not recall" (*CF* 1.414). The language here raises all sort of interesting problems.

First, it is clear that interstitiality is really the source of the horror here; one can scarcely imagine the narrator's being quite this disturbed, had the creatures emerging from the cavernous dark possessed "altogether" any one of the categorical descriptions given—had they been merely moles, or merely ants, or whatever, unalloyed, then they would scarcely have been the mind-numbing monstrosities they evidently were. It is their hybrid nature that unsettles the narrator's wits. (Hybridity as such is expressly a widely notable concern in Lovecraft's fiction; listen, for example, to the narrator of "Under the Pyramids" when he broods: "*Hippopotami should not have human hands and carry torches . . . men should not have the heads of crocodiles*" [*CF* 1.446; emphasis in original].) And it is dizzying to contemplate the implications of what the narrator of "The Festival" says about a sound eye's being unable to grasp, or a sound brain's being unable to remember, the impact of such hybrid horrors; in effect, the text is saying that we are so deeply dependent upon the integrity of our cultural categories, so dependent upon seeing the world as divided up into the sorts of pigeonholes we devise, that we cannot even clearly register a radically interstitial perception. Yet of course the text sports with us here, in that it purports to present to us, through its veiled descriptions, just such a hybrid perception as that which it says cannot be registered; it says, in effect: try to read me if you can, but the very reading will imply, paradoxically, that you cannot. Of this text we must say, then, that like the horrific book described by "Poe's German authority" as mentioned in "The Horror at Red Hook," "es lasst sich nicht lesen" (*CF* 1.483).

Even the final words of "The Festival," a quotation from the *Necronomicon,* will be seen to reinforce this pervasive concern with horrific failure of categorical integrity: "Great holes secretly are digged where earth's pores ought to suffice, and things have learnt to walk that ought to crawl" (*CF* 1.417). Here we have, in the statement that things "that ought to crawl" may have learned to walk, the notion of invasion of one category by the supposed occupants of another. If categories are defined by their contents, then surely categorical borders are blurred when contents of one supposedly fixed category drift into the supposedly well-defined interior of another. Perhaps a biographical-minded reader familiar with Lovecraft might even see, in this statement, a sort of allegory of xenophobia: things have moved into the neighborhood that ought to have stayed down where they were. However that may be, the story's final words are redolent of violence to the notion of categorical fixity.

Indeed, this notion of horror as residing in the melting of categorical contents into each other, by the blurring of boundaries of definition, is one rather prominent in Lovecraft. See, for another example, the narrator's ordeal in the climax of "The Shunned House," where in the uncle's liquefaction the narrator sees his relative becoming "at once a devil and a multitude, a charnel-house and a pageant" and showing in its dissolving face "a dozen—a score—a hundred—aspects" (*CF* 1.476), a churning turmoil admixing the faces of the ill-fated Harris line, until at the end "it seemed as though the shifting features fought against themselves, and strove to form contours like those of my uncle's kindly face" (*CF* 1.476). Here we have a veritable epitome of endangered categorical definition; the very integrity of the individual human form is perturbed, subverted, displaced—not only do the Harris faces (by and large, people originally similar to one another and thus not wholly odd in combination) coalesce in the moiling shape in the cellar, but the uncle's face—not a Harris face—emerges among the rest, calling into question not only the very cellular integrity normally separating one Shunned House resident from another, but even the distinction between themselves and outsiders. We could have no more eloquent statement of the horrific nature of category failure.

This imagery of dissolution finds another, if different, expression in "The Colour out of Space," where the strange external influence arriving with the meteor not only raises obvious questions of what happens when the category "extraterrestrial" confronts the category "terrestrial," but also works, throughout the tale and in insidious stages, to confound terrestrial categories, bringing down definitional borders that one in ordinary human terms would have thought unassailable. The creeping blight, the "grey brittle death" (*CF* 2.390) spreading through the soil from the meteor, attacks first the vegetation, then the farm animals, and finally the Gardner family itself. The vegetation "was fast crumbling to a greyish powder" (*CF* 2.381), and of the cattle we are told that the "swine began growing grey and brittle and falling to pieces before they died" (*CF* 2.382); and when the subnarrator Ammi Pierce enters Mrs. Gardner's attic confinement and sees the poor woman in her late stage of dissolution, we hear of her as a "blasphemous monstrosity . . . which all too clearly had shared the nameless fate of . . . the livestock," and we are told that "the terrible thing about this horror was that it very slowly and perceptibly moved as it continued to crumble" (*CF* 2.385). The first-person narrator sees the end result of all this corruption, of course, before he hears the tale from Ammi, and notes, on the Blasted Heath, "only a fine grey dust or ash" (*CF* 2.369), so that the effect has been to break down all boundaries, all integrity of definition separating plants, cattle, and people. Somehow this fictional configuration seems a great deal more potent in its horrific effect than would have been, e.g., a similar story involving dissolution of the people only; vegetation, farm animals, and farm family members alike have become category-problematics here, in merging so unthinkably with each other and ending up undifferentiated in the swirling grey ash of the Heath.

Clearly, this whole problem of categories and categorizability finds further, and especially striking, articulation in "The Dunwich Horror," with the account of Wilbur Whateley and his twin brother. Here again we have the motif of hybridity, a fictional concern much in evidence in Lovecraftian texts as we have noted. The Whateley twins, of course, are partly human (from their mother Lavinia) and partly nonhuman (from their having been sired by Yog-Sothoth). The description of Wilbur as he lies dying in the Miskatonic library makes his hybrid nature clear enough: "It was partly human, beyond a doubt, with very man-like hands and head, and the goatish, chinless face had the stamp of the Whateleys upon it. But the torso and lower parts of the body were teratologically fabulous" (*CF* 2.439).

Wilbur himself ponders the proportions of his and the brother's mixed parentage in his diary, when he speculates, of the coming time when the earth would be cleared off: "The other face [referring to the brother's partly human face] may wear off some. I wonder how I shall look . . . He that came with the Aklo Sabaoth said I may be transfigured, there being much of outside to work on" (*CF* 2.451). Ironically, from a human standpoint, it is evidently the human side of the mixed genetic structure that Wilbur is ashamed of. In the end, when Curtis Whateley views the fleetingly visible twin brother through the telescope, he gives further expression to the concern of hybridness in seeing in the entity "that haff face on top of it . . . that face with the red eyes an' crinkly albino hair, an' no chin, like the Whateleys. . . . It was a octopus, centipede, spider kind o' thing" (*CF* 2.465). Clearly, it is the interstitial nature of this creature, and of Wilbur, that makes for horror. The weakest kind of horror here would have been (e.g.) for Curtis to see merely an octopus-kind-of-thing on the mountain; an enhancement would have been for him to see merely an "octopus, centipede, spider kind o' thing" in what Mary Douglas would call an impurity-generating category violation but without the human aspect; the strongest horror is of course all this together with the human face. Wilbur and his brother are walking category mistakes; they are, needless to say, not proper human beings (the brother is not even close), yet they are not proper "outer beings" either, having human features that they are even expressly ashamed to bear.

But we should also note, here, that there are problems even with the categories human/non-human in terms of sources of horror-response. In the story's opening descriptions of Dunwich as a squalid place with a sordid and inbred populace, we see that quite a lot of horror resides in the human side of the opposition; horror does not come from the outside influence alone. Conversely, how entirely preterhuman can the outside influence be, if it is capable of siring a child in coital union with Lavinia? Even rather closely related animal species are often incapable of producing offspring; this is, of course, a problem in general with literary accounts of such matings—in, e.g., stories of the Greek gods' sexual unions with human women, producing demigods, we must wonder whether the gods do not by implication have more commonality with humankind than is often supposed. It is not without significance that the gods—see Goya's *Il Saturno,* for example—are often portrayed in anthropomorphic terms. In any case, the commonly assumed integrity of categories is seriously questioned here.

Such perturbing and interrogating of categorical integrity occurs in even stronger form in "The Thing on the Doorstep," where the text unsettles and displaces not only such categorizations as male/female and presence/absence, but also perhaps the most fundamentally cherished category of all: the identity of the self. Arguably, the common notion of the autonomous self, the supposedly well-defined and unitary "I" with which one tends to equate oneself, may well in the end be more a linguistic construct than anything else; nevertheless, even as the illusion of a stable category (oneself as opposed to everything and everyone else) it permeates not only the thinking of the reader, but presumably the thinking of the story's characters as well, and is thus a categorical device whose displacement is extremely effective in narrative terms; indeed, the resulting horror in this well-wrought tale is unforgettably potent.

The horror here centers around the notion of a mind's being able to inhabit a body other than the one to which it has been born. The problem, for purportedly stable categories, is obvious: if the mind of X inhabits the body of Y, displacing Y's own mind, then who or what is it that appears to be Y walking among us? Clearly, a body inhabited by an invading mind is an interstitial being, a category mistake. In particular, in this tale, Edward Derby's body at times is taken over by his wife Asenath's mind, whereupon Edward's own mind is imprisoned in Asenath's body so that the "mental Asenath" can run about in Edward's form. One of several concerns is: would the being to whom Edward is married be called a man or a woman, if it has a woman's body but a man's mind? But the problem is a great deal more intriguing than that, because from the outset there are at least two added complications.

The first of these is that the original Asenath, daughter of Ephraim Waite of Innsmouth, was the product of Ephraim (himself a shadowy figure as to origins and nature, though presumably human) and "an unknown wife who always went veiled" (*CF* 3.329). One infers that the veiled mother of Asenath is one of the Deep Ones well known in Lovecraftian Innsmouth lore,[2] so that Asenath herself is an interstitial or category-problematical being: partly human, partly aquatic, but not a "healthy" (unalloyed) example of either. The second complication is that, as the reader and the narrator Upton gradually learn, Asenath's father Ephraim has, prior to the events of the main narration, usurped his daughter's body with his own mind, placed her mind in his aging body, and killed the Ephraim-body containing the Asenath-mind. Thus it is really (mentally) Ephraim that stands beside Edward; this fact alone makes for a categorical taboo-violation, obviously: Edward has really married a man. The overall picture of course is that of a multi-level failure of categorization. The creature whom poor Edward marries is a multiple category-collapse, a multiply interstitial monstrosity: it has a female body that is half-human and half-aquatic in its cellular inheritance, and it has Ephraim's male mind. (When Derby tells Upton that Asenath "wanted to be a man—to be fully human" [*CF* 3.339]—a remark destined, no doubt, to raise many a feminist eyebrow upon casual reading—one must realize that Eprhaim's mind knows full well that in fact the Asenath-body that he inhabits is not "fully human," but rather half-batrachian and destined to become more aquatic with age, acquiring the well-known Innsmouth look.) And when "Asenath" takes over Edward's body, forcing his mind into the female frame, what sallies forth as "Edward" is Edward corporeally, but Eprhaim mentally: a usurping

2. "The Shadow over Innsmouth" of course provides yet further interstitial suggestions. The hybrid offspring of the human Innsmouth denizens with the aquatic Deep Ones are clearly beings who slip into the cracks between categories; here we have the spectacle of living creatures who gradually slide from one supposedly inviolable category into another (humans growing more aquatic with age), blurring and denying the integrity of borders. Characteristically, the effect here is especially potent; we could countenance, perhaps, the Deep Ones themselves, unmixed with human blood, as being merely an alien race; but the hybridization makes true shambling horrors of the creatures who walk the streets of Innsmouth.

mind masquerading, as it were, for what Edward (the mental Edward) thinks has usurped his body: Asenath's mind. What remains behind, imprisoned, is Edward's mind in the half-human, half-batrachian body. Here again we have multiple levels of category violation.

And as if all this were not enough, the text in question also deals, in self-subverting fashion, with another categorical matter: the opposition of presence versus absence. The text seems to deal with a very vivid character named Asenath—it is always "she," "she-devil"—and seems to portray this character as a powerful presence in Edward's life; a great deal of the narrative energy of the text is expended to this effect. Consequently, it is only with some difficulty, unraveling the labyrinthine exchanges and category-violating substitutions of the tale, that the reader realizes that Asenath has never really been present in the story at all; her demise has occurred, we eventually learn, well before the "present" narration's events. One has the vivid impression of a sort of wicked, wayward, scheming woman named Asenath; but in reality we know very little of the original Asenath, and have no compelling reason to assign any objectionable qualities to her, other than, reportedly, her having been interested to some extent in her father's magic. Asenath is an absent figure in the tale masquerading, in effect, as a present figure.

In the end, of course, when Edward has killed "Asenath" but succumbed to "her" (really Ephraim's) mind-exchange again, whereupon Edward's mind is imprisoned in his "wife's" rotting corpse, we have the strongest category-failure of all: Edward's mind in a body now not only half-human and half-aquatic but also in the process of necrotic dissolution (it gets up and walks and is therefore no more a proper corpse than it is a proper living entity), while the Eprhaim-mind resides in Edward's real body in the sanitarium. Category failure abounds, and promises to continue to do so; Ephraim's mind, we are told, will, if not stopped, go "on and on" (*CF* 3.356) (and what was it originally?—another problem) from body to body; Upton, after shooting "Edward" (Ephraim), is even afraid that his own body will be the next category mistake, the next host to the physical-death-surviving intelligence that has already come back from the cellar-grave to claim Edward's body. This tale provides one of the most striking of all models, in the Lovecraft canon, of the principle of horror in interstitiality.

In their shifting and blurring of distinctions, their violation of categorical boundaries, the characters in this work provide a veritable tour de force in the deconstruction of the unitary self.

Further examples could be spun out indefinitely; I shall briefly mention only a few others before passing along to the matter of Lovecraft's themes. In "The Shadow out of Time," one notices that Nathaniel Peaslee, in experiencing those dreams that come increasingly to take on the aspect of memory, does not find the image of the cone-beings overwhelmingly horrific until he glances down, in one such dream, to find himself (his mind) in a cone-shaped body—it is not the physical aspect of the Great Race itself that bothers him, but rather, as in "The Thing on the Doorstep," the loss of integrity of definition of the self, in this case as given by the interstitial or hybrid situation of a cone-being driven by a human mind, a creature thus not properly human nor properly belonging to the Great Race. This notion of the dissolution of defining boundaries, with resulting violence to categorical schemes, is perhaps ultimately epitomized by the description in *At the Mountains of Madness* of the shoggoths: protoplasmic monstrosities capable of infinite amounts of shape-changing, shifting, unsettling, resettling, radical metamorphosis; here the borders between categories waver and vanish altogether. And in a more subtle way Lovecraft again, late in his career, deals with such categorical dissolution when, in "The Haunter of the Dark," he has Robert Blake undergo a coalescence with the Haunter, the horror winging its way across town from the dreaded church tower: "I am it and it is I" (*CF* 3.477).

But perhaps the most enduring effects of interstitiality and category-violation are to be found in consideration of Lovecraft's broad thematic concerns, which themselves pose serious questions of definition and categorical integrity.

One of Lovecraft's major recurrent themes is what I have called the theme of denied primacy: that we humans are not, were never, the first or foremost tenants of this planet. Clearly, the human desire to maintain such an illusion of being first and dominant is a matter of categorical thinking; one constructs the category "first intelligent race" and presumes to occupy it. At first glance, one might think that there is no question of categorical integrity here, since the category itself is well-defined and the only question is who makes up its contents. But the category of "firstness" or primacy is not so unproblematical as one might suppose. There are a number of instances in Lovecraft's fiction in which even the older occupants of the category are of ambiguous primacy; in "The Shadow out of Time," for example, we learn that the Great Race, as a race of cone-shaped bodies, are actually an older alien intelligence having occupied those bodies, and that they themselves fear another, more shadowy race lurking underground. One often gets the sense of lines of mental heritage stretching not just back to some earlier time in earth's history, but back and back into primordial mists unimaginable. The whole notion of categorical primacy is problematised by the unsettlement of beginnings and origins.

The Lovecraftian theme of illusory surface appearances—that things are not as they seem to be, that the surface of things masks some unsuspected and more dreadful reality—ties in well with this notion of problematical categories; just as such a category as "earth's first and primary lords" turns out not to be what it appears when we learn that we do not belong to it, many other things in Lovecraft's fiction turn out to be illusory as well, sometimes through such fictional devices as masks or other disguises (e.g., the waxen mask in "The Festival," or the face/hands disguise in "The Whisperer in Darkness"). Often what is masked is something that points up another Lovecraftian theme, that of unwholesome survival: the survival into present times of things from a distant past that ought to lie still but will not. Here, categories as fundamental as historical periods themselves are violated, unsettled, blurred as to boundaries. The survival of such denizens of the past is often a matter of—another pervasive Lovecraft theme—forbidden knowledge, or merciful ignorance (as articulated, e.g., in the well-known opening lines of "The Call of Cthulhu"): the theme that in the case of certain species of knowledge, it is best not to know, for awareness of such information can unsettle the mind, and the reason is that the mind is tethered to comforting modes of categorical thinking, whose violation can spell profound horror. What is an unnatural survival into the present from the past, if not an interstitial entity, a presence not sufficiently well-behaved to fit into any convenient time-category?

Even aside from this concern with time, we have similar category problems with yet another Lovecraft theme, that of oneiric objectivism: the theme that the distinction between dreaming and "reality" is, at best, ambiguous. In a shared dream-world such as that which we find in *The Dream-Quest of Unknown Kadath*, where is any firm, stable border between dreaming and wakeful reality? Randolph Carter's whole experience in that novel is (anti-)categorically interstitial: it belongs to the realm of dream, yet it obtrudes, we may infer, upon his wakeful life as well. It is neither simply dream nor wakeful "fact."

But all these major Lovecraftian themes are confluent, running into what we may call Lovecraft's macro-theme, as it were: the theme of the ruinous nature of self-understanding, or the crisis of self-knowledge, the crisis of coming to knowledge of one's place on the cosmic canvas. Time after time throughout the Lovecraft fictional canon, from the Outsider's touching the epistemologically fateful glass to Nathaniel Wingate Peaslee's opening the dreaded notebook in the vaulted chamber under the Australian sands, Lovecraft characters arrive at this ultimate crisis, discovering that they are evanescent dust-specks in an uncaring universe. The opposition to which this crisis gives birth is that of humankind (full of longing to be significant) versus the universe (wheeling blindly along, indifferent to human concerns). Yet serious complications reside in this supposedly categorically stable opposition.

Clearly, if Lovecraft's fiction has any force at all (and it is impossible to deny that it does), the universe in Lovecraft's fictive world is the uncaring and impersonal cosmic environment in which we find ourselves orphaned; Lovecraft's stories postulate and develop this predicament over and over, to high effect.

But one notices that in the very language with which we may most strenuously attempt to de-anthropocentrize or un-personify the universe to make of it what the Lovecraftian Weltanschauung insists on making of it, we but find ourselves re-personifying the universe. When we call the cosmos "blind," "indifferent," "uncaring," etc. we reimpose anthropocentrist and personifying characterizations, for these are all highly human qualities and concerns. One does not bother to say that a stone is blind, because there has never been any question of its being otherwise; yet we say that the universe is blind, suggesting, in spite of everything, that it might have seen. We do not say that a can of tomato soup is "uncaring," since any thought of its even conceivably being compassionate is absurd in the extreme—yet we say that the universe is "uncaring" and "indifferent," suggesting (at the very site of our language's most ardent efforts to do the opposite) that it might have cared; either such a remark is trivial (like saying that the stone is blind or the soup is indifferent) or is, to escape triviality, capable of generating the effect opposite to that which was intended. To call the universe "blind," "impersonal," etc. is a self-deconstructing gesture: it re-personifies the universe. It is difficult to imagine what could be meant by an "impersonal" universe without the presence of persons.

The result is that the universe itself—when we deal with it through language, as we must—is neither simply personifiable (as Lovecraft's fiction amply illustrates) nor simply un-personifiable. Recalcitrant, it resists these attempted categorizations. That is to say, Lovecraft's universe itself is interstitial. And to the extent that monstrousness springs from interstitiality, Lovecraft may well then have created the ultimate monster of all: his universe, a universe neither simply caring, certainly, nor simply one in which humankind (part of that universe, after all) can ever quite see the cosmos as one in which the lost hope for compassion is beyond all imaginable recall. Lovecraft places us in an unthinkable position—from most monsters in horror literature, we can flee; but when we are, in our very tissues, woven into a monstrous universe, then so long as we live and breathe and think, there is nowhere we can run. As writhing nerve-endings through which a conceptually teratological universe experiences itself, we are ourselves categorically benightmared dwellers of crevices.

Lovecraft and Gender

What of gender in the fiction of H. P. Lovecraft? What of woman?

As readers of Lovecraft well know, his fiction is not notable for giving expression to major female characters, overall; men, by and large, seem to dominate the stories. (One reflects that there is even a story whose title is "He.") But things can scarcely be so simple, and indeed this observation does not begin to address the general textual question of gender, which arises in far other ways.

Let us chose, as a departure-point, another writer.

In his well-known diatribe about "quibbles" (puns, and instances of extravagantly figural language generally) in Shakespeare, Samuel Johnson remarks that the tendency toward figurality, on Shakespeare's part, "has some malignant power over his mind," and that this tendency "was to him the fatal Cleopatra for which he lost the world, and was content to lose it"[1] (68)

Dr. Johnson, by his own metaphorical reference to Cleopatra, thus makes an interesting connection: woman-as-seductress comes to sym-

---

1. It is interesting to note that when Dr. Johnson's language most endeavors to inveigh against figurality, it becomes, itself, the most spectacularly figural, as in this very quote metaphorizing Cleopatra. One thinks of his well-known complaint against the metaphysical poets: "The most heterogeneous ideas are yoked by violence together." Here the imagery of the yoke makes the good doctor an accomplice in the very art of figurality that he seeks to disparage; since one commonly associates a yoke with oxen, but now hears it spoken of as joining "heterogeneous ideas," one finds, indeed, heterogeneous ideas—namely, oxen and ideas—"yoked by violence together" by the very language that purports to disallow the yoking-together of heterogeneous ideas by violence. The very language—like MacLeish's famous line "A poem should not mean, but be"—manages to *do* the opposite of what it *says*. The passage could be regarded as parodic, of course, but then there is still a broad element of *self*-parody in it as well. In any case, T. S. Eliot many years later took Samuel Johnson's disapproval of the metaphysical poets seriously enough to go to considerable trouble to rescue them from his clutches.

bolize figurality, metaphoricity, in literary language. One readily extends this metaphor, of course, to a pervasive schema for describing textual language in terms of gender. If literary femininity is figurality—metaphor, extravagance, displacement, seduction, any gesture of *swerve* from, or subversion of, "linear" or "literal" linguistic systems—then literary masculinity is linearity and literalness: systematicity, classical decorum, straightforward (and the phallomorphic imagery is suggestive) perpetuation of a system of propriety maintained essentially by structures of tradition and power. Textual Man, in this schema, is Augustan, proper, forthright, insistent upon preserving the integrity and stability of received systems of meaning; Textual Woman is indirect, covert, subversive, insistent upon displacing the settled assurance of systems of meaning—she is *femme fatale* to facile notions of semantic fixity. (In Lovecraft's "That is not dead which can eternal lie," from the *Necronomicon,* it is the settled masculine principle, the *yang,* that insists on reading "lie" only as "being recumbent," while it is the unsettling feminine principle, the *yin,* that allows "lie" in a perverse but intriguing way to suggest "prevaricate.") No doubt Dr. Johnson thought it *unfortunate* that literal, stable (male) language got subverted by figural, freewheeling (female) language; we shall feel free to draw other conclusions.

The binary opposition of masculine literalness versus feminine metaphoricity is one, as we shall see, that deconstructs itself, but in any event it provides a paradigm in terms of which it will be possible to examine, briefly but with an eye to making some real inroads, the question of gender in Lovecraft's fiction. (I should like to presume to think of this inchoate inquiry as a sort of preface to many future essays, perhaps by critics not yet born. Like deconstructive thinking, the issue of gender is not going to go away, nor should it.)

The metaphoricity/literality problem, as we have formulated it, suggests that the notion of gender in literature does not restrict itself to residence in so simple a domain as the sexual identity of fictional characters, nor even the overt philosophical treatment of gender in works of fiction. Rather, literary texts *themselves,* in terms of the schema that we have derived from Dr. Johnson's remarks about Shakespeare, possess ways of reflecting gender distinctions, on the level of allegory. Let us see another quotation from Dr. Johnson, this time *Barbara* Johnson, the deconstructionist critic: "Literature itself becomes inextricable from the sexuality it seeks to comprehend. . . . Literature is not only a thwarted investigator but also an incorrigible *perpetrator* of the problem of sexuality"[2] (13; my emphasis).

It is possible to maintain such a view, of course, precisely to the extent that the question of gender intertwines itself with the question of the tropic or figural workings of literary language. But the schema described—wherein femininity aligns itself with the unsettling wiles of metaphoricity, and masculinity aligns itself with those decorous systems of literality which a more wayward figurality works to displace—finds corroboration even in biological terms. The female of the species is generative in a primal, pervasive, inalterable way; the male is generative in only a limited way. To hazard a comment on the obvious: subsequent to sexual union and fertilization, if, say, the male dies the next day, birth can still occur when the time comes, while if the female dies the next day, this future event is canceled. The male is "disseminative" (in both biological and textual/metaphorical senses of the word) only in this limited fashion, while the female is genuinely, fully generative—like Lovecraft's fertility figure Shub-Niggurath, she is capable of "a thousand young." The parallels for textuality are obvious: in terms of our paradigm, the linear, univocal, authorial-intention-presuming literal strictures of a decorous "classical" reading are productive of meaning in only a sharply limited way—it is the license of the feminine principle, the freeplay of a reading that thrives on the fecundity of figural language and interpretative openness, that proves to be *truly* productive, that generates ever outward-spiraling realms of meaning, meaning that lives even when "original" or "intended" or "seminal" levels of meaning (father-meaning, as it were) are irretrievable.

What are the implications for the fictional texts of H. P. Lovecraft?

One is tempted to say that among the characters in Lovecraft's

2. Barbara Johnson, a poststructuralist who studied with the late Paul de Man at Yale University, taught at Yale herself, and then moved on to Harvard, is in my estimation one of the most brilliant and readable literary critics writing in the English language today; I have continually maintained that her remarkably "canny" commentary is the perfect answer to any charge against deconstruction as being nihilistic, wrong-headed, and the like. Her deconstruction of *Billy Budd,* for example, is quite possibly the best piece of Melville criticism ever written.

stories, the most outstanding woman is Asenath Waite, in "The Thing on the Doorstep." In a sense the very opposite is true; from the tale's narration one infers that Asenath does not stand out at all. Her place has been usurped; *she*—mentally—does not even appear in the story. But the paradox (or one of the paradoxes) here is that after a fashion she does manage to be present in the text, in the sense that she brings alive—as only women are capable of bringing things alive—the textual question of gender.

Perhaps the salient feature of this text, besides its treatment of the theme of usurpation, is the motif of *masking*, concealment, disguise: Asenath's mind has been displaced by that of her sorcerer father Ephraim, so that a man's mind is secretly ensconced in the body of a woman. Naturally, all kinds of questions—about gender, about appearances and reality, about texts and subtexts—raise themselves here.

What do we make of this man-concealing womanly exterior, this woman in whom—the interiority here is clearly suggestive of the fact that Eprhaim has "raped" his daughter in the most extreme way, usurping her very mental identity; he is illicitly inside her—in whom lurks a concealed male presence? The text makes it clear that it is Eprhaim's plan to go on usurping body after body, perpetuating himself unnaturally. It is also clear from intertextual reading of this tale with "The Shadow over Innsmouth" that the original Asenath was herself the product of the union of human and aquatic progenitors. Thus when Edward Derby says, of his wife's intermittent possession of his own body, that she "wanted to be a man—to be fully human—that was why she got hold of him" (*CF* 3.339), no feminist critic need see in this any remark to the effect that a woman's humanity is in question; "she" is really Eprhaim in Asenath's body, and he wants to move from her body to Edward's, eventually permanently, indeed to be "fully human"—because Asenath's body, from her partly nonhuman Innsmouthian parentage, is in truth *not* wholly human, so that in stealing her body, Ephraim has stolen a vessel that is not going to serve him as he would have wanted.

But in all this obfuscation of identity and gender, the real problem lies in the figural/literal schema that we have described. What part of the schema does Asenath occupy? In her original identity, she is plural, displaced, a product of human/nonhuman miscegenation, and thus seems to epitomize—by this very plurisignification, this mixed "etymology," so to speak—the feminine principles of proliferation and variegation. But, strange creature though she was before her father's incursions into her being, she no doubt would have preferred to resist him, to remain in her own body, to live her own life; and to the extent that she is in this sense a normal victim of an abnormal victimizer, she represents settled, stable systematicity: the male principle. Ephraim, on the other hand—male though he is, and although he has a linear, systematic plan (to go on "body to body to body" and live forever) characteristic of the male principle—Ephraim is clearly an anomalous being, a bizarre creature representing in every way a departure from normality, a perturbation of accepted systems; in this role, that is, he represents the feminine principle, the principle by which he may give birth—to himself—over and over. (His Hebrew name, after all, means "very fruitful.")

The masking of a male presence by a female exterior is thus multiply problematical; the occupied body of Asenath, though biologically female at least in part, represents the *yang* of a given systematicity, while the usurper, the mind of Ephraim, though male in its own origins, represents the *yin,* the feminine principle of uncertainty, openness of potential, deviation from received systems of normality. With reference to textual language and the paradigm of feminine nonlinear figurality versus male linearity, then, the enigma casts itself in terms of uncertain relations between metaphor and literalness; in effect, the text is covertly saying that there can be no clear distinction between the two. What "meaning" is masked, what unmasked? What is "really" there, underneath? The matter is indeterminate. But this very indeterminacy is characteristic of the feminine principle, the *yin* aspect of the schema, so that the indeterminacy itself is interrogated, made indeterminate—the text questions whether it questions itself. The very motif of masking, or disguise, in "The Thing on the Doorstep," operates on the level of allegory; the text sports with us, coyly withdraws behind masks, half covers its face, over the questions of male versus female, literal versus metaphorical, systemic versus contrasystemic, and thus allegorizes its own troubled workings.

Asenath has proven to be a particularly knotty problem; what other Lovecraftian women are there? Mollie L. Burleson, herself a Lovecraftian woman, has argued with much cogency ("The Outsider: A

Woman?") that the carrion wraith in "The Outsider," a first-person narrator not directly identified as to gender but long assumed to be male, is probably a woman. In our present schema, what of the Outsider, then? She certainly represents anomaly, disturber of conventions, waywardness, externality to received systems, and thus indeed aligns with the feminine principle, though she is masked by the asexual pronoun "I." Woman thus comes to be seen, here, not only as a wayward, vertiginous force disturbing the complacency of systems, but as externality per se—woman as *other*. The opening paragraph of "The Outsider" actually has the Outsider reflect that her mind "momentarily threatens to reach beyond to *the other*" (*CF* 1.265; emphasis in original), expressing a central thematic concern in all Lovecraft's fiction: the threatening nature of self-knowledge when one oneself *is* other.

At first glance, it would seem that this is nothing new: woman, historically, has always been relegated to that position, the position of the other. But what *is* otherness, alterity, externality, in the Lovecraft text at hand? The obvious answer is that it is the heart of the text itself; there could be no story at all without the Outsider's *being* the Outsider. Alterity is of utmost importance, in fact, in the entirety of Lovecraft's fiction. The point is that alterity need not be understood in pejorative terms. While one rejoices at the collapse of sociopolitical institutions that have marginalized women, one also sees that otherness is a kind of *sine qua non,* a kind of distinction that deconstructs the opposition between centrality and marginality. Does the *other,* in the scheme of things, matter? In a manner of speaking, otherness is all that *can* matter, all that can be remarked; anything that can be re-marked (iterated, inscribed again as a sign, given the function of signification) is only remarkable by its being "other" to what is *not* remarkable. What is music but an "other" to noise? Literature, but an "other" to common nonliterary language? Poetry, but an "other" to prose? The sonnet form, but an "other" to non-sonnet poems? The Miltonic sonnet, but an "other" to sonnets not of this form? Alterity operates as a positive force at all levels of specificity. Or generality: what is knowledge, if not an "other" to a featureless backdrop of undifferentiated ignorance? If, in textual terms, woman (as metaphoricity, displacement) is "other" to classical decorum and the stultifyingly univocal "propriety" of literal, referential language, then she should re-joyce; like Molly Bloom at the end of *Ulysses,* she is textual affirmation. We read, in "The Outsider," an odd and painful but nonetheless resounding affirmation: of alterity, of woman.

Let us inquire after another Lovecraftian woman: Lavinia Whateley, in "The Dunwich Horror." The nonhuman force Yog-Sothoth has sexual union with her to sire a pair of twins; we do not see the conception scene, we do not know if it amounts to cosmic rape. Possibly not; she does do apparently willing homage later, upon Sentinel Hill, to the forces with which the birth of her twins are allied. What has sired the twins, in any case, is alien, unsettling, a swerve from prosaic normality, and thus perversely insists upon characterizing itself not as the male principle (the father) in the Johnsonian schema but the female. Lavinia herself, in this schema, is of ambiguous sexuality; she is human, though of weird inclination—she is a sort of given normality-in-place (the male principle) waiting to be perturbed. Lavinia is generative, but of *hybrid* issue: Wilbur Whateley, though passing himself off as fully human for a while, is partly teratological, and his sibling is worse: an "octopus, centipede, spider kind o' thing" (*CF* 2.465; emphasis suppressed). It is interesting that even in the more nearly human Wilbur, who, early on, is assumed to be male, the teratology of his makeup below the waist prevents any real determination of "his" gender; and of course the "brother" is altogether indeterminate as to sex. Thus Lavinia is generative of uncertainty, ambiguity, undecidability, and thus ends up aligning herself strongly, in *this* respect, with the feminine aspect of our schema, though, as we have noted, she also plays the "normal" role in a normal/nonnormal sexual union and thus partakes, symbolically, of the male aspect. But then the very uncertainty that she thus generates makes her all the more female, allegorically.

There are places in Lovecraft's fiction where women as characters are directly associated with mysteries of language, much in keeping with the Johnsonian "Cleopatra" paradigm. In "The Colour out of Space," when Nahum Gardner's wife falls victim to the grey blight that is spreading over the Gardner farm, we read: "In her raving there was not a single specific noun, but only verbs and pronouns" (*CF* 2.380); language, here, is characterized as open, disseminative, with no nouns to pin things down. In "The Shunned House," it is a woman, Rhoby Dexter Harris, "educated only in the rudiments of French," who "shouted for hours in a coarse and idiomatic form of that language" (*CF* 1.459); here symbolically we have disseminative-text-as-woman, textuality that cannot know, ahead of time, what it will say or mean in future contexts, because language oversteps boundaries, carrying messages not even known by the sender. There are subtler examples. In "Cool Air," it is interesting that the only character *shown* directly as speaking is the landlady Mrs. Herrero: "Doctor Muñoz, he have speel hees chemicals" (*CF* 2.12)—the feminine voice, and only that voice, speaks, and with an accent, suggesting alienage, alterity, the "other" possibilities of language. In "The Call of Cthulhu," it is Captain Johansen's *widow*, woman as survivor, who releases his diary to the narrator, a diary that she thus disseminates without reading it herself (it is in English, and she apparently knows only Norwegian); here again we have the feminine principle, linked to the promulgation of linguistic mystery. The question of textuality continually interlaces itself with the question of woman.

And these questions are certainly not simplified by the fact that the basic textual bipolarity here—male literalness versus female metaphoricity—is one that deconstructs itself. Classical (male) decorum is the downplay of figurality, often in fact only the seeming or unsuccessful downplay; as Nietzsche and Derrida have reminded us, even the most apparently straightforward and rigorous philosophical language is laced with metaphor. Conversely, figural displacement has to maintain a sense of the *distance* across the gap by which the displacement occurs, a distance from the linear language or "ordinary" meaning displaced; metaphor only *feels* like metaphor when we sense its indwelling difference from some more simply referential use of language. Thus each pole of the bipolarity at stake here covertly contains the necessary, enabling trace of the supposedly opposite pole. Gender issues, to the extent that they interact with linguistic issues, must therefore be perpetually aporetic and irresolvable.

By dealing in such issues allegorically—figurally reversing such oppositions as male/female as normal/abnormal, and thus questioning their propriety, threatening to displace natural or "proper" notions with more wayward ones—the Lovecraft (inter)text practices an *overall* swerve from simply "literal" language and enters the gender schema on a high level, enacting the feminine principle of linearity-subverting swerve, so that an apparently male-dominated Lovecraftian canon is only apparently so.

Nietzsche once asked: "Supposing truth to be a woman—what?"[3] (*Beyond Good* 13). It is, of course, "truth" that we ultimately *find* the least of, in texts. Literary language abounds in artful indeterminacy, and if truth is a woman, then this woman forever dodges, shifts, hides herself in the labyrinthine world of the text; truth is not simply "in" a text, and if truth is a woman, then woman is thus absent. But paradoxically it is by this very absence that she is most present—not, in the Nietzschean sense, as truth, but as the ever-incomplete search for it, the ever-receding glimmer of it like Keats's "bride of quietness" on the urn, the ever-intriguing call, to us, of language out of the abyss. In the texts of Lovecraft, woman flickers in and out of focus, yet epitomizes the textual energies of uncertainty, of open reading, of figurality, of the fecund capacity of the texts to give birth to themselves without end. Whether truth is a woman or not, it would seem that textual dissemination *is* a woman—and in Lovecraft's textual universe, that is a dark and fascinating lady indeed.

---

3. Jacques Derrida has examined this notion of the feminine principle in literary textuality as aligning with the mysterious indeterminacy of language, and with the elusiveness of "truth" in texts; see his *Éperons: Les Styles de Nietzsche*.

H. P. Lovecraft: Textual Keys

Perhaps no imagery in H. P. Lovecraft's fiction operates so powerfully as the image of keys—with reference to their tantalizing power, to the doors that they physically or metaphorically unlock, to those doors themselves as a thematic concern pervading the canon: the concern of almost-unlocked barriers and of those aspects of reality that they both separate and threaten to conjoin. Indeed, the striking thing about these keys, and about the doors that they may unlock, is the double gesture inherent in the very notion of a key and, correlatively, the very notion of a door—the duplicitous gesture by which a key may both unlock and lock, may both allow and forbid passage, may lock in or lock out, may both invite and repel; the gesture by which a door, like (to use one of Jacques Derrida's favorite images) the tympanum in the ear, may self-opposingly function both as a barrier separating two realms and as a conduit back and forth between them. It is intriguing that the same Indo-European root *kagh-* ("to hold," "enclosure") yielding *key* also gives us the Greek *hexe* ("witch") and of course the English *hex,* suggesting a certain witchery in the very notion of a key, with its proclivity toward seemingly contradictory alternatives: locking in/locking out, admitting/barring. Herein lies, allegorically, the double movement of texts, the uncanny facility with which they move against themselves, problematizing but enriching their own textuality as they go.

The motif of the key appears nowhere so conspicuously in the Lovecraft canon, of course, as in "The Silver Key," in which the key functions both metaphorically and literally. Randolph Carter has "lost the key of the gate of dreams" (*CF* 2.73), i.e., has lost the youthful ease with which he has always slipped away into regions of dream to escape "things as they are" (*CF* 2.73), the things of a prosaic world bereft of wonder and magic; he has enjoyed, but has lost, the insight "that all life is only a set of pictures in the brain, among which there is no difference betwixt those born of real things and those born of inward dreamings" (*CF* 2.73). Thus the metaphorical key that Carter has lost, functions as the possibility of unlocking and opening the door between two realms whose separation cleaves Carter's world in half—the beautiful, longed-for realm of dream and the garish world of "things that are."

Yet in the remarkably phenomenological passage cited, the text deeply problematizes the very division over which the symbolic key presides. The text works sedulously to value Carter's dream-realm over the stultifying world of "real things," yet maintains here that "there is no cause to value the one above the other" (*CF* 2.73). If one reads in parallel structure, so that "the one" points to the world of "real things" while "the other" points to the world of "inward dreamings"—i.e., if one infers that the text is really only saying that the real world is not superior to the world of dreams—one must still account for the text's claim, in the same passage, that "there is no difference," so that the refusal to overvalue works both ways. And if there really were no difference, Carter's quest for his "twilight realms" would be misguided—he would be (but, one feels, would not *really* be) wise to content himself with the "pictures in the brain" derived from a poet's contemplation of his real surroundings. The old Lovecraftian theme of "oneiric objectivism" (see Burleson, "On Lovecraft's Themes" 136, 142) arises with force here; the relation between waking and dreaming is forever unsettled and unsettling. But then what does one make of a metaphorical key that purports to rule this problematic relation? It is a key that may or may not be available to unlock a door that may or may not be there. More precisely—for binary logic falls by the wayside in considerations such as these—the door is and is not there, and its key, accordingly, is a remarkable symbol indeed.

Further, what of such a profoundly disturbed symbol, this key, when it becomes a physical implement? Carter, fortified against the dullness of the "real" world by arcane studies, experiences horrors that "[take] him only to the edge of reality, and [are] not of the true dream country he [has] known in youth" (*CF* 2.78), and once again the text moves against itself over the question of what is "real." Carter has a dream—he is apparently not wholly barred from the dream world—in which his grandfather reminds him of an actual silver key hidden in an attic; he finds the box that holds it but, ironically, no key exists for "the formidable lock" (*CF* 2.80), which must be forced open. The "huge key of tarnished silver" (*CF* 2.80) is wrapped in an unreadable parchment that might well be the story itself, unreadable in the best poststructuralist sense of eluding facile, single-minded interpretation. (Do we then force the lock, as it were, in approaching the text? It may be that we do; but to do so is to encounter not mastery within, but mystery.)

When Carter returns to "the lonely rustic homestead of his people" and seems to slip back in time, to his childhood, he has the silver key in his pocket, but his memory of finding it, as a child "bribing Parks with half his week's allowance to help him open the box" (*CF* 2.83), is mixed up with the adult memory. He muses, in this cherished place of his youthful self, that the "trees and the hills [are] close to him, and [form] the gates of that timeless realm which [is] his true country" (*CF* 2.84), and one reflects that as such, these gates need no key. Yet, entering a cave, the young-again Carter does make use of the silver key, some esoteric use that we do not see in the text. This use of the key can scarcely be to return him to his youth, for he is already there. Or is he? We read that the boy, in his tenth year, seems "to have picked up an odd gift of prophecy" (*CF* 2.85), i.e., seems to have lived before and to have remembered, as prophetic vision, the experience of things to come. The usual paradoxes of time travel prevail here; the narrator finally tells us that "There are twists of time and space, of vision and reality, which only a dreamer can divine" (*CF* 2.86), and once again we are left with a necessary but impossible distinction between "vision" and "reality." The tale of the key—a key needed and not needed by a man who is and is not again a boy to unlock and not unlock a door that is and is not there separating and not separating realms that are and are not distinct—the tale of the key is indeed like the "queer parchment whose characters no linguist or paleographer has been able to decipher" (*CF* 2.86); we will never wholly read it.

But key-imagery emerges elsewhere in the Lovecraft canon as well, in places not so obvious. Keys, to have even the appearance of a reason for being, need locks, and locks need doors; and doors (barriers, screens) pervade Lovecraft's work as powerful recurrent images, in that the whole Lovecraftian Weltanschauung is one in which barriers forever raise themselves or threaten to come down—barriers not only between dreaming and waking, but between purposelessness and perceived purpose in the universe; between apparent dominance but real meaninglessness of humankind as a life form on earth; between the present and a past that will not stay dead; between surface appearances and hidden realities; between merciful ignorance and soul-annihilating knowledge. Wherever such a barrier rears its monolithic form, some figural key promises or threatens to unlock the door and let space flow into space, realm into realm. In deconstructionist studies it is well known in general that doors and barriers have this flickering, now-you-see-it-and-now-you-don't kind of quasi-existence, for to erect a barrier one must think on both sides of it, thus dismantling it; Lovecraftian barriers are all the more tantalizing in this respect, for the realms (imperfectly) separated by a Lovecraftian barrier always partake of the cosmic vision that pervades his work, even when—perhaps especially when—the door and its key are metaphorical images.

In fact, one of the most striking metaphors of this kind in all of horror literature occurs at the moment in "The Shadow out of Time" when Nathaniel Wingate Peaslee's imperfectly expunged memory of his alien experience threatens to break through into his conscious mind. He says: "Something was fumbling and rattling at the latch of my recollection, while another unknown force sought to keep the portal barred" (*CF* 3.422). Here the realms to be separated by the metaphorical "portal" are the narrator's familiar, comfortable world on the one side and, on the other, that nightmare world of pseudomemory that endeavors to become memory. And here one observes that when a lock is of the sort known as a latch, the "key" to that lock, its potential opener, is simply the hand or the motion that would unfasten the latch: the "something" feared by the narrator, the mass of repressed memory that threatens to break through. (Yet at the same time that same repository of horror works to keep the "portal" closed and locked.)

But then the key becomes not just the implemental means for one of the separated realms to break through and obtrude upon the other, but rather the very force and presence of that realm itself; it is as if the key to be turned in the lock of a door separating us from a dark room beyond were that room itself, opening (or holding closed) its own door, and this notion of such a shadowy realm functioning itself as the "key" that would turn to bring that realm forth into our own space is a ponderous and frightening one indeed, especially in the context of what we have been observing here about the double gesture of the key, the simultaneous promise and denial of passage, the radical and perpetual uncertainty attendant upon the whole matter of keys, doors, and locks.

With regard to the example cited, where the Lovecraftian door or barrier is a "portal," one may observe that *portal,* like the Latin *porta,* "gate," derives from the same source (the Indo-European *per-,* "crossing," "passing over," "carrying over") as such words as *portage,* with their imagery of carrying through or across. If one carries something through a door or across a threshold, one partakes of that aspect of doors that assumes openness, pass-ability, the condition of being unlocked; yet in the citation from the text we have the portal "barred," locked, the key turned against us, as if once again the text were sporting with the duplicitous nature of doorways and keys, both describing and denying the sort of passings-through inherent in the etymology of the term *portal.* Allegorically, there is textual self-reference here as well, since in saying that the "portal" is "barred" the text pretends to be clear (simple, open, unlocked) yet really is problematized (barred, locked) by the use of a term, *portal,* whose etymological connections belie the description "barred" in a manner antithetical to, say, what would have happened if the term had instead been *barrier,* which would etymologically have been consistent with its being "barred." This is not, of course, to suggest that *portal* is an error in diction, given its description in context; rather, the text's use of *portal* delectably problematizes what otherwise would be a less interesting description.

This sort of effect heightens and takes on yet other lineaments when one considers another passage, this time from Wilbur Whateley's readings from the *Necronomicon* in "The Dunwich Horror": "*Yog-Sothoth* is the gate. *Yog-Sothoth* is the key and guardian of the gate" (*CF* 2.434). Here we have not only a linkage between keys and portage (by way of "gate": Wilbur's text is in Latin and would actually say *porta*), but a conflation of the gate and the key and the guardian: Yog-Sothoth is all of them, a composite being like his hybrid "octopus, centipede, spider kind o' thing" offspring. And here again the imagery of keys and doors partakes of ambiguous directionality; the etymologically underscored notion of portage would suggest openness of passage, yet the gate has a guardian, and it is the function of a guardian to prevent, or at least control, passage, keeping the portal closed in effect, making the portal as much barrier as conduit. One clearly sees Yog-Sothoth here as the double-faced Janus, presider over gateways, looking both forward and back. Janus is related to the Sanskrit *yana* (as in *Mahayana*), "way," "vehicle," "mode of knowledge"—but, one must ask, is the way open or blocked? Is the gateway a way, or is the gate in the way? It is of course both; here as always, keys and doors are multifold, self-opposing entities, both promising and forbidding passage. (It is interesting, in this context especially, that one speaks of a patch of text as a "passage," suggesting figurally that texts allow us to pass through, penetrate them, when their very workings forbid any facile possibility of doing so.)

One may note that this multiple directionality of keys and doors shows up again in Lovecraft's sonnet "The Key" (*AT* 81), the third in the *Fungi* sequence, when the poem's persona speaks of holding the book "that told the hidden way" (again, the connection with Janus and *yana*) "[a]cross the void and through the space-hung screens" between the worlds; here, the "screens" function both as a barrier and as a portal that one may pass through. The persona proclaims, "The key was mine," but of course the key is never wholly one's own.

But Lovecraft employs the imagery of keys in yet another way, in connection with cryptography, a pervasive motif in his works. In cryptography, a key is a device whereby the cryptographer can encipher a given "plaintext" message and whereby the intended recipient can turn the "ciphertext" back into readable text; or the cryptanalyst, an unintended recipient, may analytically recover the key and thereby come to read the message, as in the case of Henry Armitage in "The Dunwich Horror": Armitage dealt with a Vigénère cipher, a polyalphabetic cipher with "the message built up with arbitrary key-words known only to the initiated," and in his labors he "now and then halted maddeningly as a reapplication of the complex key became necessary" (*CF* 2.451). Here again the motif of the key is an interestingly duplicitous one, confounding any simple sense of direction or purpose, in that a cryptographic key, like a physical key, both forbids yet potentially allows passage, moving in sub-currents against itself.

Allegorically, such a key—sometimes turned in the lock against us, sometimes inviting us to turn it in the lock—reflects textuality itself. Texts invite our reading them but turn out to be unreadable, in that no particular reading ever saturates them, ever conquers or exhausts them. Like all literary texts, Lovecraft's are a double gesture of passage and denial, of portal and barrier. "The Silver Key" might as well be speaking not only of itself but of literary textuality generally when it describes the parchment in which the silver key is wrapped as holding "only the strange hieroglyphs of an unknown tongue written with an antique reed" (*CF* 2.80).

SOURCES AND INFLUENCES

H. P. Lovecraft: The Hawthorne Influence

Howard Phillips Lovecraft, the Rhode Island fantaisiste whose cosmic mythos of primordial gods has moved some critics to proclaim him a unique figure among creators of supernatural horror, came to admire Nathaniel Hawthorne greatly but did not seem to consider him a major influence on his own work. Lovecraft perceived his primary sources as residing in Poe and Lord Dunsany, and indeed the influence of these writers is readily recognized, especially in Lovecraft's early tales—for instance, the Poesque tales "The Outsider" (1921) and "The Hound" (1922), and the Dunsanian tales "Celephaïs" (1920) and "The Quest of Iranon" (1921). But a Hawthorne influence can also be clearly discerned—an influence more thematic than stylistic, to be sure, but a lasting influence and one ranging over so many common themes and images that its effect on the Lovecraftian oeuvre is striking. The dark dreamer from Providence had, certainly, his own ways of working out his chosen themes, including a "personal myth" that differed radically from that of Hawthorne. While Hawthorne's inner life of allegory gave utterance to brooding concerns with good and evil in the world, Lovecraft had a Weltanschauung by which his writings were expressive symbolically, though not didactically, of an indifferent and purposeless cosmos in which such Hawthornian matters as the Unpardonable Sin would be well-nigh meaningless. Nevertheless, Hawthorne in some respects assumes a central importance in the fabric of Lovecraft's creations.

By the time he wrote his critical survey, "Supernatural Horror in Literature" (1925–27), Lovecraft had reread Hawthorne intensively and devoted considerable space to him in the survey, describing him—albeit with a tone of distaste for Hawthorne's allegorical didacticism—

in terms of genius. This survey, far from being "a piece of frivolous self-indulgence" as remarked by L. Sprague de Camp in his *Lovecraft: A Biography* (1975), is an indispensably useful source for the student of Lovecraft's critical views, and it sheds light upon an important aspect of Lovecraft's interest in Hawthorne: the regional aspect. With his own love for the dark side of New England history and folklore, Lovecraft found endless fascination with Hawthorne's shadowy interest in and ancestral connection with New England Puritanism and witchcraft persecution. The inclination of Hawthorne to be led by this state of mind to plant his creations in his own native Novanglian soil is reflected in Lovecraft's developing preference for such settings. Prior to his serious study of Hawthorne, Lovecraft's tales show no particular tendency to concentrate upon New England; but as his style ascends to its maturity in the late 1920s and early 1930s, he weaves the byways and accumulated lore of his native region into the heart even of his most sweepingly cosmic conceptions. And so many are the thematic and imagistic echoes of Hawthorne in Lovecraft's work that the two writers, for all their differences in outlook and purpose, are remarkably similar in their use of New England terrain and culture as a canvas on which to try to suggest the hues of their respective personal visions.

Sometimes similarities are evident even with respect to Lovecraft's early writing. Hawthorne, with ever an eye on the past, was fond of darkly personifying old New England houses in his fiction, saying, for example, of the House of the Seven Gables: "The aspect of the venerable mansion has always affected me like a human countenance, bearing the traces not merely of outward storm and sunshine, but expressive, also, of the long lapse of mortal life, and accompanying vicissitudes that have passed within. . . . The deep projection of the second story gave the house such a meditative look that you could not pass it without the idea that it had secrets to keep, and an eventful history to meditate upon" (*Novels* 245, 248).

It would be difficult, for one familiar with Lovecraft's work, to read these passages without thinking of his story "The Picture in the House" (1920), in which the narrator says of certain old New England farmhouses remote from traveled roads:

> Two hundred years and more they have leaned or squatted there, while the vines have crawled and the trees have swelled and spread. They are almost hidden now in lawless luxuriances of green and guardian shrouds of shadow; but the small-paned windows still stare shockingly, as if blinking through a lethal stupor which wards off madness by dulling the memory of unutterable things. (*CF* 1.207)

This passage has an alliterative style not unlike Hawthorne, and a feeling for the sentient nature of *place,* a characteristic tendency in Lovecraft and one also shown by Hawthorne in such tales as "The Hollow of the Three Hills" and in such scenes as the forest meeting in *The Scarlet Letter* (1850). Referring to the Puritan gloominess and furtive isolation in which the history of many such houses is steeped, Lovecraft's narrator further observes: "Only the silent, sleepy, staring houses in the backwoods can tell all that has lain hidden since the early days, and they are not communicative, being loath to shake off the drowsiness which helps them forget. Sometimes one feels that it would be merciful to tear down these houses, for they must often dream" (*CF* 1.207).

Both writers make repeated use of the "window-eye" metaphor in the personification of houses—as, of course, does Poe also, for example, when he speaks of the House of Usher as having "vacant and eye-like windows." In *The Blithedale Romance* (1852), Hawthorne's narrator Coverdale sees that "some of the windows of the house were open, but with no more signs of life than a dead man's unshut eyes" (562). Lovecraft, in "The Shadow over Innsmouth," a tale of a decayed Massachusetts town concealing monstrous human matings with ichthyic creatures, invests the houses, by metaphorical transferral, with a life worse than death when he describes their "fishy-eyed vacancy" (*CF* 3.181). This tale, with its treatment of the "Innsmouth look"—an unblinking, fishlike appearance gradually assumed by Innsmouth denizens because of their partly nonhuman ancestry—also seems thematically to echo a Hawthorne notebook entry of January 4, 1839: "A mortal symptom for a person being to lose his own aspect and to take the family lineaments, which were hidden deep in the healthful visage. Perhaps a seeker might thus recognize the man he had sought, after long intercourse with him unknowingly" (*American Notebooks* 209–10). Indeed, in Lovecraft's tale, the narrator experiences just such a delayed recognition—of himself, when he discovers that his own genealogy contains the tainted Innsmouth blood.

There is another Lovecraft story in which the author's tendency to deal with gloomy or sinister interiors reminds one of that tendency in Hawthorne, especially in view of parallel imagery. When Lovecraft wrote "The Shunned House" (1924)—based on a real house in Providence just as *The House of the Seven Gables* (1851) is based on a real house in Salem—he was still very Poe-conscious, even mentioning him in the story (in the connection that Poe in real life had walked by the Shunned House's prototype on Benefit Street); but the presence of Hawthornian elements is clear. Hawthorne says that Colonel Pyncheon "was about to build his house over an unquiet grave" (*Novels* 247), and Lovecraft extends this notion into the literal. His Shunned House is built, as was the real house, over the graves of an earlier family of French settlers (of whom, like Chillingworth in *The Scarlet Letter,* there are evil rumors from abroad), and their grave site is "unquiet" indeed in its vampiristic effects on subsequent dwellers there, who waste away and die, sometimes beset with mad visions of a presence in the house gnawing at them. Other imagery relates the two works as well. At Hawthorne's Seven Gables, "the street having been widened about forty years ago, the front gable was now precisely on a line with it" (*Novels* 259); at the Shunned House, "a widening of the street at about the time of the Revolution sheared off most of the intervening space" between the house and the road, so that by the time a sidewalk was laid by the cellar wall exposed at street level "Poe in his walks must have seen only a sheer ascent of dull grey brick flush with the sidewalk and surmounted at a height of ten feet by the antique shingled bulk of the house proper" (*CF* 1.452). The image in each case is that of an ancient edifice nuzzled by the encroachments of a growing, changing community knowing little of the depths of horror still lingering there. Further, when Hawthorne describes the Pyncheon looking-glass said to be connected with the Maules in such a way that "they could make its inner region all alive with the departed Pyncheons" (*Novels* 254), the reader of Lovecraft is reminded of the scene near the end of "The Shunned House" where, as old Elihu Whipple is attacked in the moldy cellar by the house's vampirelike presence, the narrator sees in the vortex of dissolution a shifting display of the house's ill-fated occupants over the centuries. It is not surprising that a Lovecraft work would contain imagistic echoes of Hawthorne's Salem novel, for Lovecraft expressly admired the work; in his critical survey he refers to the novel as "New England's greatest contribution to weird literature" and to the fictional house as a place of "overshadowing malevolence . . . almost as alive as Poe's House of Usher, though in a subtler way" (*CE* 2.106).

Lovecraft, in the survey, expressed fascination with the psychopomp motif in Hawthorne's novel, remarking that

> the dead nocturnal vigil of old Judge Pyncheon in the ancient parlour, with his frightfully ticking watch, is stark horror of the most poignant and genuine sort. The way in which the judge's death is first adumbrated by the motions and sniffing of a strange cat outside the window . . . is a stroke of genius which Poe could not have surpassed. Later the strange cat watches intently outside that same window in the night and on the next day, for—something. It is clearly the psychopomp of primeval myth . . . (*CE* 2.106)

Lovecraft himself uses this motif, the notion of the psychopomp or ghastly catcher of departing souls. In a form transmuted by local folklore which Lovecraft absorbed during a 1928 visit to North Wilbraham, Massachusetts, he presents (in "The Dunwich Horror," 1928) the psychopomp in the guise of whippoorwills, who gather outside the death-chamber window and time their cries in unison with the dying person's breath, waiting to capture the fleeing soul.

Another notable motif in *The House of the Seven Gables* is that of the long-lost family papers concealed in a recess, constructed for the purpose, in the wall behind the portrait of old Colonel Pyncheon. A similar use of this motif occurs in Lovecraft's 1927 novel *The Case of Charles Dexter Ward,* in which young Ward finds the papers and notes of his unwholesome ancestor Joseph Curwen in a recess behind the paneling on which the ancestor's portrait has been painted. The two situations differ in that, in Hawthorne's novel, the discovered papers, though having caused much misery during their concealment, are finally without real worth or effect, while in Lovecraft's novel the discovered papers are of momentous import, leading to Charles Ward's ruin. But in each novel there is the theme of the modern character whose family past reaches forward, through centuries in time, to engulf him. The modern scion is culpable in Hawthorne, innocent in Lovecraft; but each one physically resembles his evil ancestor to an uncanny degree, suggesting atavistical exhumation of family woes long buried. And it is interesting to note that Lovecraft's Curwen is a name-echo of the Salem witchcraft judge Corwin, a colleague of Hawthorne's witchcraft-judge ancestor Hathorne.

Another Hawthorne novel much admired by Lovecraft is *The Marble Faun.* Lovecraft makes a revealing remark, in his "Supernatural Horror in Literature," about what it is in this novel that catches his fancy: the hint of "fabulous blood in mortal veins" (*CE* 2.105)—Donatello's resemblance to the Faun of Praxiteles. Lovecraft employs this motif in his 1926–27 novel *The Dream-Quest of Unknown Kadath,* where, in a passage recalling also Hawthorne's "The Great Stone Face," he says (of an ancient dream-priest advising the narrator on his dream-quest of the gods called the Great Ones):

> Atal babbled freely of forbidden things; telling of a great image reported by travellers as carved on the solid rock of the mountain Ngranek . . . and hinting that it may be a likeness which earth's gods once wrought of their own features. . . . It is known that in disguise the younger among the Great Ones often espouse the daughters of men, so that around the borders of the cold waste wherein stands Kadath the peasants must all bear their blood. (*CF* 2.106)

Lovecraft also flirts with this theme in his early tale "Hypnos" (1922), in which the narrator's Hellenically statuesque companion may have been either a living human or the godlike statue finally perceived—or may have been a god among humans. He is even described as "a faun's statue out of antique Hellas" (*CF* 1.326). This story, like Lovecraft's other Hellenic piece "The Tree" (1920), is thematically and tonally very Hawthornian in flavor, though both tales were written during the period of Lovecraft's strongest infatuation with Poe.

Lovecraft, in his 1922 essay "A Confession of Unfaith," acknowledges a significant early debt to Hawthorne. He relates that at the age of six his philosophical development took an important turn when he read *A Wonder Book* and *Tanglewood Tales,* which gave him an early awareness of Graeco-Roman thought and charmed him with the beauty, even in retold form, of Hellenic myth. This germinal glance led to more extensive reading and a lifelong love of classical antiquity. It is significant that Lovecraft so early thus imbibed a sense of myth, for he was later to develop his own mythos: a symbolic pantheon of primordial gods and, surrounding them, a cycle of myth that runs as a sable thread through virtually all his later work. Frank Belknap Long, in his memoir *Howard Phillips Lovecraft: Dreamer on the Nightside* (1975), has remarked that this mythos "is simply without parallel in the whole of literature" (21). And it seems probable that its development—while more directly showing the influence of Lord Dunsany—owes much, in its incipient stirrings, to the view of Argos and Sicily seen by a six-year-old through the storyteller's eye of Hawthorne.

But there is a much more direct and striking way in which Hawthorne seems to have left his mark upon the Lovecraft mythos. Lovecraft is known to have read Hawthorne's notebooks as early as 1919, for in that year he writes in his own commonplace book—a compendium of impressions and story ideas very similar in overall tone and flavor to many of the most somber Hawthorne notes—this entry: "Hawthorne—unwritten plot. Visitor from tomb. Stranger at some public concourse followed at midnight to graveyard where he descends into the earth" (*CE* 5.222). This note, besides showing (if there were any doubt) that Lovecraft early in his writing career had read Hawthorne thoroughly enough to know the plot to be unwritten, establishes that Lovecraft by 1919 could hardly have missed the following Hawthorne note dated October 17, 1835: "An old volume in a large library,—every one to be afraid to unclasp and open it, because it was said to be a book of magic" (*American Notebooks* 26). This entry is remarkable for its similarity to the description of Lovecraft's mythical book, the abhorrent *Necronomicon,* which plays so central a role in his major works. Lovecraft's reading of Hawthorne's notebooks in 1919 would have been early enough for the *Necronomicon* to be suggested, at least in part, by Hawthorne's note, for Lovecraft first quotes from his imagined tome in a story in 1921 ("The Nameless City ") and first refers to it by name in a story in 1922 ("The Hound"). The *Necronomicon,* in the Lovecraft mythos, is seen as an ancient and forbidden volume containing the means of invoking, by sorcery, certain Old Ones or gods—chief among them being Yog-Sothoth, whose name is shrieked atop a mountain in "The Dunwich Horror" by a wizard holding the dreadful volume open before him. Lovecraft invented a whole history of printings, translations, and suppressions of his rare and forbidden book, from its composition circa A.D. 700 by Abdul Alhazred, to its modern-day presence, under lock and key, in a certain few university libraries—including the Widener Library at Harvard and the library of Lovecraft's imaginary Miskatonic University. The fabulous tome lurks tenebrously in the mythos stories and is a key to their understanding, as in "The Whisperer in Darkness," for example, when Lovecraft's narrator says, "I started with loathing when told of the monstrous nuclear chaos beyond angled space which the 'Necronomicon' had mercifully cloaked under the name of Azathoth" (*CF* 2.521). Lovecraft thus reveals the symbolic nature of his god. A Hawthorne notebook entry, then, may well have played a part in generating a pivotally important aspect of the Lovecraft mythos. Lovecraft makes it clear in a late February 1937 letter, written only a few days before his death, that the direct source of his *Necronomicon,* or at least of its title, was a dream encompassing even what Lovecraft (erroneously) believed to be the Greek etymology: "Image of the Law of the Dead." But it seems highly probable that the Hawthorne note, with its similarity to the notion of Lovecraft's shunned and guarded volume, was a part of the assimilated lore out of which the oneiric image was born.

Many other comparisons can be drawn, even with respect to Hawthorne's short works, many of which Lovecraft admired. The patterns of similarity and possible or probable influence become complex. For example, in "Roger Malvin's Burial," Hawthorne describes a gravestone-like granite slab "upon which the veins seemed to form an inscription in forgotten characters" (*Novels* 1125). Lovecraft, always taken with the notion of haunting, elusive pseudomemory—of hidden meanings lying just beneath the surface of things—similarly writes of the Vermont landscape in "The Whisperer in Darkness": "I felt that the very outlines of the hills themselves held some strange and aeon-forgotten meaning, as if they were vast hieroglyphs left by a rumoured titan race whose glories live only in rare, deep dreams" (*CF* 2.511). These hill outlines, like Hawthorne's rock veins or the tattoos of Melville's Queequeg in *Moby-Dick,* are hauntingly inscrutable, almost-readable characters. This notion can be extended to that of ciphers, a common motif with Lovecraft ("The Dunwich Horror," "The Haunter of the Dark," "The Whisperer in Darkness," *The Case of Charles Dexter Ward*) and one that plays a part in Hawthorne's *Septimius Felton.* The latter, unfinished work has a character named Aunt Keziah, who boasts that she has resisted the temptations of the Black Man; Lovecraft's story "The Dreams in the Witch House" (set in Hawthorne's own Salem, called Arkham) deals with a witch named Keziah Mason consorting with the Black Man of witchcraft lore. The Hawthorne influence here is clear, though Lovecraft goes far in his use of the Black Man motif, boldly absorbing the whole of Salem witch-lore into his own mythos. *Septimius Felton* also deals with the motif of a silver key that leads to ancestral papers in a chest; Lovecraft's story "The Silver Key" treats of these things also, but (especially when considered together with the sequel "Through the Gates of the Silver Key") with a cosmic scope far beyond anything suggested by Hawthorne. This latter work is thematically related to another unfinished Hawthorne novel, *Dr. Grimshawe's Secret,* whose motif of the bloody footprint brings to mind the cloven hoofprint of Lovecraft's tale "The Unnamable," a story whose setting is the very Charter Street Burial Ground (in Salem) employed in the Hawthorne work. The configuration of comparisons and apparent influences comes to be, after a while, labyrinthine.

Many other examples could be cited. But it is clear that although Lovecraft did not greatly care for Hawthorne's style (at least as a style generally to emulate) or his allegorical moralizing, he was thematically influenced by Hawthorne to a considerable extent. Lovecraft, of course, worked out his chosen ideas in a way uniquely Lovecraftian; he was, for all his delvings into Poe, Lord Dunsany, and Hawthorne, a highly original thinker and writer, one who developed his oeuvre with a sense of cosmic horror more profound than that of Hawthorne (whose work pointed in rather different directions) but with a relation to Hawthorne very much in evidence. If the Custom House dreamer could read the tales of the dreamer from Providence, he would find old familiar images and themes, but would find them cosmically transmuted—not "shrouded in a blackness, ten times black," but shrouded in the blackness of the abyss.

Strange High Houses: Lovecraft and Melville

Readers familiar with H. P. Lovecraft's Dunsanian tale "The Strange High House in the Mist" may be surprised, upon reading Herman Melville's story "The Piazza," to find a number of striking parallels of plot and detail.

Melville's first-person narrator moves to the country to occupy an old farmhouse offering a northerly view of nearby mountains: "ranges, here and there double-filed, as in platoons, (which) shoulder and follow up upon one another, with their irregular shapes and heights" (92). The Lovecraftian textual parallel is of course Thomas Olney's arrival in Kingsport, where he sees "the crags climb lofty and curious, terrace on terrace, till the northernmost hangs in the sky like a grey frozen windcloud" (*CF* 2.88). Melville's narrator, having a piazza or semi-enclosed porch built on the north side of his house, espies in time what seems to be an unaccountable structure on the mountain, "the first peep of a strange house" (92); Lovecraft's Thomas Olney of course sees his own "strange house," and speaks with Kingsport natives about it just as Melville's narrator makes fruitless inquiries of his country neighbors. In "The Piazza" the narrator, like Thomas Olney, resolves to make a trek up to the strange house, and does so, meeting someone up there who changes him forever.

The descriptions of the respective houses are remarkably similar. Melville's "fairy" house (echoic with Lovecraft's "aether of faery") is a "low-storied, grayish cottage, capped nunlike, with a peaked roof" (97), "a roof newly shingled" (94), while Lovecraft's strange high house has "a grey primeval roof, peaked and shingled, whose eaves come nearly to the grey foundations" (*CF* 2.88), and is an "abnormally antique grey cottage in the sky" (*CF* 2.90). Melville's narrator first sees his faraway house on "a mad poet's afternoon" (93), and Lovecraft's opening paragraph tells us that "in still summer rains on the steep roofs of poets, the clouds scatter bits of those dreams" (*CF* 2.87) that the morning mists bring from the sea.

Clearly, if one wishes to make an argument for influence in the traditional sense, one finds the textual evidence here fairly strong; parallel passages of course do not prove influence absolutely, but it would seem not unlikely that Lovecraft (though he does not mention the story in any letter I have ever seen) read "The Piazza" and that it made its imprint upon his own "Strange High House." But the matter is not so simple as all that, when one considers these texts to have grafted themselves together to make intertext. Here, with a radicalized sense of the term "influence" not contingent upon causality or temporal priority, "influence" runs both ways; the texts, as on-going reader-participatory creations, write each other.

Indeed, the present reading is a good case in point; when I first read Melville's "The Piazza," I had already read Lovecraft's "The Strange High House in the Mist" many times over (finding it, of course, a different text each time), and there is no denying that in my own readerly re-creation of (and recreation in) the "Piazza" text, that text was influenced by Lovecraft. As a reader, one generally does not come to a text, after all, with amnesia; one comes to a text, rather, with the power to imprint upon that text all sorts of other textuality—each text becomes a palimpsest many times written over (like impressions on a child's magic writing-pad) by other texts. As Jacques Derrida says, each text is a set of multiple reading-heads for reading (and thus writing) other texts. Melville's and Lovecraft's "strange high houses" are mutually implicative constructs.

It is obvious, when one reads these tales, that each deals, in a way, with vampirism. Melville's narrator makes his pilgrimage to the "fairy" house and meets a mountain girl there named Marianna, whose face haunts him endlessly when he comes back down the mountain to his home. Lovecraft's Thomas Olney comes back down his own mountain having also been changed, perturbed, subtracted from. But the two vampirisms compare problematically. What Olney has lost is his sense of wonder, while Melville's narrator has lost his complacency and peace of mind. Olney starts out ill at ease with his lot, unsatisfied with common existence, and comes back robbed of this wanderlust: "The sameness of his days no longer gives him sorrow," we read, and "well-disciplined thoughts have grown enough for his imagination" (*CF* 2.95); Melville's narrator starts out at peace with his country solitude—"for what but picture galleries are the marble halls of these same limestone hills?" (90)—and comes back restless and starstruck.

As an intertextual figure, the wanderer—Lovecraft's, Melville's—is thus a figure divided against himself. When we read these texts as fully conflated intertext, peculiar questions arise as to who or what is vampire, who or what is victim. The intertextual wanderer has (as Olney) original discontent taken away by a text that substitutes contentment, and has (as Melville's "I") original contentment taken away by a text that substitutes discontent. The wanderer, himself an eternally unstable and self-deconstructing vampire/victim figure, vampirizes and is vampirized by both texts. The texts make vampiric incursions upon each other; Melville's Marianna (who robs the narrator of peace of mind) has her function usurped by the Lovecraft text (which substitutes discontent for contentment), and Lovecraft's high-mountain-house presence (who robs Olney of his visionary discontent) has its function usurped by the Melville text (which substitutes contentment for discontent). In each case, then, the supposed vampire—Melville's Marianna, Lovecraft's crag-presence—becomes a victim: of usurpation, of vampiric invasion by the other text. (It is as if each mountain-gazing wanderer, in journeying toward what will be a vampiric effect, journeys toward the other text—so that the texts strain toward each other, suggesting self-referentially the appeal of their own intertextuality.) In making such incursions, each text allegorizes its own content, since it not only deals narratively with vampirism but practices it as well! The intertext is thus an eerie mirror—dance of vampires and victims, a Nietzschean "dance of the pen" that becomes more intriguingly complex with every new reading.

Those traditionalists who are uncomfortable with such modes of reading may comment smilingly that it is intertextual-deconstructive reading itself that vampirises the text(s)—that deconstructionist denial of boundaries between texts becomes, itself, a vampiric incursion upon each text, draining each text of its "sanctity" or "integrity." And there would be a certain truth to this—albeit, I would claim, to the effect that the allegorization that we have mentioned moves to new levels then, so that the texts themselves, in their narrative and performative dealings with vampirism, always already adumbrate our "vampiric" readings. And as before, the effect cuts both ways, disturbing the opposition between vampire and victim, for not only does deconstruction "invade" the texts—the Melville/Lovecraft intertext makes its own incursion upon deconstruction, which is, after all, a developing matrix of textuality itself, continually modified by, rewritten by, all that with which it interacts.

Ambrose Bierce and H. P. Lovecraft

Samuel Loveman was in the enviable position of corresponding with Ambrose Bierce over literary matters for several years, up to the very time of Bierce's disappearance. Loveman was also a close friend to Howard Phillips Lovecraft, during a period later than the Bierce correspondence. One finds an interesting interweaving of relationships in these facts, together with the facts that Bierce influenced Lovecraft, that Lovecraft wrote important literary criticism on Bierce, and that Bierce and Lovecraft were further "linked" through the latter's revision client Adolphe de Castro, with whom Bierce had been embroiled in a complex question of collaboration and ascription. Had there been somewhat different timing—i.e., had Lovecraft known Loveman earlier, or better, had the Bierce-Loveman exchanges been able to occur later, when Lovecraft could have entered the circle with his own fictional plans taking clear form—we should probably have been witness at least to an exciting exchange of correspondence between Bierce and Lovecraft. But the stars were wrong; this meeting of the minds was not to be, and we shall have to be content with the web of relationships that did evolve.

Ambrose Bierce made lasting impressions on Lovecraft early, for the Providence gentleman says in the *United Amateur* (January 1920): "No formal course in fiction-writing can equal a close and observant perusal of the stories of Edgar Allan Poe or Ambrose Bierce" ("Literary Composition," *CE* 2.44). Later Lovecraft would evaluate Bierce in "Supernatural Horror in Literature," even quoting Samuel Loveman, who had said of Bierce that he had had an uncanny knack for conveying unusually powerful horror through what in less skillful hands would be simple, hack-like language. (One is reminded of the fact that Ben Jonson and Shakespeare have both been praised by critics for their masterful uses of "the little word.") In the essay cited, Lovecraft himself delivers perceptive critical comment on Bierce, noting his "sardonic comedy and graveyard humour," and concluding that although Bierce's writing was uneven, bothered as it sometimes was by a mechanical and journalistic style, Bierce must still loom large in American weird fiction, so that "his greatness is in no danger of eclipse" (*CE* 2.107–8). This view is somewhat more generous than that of Clifton Fadiman, who said, "Bierce is not, of course, a great writer" but conceded that Bierce was, "in his own constricted way, an artist" (xix).

Lovecraft's critical view of Bierce shifted somewhat as his own view of weird fiction developed. He had been willing to say of Bierce's stories, in "Supernatural Horror in Literature," that "a substantial proportion" of them could be said to "admit the malignly supernatural" (*CE* 2.107). But by 1930 he could write: "In literature we can easily see the cosmic quality in Poe, Maturin, Dunsany, de la Mare, & Blackwood, but I profoundly suspect the cosmicism of Bierce, James, & even Machen" (*SL* 3.196). Lovecraft came to feel that few writers of weird fiction achieve a truly cosmic scope in their work, and evidently saw Bierce as falling outside the inner circle of masters in that regard.

Nevertheless, it is clear that Bierce had his influence upon Lovecraft, who wrote in certain letters of 1919 and 1920 that Bierce had given shape to some of his more vivid dreams. Indeed, Bierce has been said to have influenced many writers, including William Faulkner, Sherwood Anderson, Ernest Hemingway, and Stephen Crane. In the case of Lovecraft one may point to a number of specific matters. Lovecraft discovered Bierce in 1919, and it may not be coincidental that, as S. T. Joshi has pointed out to me, Lovecraft's 1919 title "Beyond the Wall of Sleep" seems to echo Bierce's "Beyond the Wall," in *Can Such Things Be?* Lovecraft speaks at length, in "Supernatural Horror in Literature," of Bierce's oft-anthologized tale "The Damned Thing," and this tale seems to have left its mark on his own work. It is difficult to miss the imagistic similarity between the Bierce tale and Lovecraft's "The Unnamable," which also contains the character name Manton, possibly reflecting Bierce's use of that name in "The Middle Toe of the Right Foot," a tale of which Lovecraft has much to say in his critical survey. (Note that the amulet in Lovecraft's "The Hound" is referred to as "that damned thing" [*CF* 1.346].) Bierce's "The Damned Thing" also contains a possible impression-source in the Hugh Morgan diary entry describing the story's horror: "I am not mad; there are colors that we cannot see. And, God help me! the Damned Thing is of such a color!" This passage may conceivably be one of the impressions that provided a germinal source for Lovecraft's "The Colour out of Space."

One should note, however, that such tales as "Colour," written in the period of Lovecraft's maturing style, contain none of the biting, overtly sardonic tone of a typical Bierce tale. For a more Bierce-like sharpness in Lovecraft, one must look to such earlier tales as "The Terrible Old Man" and "In the Vault"—the latter story, in particular, is very similar to Bierce in tone and imagery. In Lovecraft's later style, one still finds cynicism and grim irony, but these narrative tones have been transmuted to far subtler form, quite unlike the heavy-handedness of, say, "The Terrible Old Man." At the same time, they have taken on a cosmicity of scope contrasting strikingly with the localism of the earlier tales, in that the ironic comment becomes directed at the mote-like place of all human history in the scheme of things. Bierce's alleged lack of such cosmic scope notwithstanding, it seems probable that Lovecraft derived at least a little of his lasting cynicism—his view of the universe as senseless and random—from reading Bierce, in whom this tone even in its more limited application sounds sharp and clear.

It should be mentioned that Bierce unwittingly contributed to what was to become the Lovecraft Mythos, in a way more tangible than that provided by his general tone of ironic pessimism. Robert W. Chambers, evidently much taken with Bierce's story "Haïta the Shepherd," borrowed the name Hastur from this story—in which it appears as the god of shepherds—for his own work "The Yellow Sign," in *The King in Yellow,* where Chambers also makes use of the name Carcosa, a borrowing from Bierce's "An Inhabitant of Carcosa." Borrowing in turn from Chambers, Lovecraft neatly absorbs Hastur into the general body of lore belonging to his Mythos, listing Hastur (and the Yellow Sign) as belonging to the traditions known to the common scholarship of Henry Wentworth Akeley and Albert N. Wilmarth in "The Whisperer in Darkness." In this connection it is well to note, however, that the Bierce-Chambers influence on the Lovecraft Mythos should not be exaggerated. Lin Carter, in his introduction to "The Yellow Sign" in *The Spawn of Cthulhu* (a collection containing his own verse "Litany to

Hastur," further echoing Ambrose Bierce), suggests that Lovecraft "quite likely" got his idea of the *Necronomicon* from reading of Chambers's fictional monstrous tome *The King in Yellow* (101). However, a more cautious look at letters and dates shows that Lovecraft, who first quoted the famous *Necronomicon* couplet in "The Nameless City" in 1921 and first referred to the mythical tome by name in "The Hound" in 1922, did not discover the horror fiction of Robert W. Chambers until 1927, when he made the discovery just in time to "make some eleventh-hour inserts in the proofs" (*SL* 2.127) of "Supernatural Horror in Literature" for W. Paul Cook. I have discovered a more likely—at least chronologically possible—source of Lovecraft's *Necronomicon* idea, in the form of an 1835 entry in a Nathaniel Hawthorne notebook, a story idea: "An old volume in a large library,—every one to be afraid to unclasp and open it, because it was said to be a book of magic" (26). Lovecraft's commonplace book shows that he had read Hawthorne's notebooks by 1919, in plenty of time to develop and use the *Necronomicon* idea in 1921. Thus, however important and fascinating may be the Bierce-Chambers-Lovecraft thread, one must exercise the proper caution of scholarship to keep such inference within its necessary limits.

Another interesting connection between Ambrose Bierce and Lovecraft resides in their common "collaborator"—in Lovecraft's case, revision client—the German Adolphe de Castro, whose real name was (Dr.) Gustav Adolph Danziger. This de Castro, to use the more familiar appellation, had translated *The Monk and the Hangman's Daughter* from the German original of Richard Voss. De Castro, as Lovecraft put it, "had Bierce work it into shape," i.e., considerably revise and polish it stylistically; but de Castro later played down Bierce's part in the work, claiming most of the credit himself, and pressing upon Lovecraft, his ghostwriter in later projects, a body of argumentative matter designed to prove de Castro the "real author" of the work. De Castro came to refer to the work as "founded on," rather than "translated from," the German original, claiming that Bierce had sent him a letter proving the minimality of the latter's part in the work. Lovecraft quotes the passage in question: "The book is almost perfect as you wrote it; the part of the work that pleases me least is my part." Lovecraft points out, however, that the letter from which this passage is excised concerns plot, not stylistics or phrasing; and that the story's "magick" is ultimately Voss's. Lovecraft makes the astute observation that the work's intimate feeling for Bavaria required the author to be *both* a German and an artist; of the three people involved, only Voss was both. Lovecraft put forth the assessment that de Castro's misused Bierce's letter, which really meant that Bierce's part in the work (chiefly linguistic) was secondary to that of Voss; de Castro was a translator, Bierce supplied the phraseology, but the story itself (plot, coloring) was Voss's (see *SL* 2.204–7). Lovecraft, in fact, deplored de Castro's prose style and spent untold amounts of time trying to revise his stories into readable form. He saw de Castro as simply capitalizing on the reputation of Bierce. The obvious ironic parallel here, between Bierce and Lovecraft, is that in both cases—Lovecraft having ghostwritten many impressive stories for his "revision" clients, some of whom treated him shabbily in return—lesser writers gained recognition from their associations with greater writers.

Again, it is truly unfortunate that Bierce and Lovecraft never met or corresponded. If the chronology of lives had been slightly different, it seems likely that they would have become acquainted through their mutual friend Samuel Loveman, with whom Lovecraft shared many travels and literary exchanges. (Unfortunately, Loveman much later in life developed the peculiar idea that Lovecraft was all the time concealing profound hatred for him because of his Jewish ancestry, although Lovecraft showed him long-abiding friendship and respect.) One may speculate endlessly what interesting exchanges a Bierce-Lovecraft friendship would have yielded, similar in various ways as the two writers were. In his letters, Bierce shows himself to be, like Lovecraft, bitterly cynical about the intelligence of some editors—but at the same time, like Lovecraft, kindly, patient, and friendly to young writers who came to him for help. It is tempting to quote from these revealing epistles, but there is no need. They can speak for themselves, and for one who has long since passed, in shrouds of great mystery, into the Ultimate Abyss.

A Note on Lovecraft and Rupert Brooke

In her reminiscences of her late former husband H. P. Lovecraft, Sonia Davis remarks, of his tastes in literature:

> H. P. loved the untrodden paths and would try to find them, always seeking the weird, the uncanny and the unusual. Although he was an ardent admirer of Edgar Allan Poe I doubt whether he was entirely influenced by his works. He may have been, in his youth, but in later years he admired Arthur Machen, Lord Dunsany, Huysmans, Pater; and Rupert Brooke was quite an idol of his. (Davis 20)

Lovecraft indeed seems to have thought enough of the English poet Rupert Brooke to mention him at times in company with such figures as John Masefield, A. E. Housman, Walter de la Mare, and William Butler Yeats ("today perhaps the greatest living poet") (*CE* 1.190). By common standards, much of Rupert Brooke's poetry can scarcely be said to measure up to that of, say, Yeats, and it may well be that Lovecraft's assessment of Brooke was colored by his own Anglophilia. There is no question that Lovecraft must have been deeply stirred by Brooke's lines, in "The Soldier,"

> If I should die, think only this of me:
> That there's some corner of a foreign field
> That is for ever England. . . . (Brooke 111)

Lovecraft even quotes these lines twice: first in his preface to John Ravenor Bullen's *White Fire* (1927), then in a letter (with "England" in capitals) (*SL* 3.363). Thus the admiration for Brooke perceived by Sonia was rather likely to have been, on Lovecraft's part, at least as much a matter of reaction to theme as to poetic quality as such.

Nevertheless, Brooke's poetry is far from being without merit, and Lovecraft may have found much in it to admire for its own sake, both in thematic and stylistic terms. The poems contain types of imagery ranging from the delicately beautiful tone of

> Tenderly, day that I have loved, I close your eyes,
> And smooth your quiet brow, and fold your thin dead hands
> ("Day That I Have Loved"; Brooke 23)

to the starkly macabre tone of

> An unmeaning point upon the mud; a speck
> Of moveless horror; an Immortal One
> Cleansed of the world, sentient and dead; a fly
> Fast-stuck in grey sweat on a corpse's neck
> ("The Life Beyond"; Brooke 67)

or of lines describing embracing lovers who are dead but do not know it:

> And then
> They suddenly felt the wind blow cold,
> And knew, so closely pressed,
> Chill air on lip and breast,
> And, with a sick surprise,
> The emptiness of eyes.
> ("Dead Men's Love"; Brooke 72)

It is clear that Brooke's variegated poetry contains much that can have caught Lovecraft's fancy for one reason or another.

The question, of course, is whether one may trace any clear influence of Brooke's poetry upon Lovecraft's own work. It is quite possible—one hesitates to say "probable" in regard to not strictly provable points of influence—that Lovecraft found something worth keeping in Brooke's lines

> Out of the nothingness of sleep,
> The slow dreams of Eternity,
> There came a thunder on the deep;
> I came, because you called to me.
>
> I broke the Night's primeval bars,
> I dared the old abysmal curse,

And flashed through ranks of frightened stars
Suddenly on the universe!

("The Call"; Brooke 41)

The similarity of all this imagery to that of Lovecraft's "The Call of Cthulhu" is obvious and striking, especially considering that Brooke's poem is even titled "The Call." Although the remaining six stanzas of the work do not bear out the initial impressions (turning the poem into one that speaks of eternal lovers), the crowding of so much evocative imagery into the first eight lines produces an effect that can scarcely have been lost on Lovecraft.

We cannot read of the "nothingness of sleep," the "slow dreams of Eternity," out of which the poem's persona is called in a "thunder on the deep," without thinking of great dead-but-undead Cthulhu, lying in His watery tomb—

In his house at R'lyeh dead Cthulhu waits dreaming (*CF* 2.34)

—and awaiting the time to emerge and claim His own. The poem's persona, who "broke the Night's primeval bars" and "dared the old abysmal curse" to "flash through ranks of frightened stars" and come "suddenly on the universe," cannot but put us in mind of the sudden emergence of the octopoid high-priest Cthulhu who has been waiting for countless ages for the stars to come 'round right, waiting to "flash suddenly on the universe," frightening, no doubt, even the stars. (The "I came because you called to me" is not exactly paralleled in the story, in which it is Cthulhu who "calls." One makes the comparison *mutatis mutandis.*) Whatever Brooke's actual intentions, it is clear that the quoted lines can only have worked powerfully on Lovecraft's fecund imagination, his sense of morbid cosmicism and vast gulfs of time.

It would appear, since Sonia mentions Brooke as an "idol" of her former husband's and must have drawn most of her knowledge of his literary interests from the New York period, that at least there is little danger of any problems of chronology in thinking that Brooke's "The Call" may well have been at least something of an influence on "The Call of Cthulhu," which Lovecraft wrote in Providence in 1926 shortly after returning from his New York "exile."[1] Whether this possible point of influence is real is, of course, uncertain, but it remains an interesting and not unreasonable speculation that in some germinal way, Rupert Brooke may have assisted as a midwife in the literary birth of Cthulhu.

1. HPL sketched out the bare plot of the story while still in New York, on 12–13 August 1925, in fact; see HPL's 1925 diary (*CE* 5.165).

Studies of Individual Tales

Iranon and Kuranes: An Intertextual Gloss

In "The Quest of Iranon," Lovecraft's purple robed minstrel Iranon wanders the earth in search of his remembered city of Aira; in "Celephaïs," Lovecraft's dreamer Kuranes wanders in dream in search of his own briefly-glimpsed marvelous city of Celephaïs. In many respects one feels that the two wanderers Iranon and Kuranes are thematically the same peripatetic soul, with different names, and it may prove interesting to meld the differently named aspects of this one mythic quester to see how, as one coalesced figure, he comments intertextually upon himself.

The wanderer, as Iranon among the stern-faced inhabitants of the granite city of Teloth, has "no heart for the cobbler's trade," preferring to sing of the beautiful memories of his childhood, but he is told that "song is folly" (*CF* 1.250). As Kuranes, caring not "for the ways of people about him," he prefers "to dream and write of his dreams" (*CF* 1.184), but those about him laugh at his writings. In both aspects, the source of his scorned art is memory—for Iranon, memory regarded as recollection of a real childhood home; for Kuranes, memory regarded as recollection of a childhood dream. Thus on this point the quester differs from himself. A valuational distinction between the "realities" of dream and of waking may ultimately be superfluous—Lovecraft's narrator in "The Silver Key" reminds us, after all, that "all life is only a set of pictures in the brain, among which there is no difference betwixt those born of real things and those born of inward dreamings, and no cause to value the one above the other" (*CF* 2.73)—but in any case the quester differs with himself over basic attitudinal and perceptive distinctions. As Iranon, he searches for his lost city only when he supposes that it corresponds to a remembered outward reality of his childhood as opposed to a memory of his childhood dreams; as Kuranes, he chooses to search for his once-glimpsed city because it corresponds to a childhood dream that he prefers to the outward realities of prosaic adulthood. The journeying quester pursues his goal tragically divided against himself, one side of his personality embracing an understanding wholly suppressed by the other side. Yet this difference is on another level dismantled by the fact that the two facets are in agreement, in that they both in their respective ways reject the "Silver Key" axiom. As Iranon, the quester would not suppress the oneiric nature of his cherished city if he believed that dream and outward reality hold equal importance; likewise, as Kuranes, if he believed so, he would not prefer dream to outward reality. Each facet takes a stand, each complementing the other like the two sides of a coin—a stand against the axiom. But there is paradox in the fact that it is by splicing the texts together that one sees this homogeneity, when the merging has the effect of grafting one text ("Iranon") in which the assumption seems to be that on a practical level the "Silver Key" axiom is false (Iranon is destroyed by the discovery that his "reality" is the memory of but a dream) with another text ("Celephaïs") in which a narrative indifference to the dream-versus-reality distinction persists to the end, where both dream and reality are treated in balance. Clearly, an interwoven web of paradox and textual self-subversion exists here, a web in which the critical process is itself enmeshed.

The quester, as Iranon, meets a young boy named Romnod, who, unlike his stern-visaged peers, seems a kindred spirit; together they search at length for the marvelous city, Romnod growing older while Iranon seems not to age. They find lodgment in the garishly festive city of Oonai, a poor parody of the city of Iranon's yearning, and Romnod grows coarse with wine and revelry and finally dies. Romnod has served textually as a kind of comparative figure; not sharing the central quester's memories of the marvelous city, he ages while the quester remains young, and not having the quester's standards, he is content with the experience of Oonai and its dissipations; he perishes, while the quester lives to quest again—but Iranon reclaims his purple rags and returns to the road only when Romnod has died; Iranon seems to have needed this experience to turn his mind back upon the quest with the conviction that Oonai has been no adequate substitute for the city of his memories. But as Kuranes, the quester has depended upon no

Romnod, no comparative object-lesson, to maintain his vision; wandering through dreamscapes, he has found lesser places than his dream-city, but has not lingered, has not really tried to content himself with them, his vision and goal remaining fixed. As Kuranes, the quester has an underlying potential for weakness (the ironic—Iranonic?—side of his personality) that he must not allow to surface and to deflect him from his steadfastness; as Iranon, the quester has an underlying strength (the Kuranes—curative?—side of his personality) that sustains him through periods of confusion.

Yet the respective sides of this complementation contain elements antithetical to themselves. Kuranes, though seemingly self-sustaining and unswerving of purpose, is tempted in the dreamland of the red-roofed pagodas to forget his Celephaïs, and he must eventually resort to drugs to maintain his quest; even as the strong side of Iranon's personality he contains seeds of weakness. Reciprocally, Iranon, though seemingly less self-sustaining, does carry on his quest without the departed Romnod, persevering though people laugh at his songs and his tattered robes; even as the weak side of Kuranes' personality he harbors reserves of strength. Thus as a unitary figure, the quester is not merely so heterogeneous as to possess a personality in which strength and weakness are mingled; in the quester's multiply complex being, there is strength in the weakness and weakness in the strength, a sort of thematic chiasmus, so that the difference between the poles of the personality dismantles itself into ways in which strength differs from itself and weakness differs from itself. Like all great fictional heroes, the wanderer is richly enigmatic.

Traditionally, the mythic hero dies in the quest and is reborn. In these present texts, to the extent that one credits their conventional boundaries, one does not find the typical mythopoeic pattern. Iranon, upon hearing the old shepherd disclose the dream-nature of the elusive city of Aira, simply walks into the quicksand (as an old man now) and dies; Kuranes, though he both dies physically and lives on in some sphere of dream, does not die and become reborn in temporal succession. It is only when one merges the texts, refusing to accept the tyranny of their artificial boundaries, that one finds the whole timeless pattern of death and rebirth. The wanderer, as Iranon the vulnerable, perishes, and we are told that "that night something of youth and beauty died in the elder world" (*CF* 1.255). The quicksand that swallows him is the dead-handed judgment of the world that dream is mere dream; it is the same stultifying judgment that has driven the quester, as the dreamer Kuranes, inward upon himself to begin with, to find a higher reality. But as Kuranes he prevails; the "Silver Key" axiom affirms itself after all in the arrival of "the cortege of knights come from Celephaïs to bear him thither for ever" (*CF* 1.190). What is confused in the seeker—the beautiful and noble but irresolute Iranon, for whom dream is not enough—has died, and what is left is strength and clarity of conviction: Kuranes reigns forever "over Ooth-Nargai and all the neighbouring regions of dream" (*CF* 1.191). The archetypal inscription of heroic death and rebirth emerges here with the recognition that as in all worthy literature, textual boundaries—boundaries between texts and critical processes—are themselves a prosaic integument of mundane illusion obscuring the wonders of dream.

On Lovecraft's Fragment "Azathoth"

In June 1922 H. P. Lovecraft wrote a piece of about five hundred words, titled "Azathoth," a reflection of plans for a novel never written. On 9 June 1922 he wrote to Frank Belknap Long: "*Imagination* is the great refuge. That is the theme of the weird Vathek-like novel *Azathoth,* on whose opening pages I have been experimenting. I even planned it long ago, but only began work—or play—on it a few days ago. Probably I'll never finish it" (*SL* 1.185). Two years later, he was still pondering it; on 3 February 1924 he wrote to Edwin Baird of what he called "my big novel idea—*Azathoth*—which will be exotic and highbrow" (*SL* 1.295). Lovecraft's editors understandably have labeled this two-page piece a "fragment." Yet at the outset with this text, as with any such text, we encounter an immensely difficult problem.

What is a "fragment"? And even supposing we settle upon some fairly workable understanding of that term, what is a "fragment" a fragment of?

The word itself derives from an Indo-European root *bhreg-,* "to prick," "to cut," "to break," and is thus suggestive of cutting away, separation, breaking off. (This same root is responsible for numerous other linguistic forms, including *fraction, fracture, break,* and *brake.*) But if a fragment is something cut away or broken off, what is it cut away or broken off *from?* It may be that we are simply hypnotized by grammar into supposing (since a preposition "needs" an object) that "fragment" leads syntactically to "fragment of" and that a fragment must be a fragment of *something,* but it would seem that only by following such a notion can we find significational function in the term: otherwise, a fragment is just a text—a conclusion that may well present itself even so.

If, then, a fragment is a cut-away or broken-off piece of something larger, then how are we to arrive at any conception of that larger entity from which it is supposedly separated? Even with works "completed" (a problematical notion, as we shall observe), we cannot of course deal in terms of authorial intent as retrievable phenomenological context; and in the case of a larger work planned but never written, we are doubly cut off from what that work "is," if it can "be" anything.

L. Sprague de Camp makes an intriguingly odd comment about the text question here: "Although Lovecraft never finished *Azathoth,* he used the same concept in some of his later stories, so the world lost nothing by his failure to finish this rudiment" (127). Here the larger text, from which the text in question is supposed to be broken off, is in effect regarded as a definite work (whatever a work never written may be) of which we can make valuational judgements: a work in whose absence "the world lost nothing," a text similar to certain specific other texts in thematic terms, a text not sufficiently different from other texts to be of literary interest. Such amount to reification: treatment of the hypothetical and the abstract as the concrete and the specific. Yet of course in rejecting the view that the *Azathoth*-that-might-have-been is in any way describable or fit to serve as the subject of a sentence and have qualities predicated of it or denied to it, we are left with the initial question: what, then, is a fragment a fragment *of?*

But this question is no more vexing than another, related one: what would it mean for a literary text to be "complete"?

Indeed, the completeness/fragmentation bipolarity amounts to a curiously self-deconstructing opposition. Fragmentation is necessarily suggestive of completeness, of some plenitude of which the fragment is a fragment; as a linguistic signifier, *fragment* points away beyond itself into a further realm that defines the fragment as a fragment—it contains the trace of the notion, at least, of plenitude. Yet, conversely, completeness contains the trace of generating fragmentation; anything described (even erroneously) as "complete" can only be so by virtue of reaching out beyond a certain fragmentation or inchoateness; reaching completeness (were that possible) would mean no longer *having* to be a fragment of some larger entity, hence completeness still contains the notion of the fragment as an enabling condition. Completeness of a literary text is, in any case, illusory; we can scarcely have a complete text, a text full and whole in every possible way, a text to which nothing may be added, a well-defined text finished and bordered in such a way that nothing of interest lies beyond its borders. Even to imagine a defining border requires thinking on both sides of it; there is no border that has nothing on its other side, and there is no text that is complete, possessed of closure, incapable of growth. (A text, of course, does not really have a border, or if it does, the border, rather than being fixed, is something that flickers continuously in and out of existence: by being put up, it collapses by drawing attention to and thus uniting both the sides that it purports to separate; and by having those sides, it erects itself anew, to collapse again, ad infinitum.)

Why do we call a story or an essay a "piece"? Paradoxically, the term for most people suggests something of completeness: a sonata regarded as finished is a "piece." To call a two-page novel-fragment a "piece" in this sense may even strike one as pretentious, though "piece" in other contexts means something like "fragment." Again, fragmentation and completeness perpetually problematize themselves. But in a very arguable way, every text is a "fragment." For example: Lovecraft, in a letter to R. H. Barlow (13 July 1931), once toyed with the notion of writing a sequel to "The Whisperer in Darkness": "I had thought of some possible later story dealing with Yuggoth, Akeley, & the Outer Ones, but may never get around to it" (*O Fortunate Floridian* 4). Clearly, then, "Whisperer" is in a sense a fragment—borderless, incomplete, formative, falling short of any imagined plenitude, inviting expansion and dissemination. But again we have the same problem: we are hard put to know by what basis of textual comparison it is fragmentary. Obviously, neither "Azathoth" nor "Whisperer" is a fragment in the same sense in which, e.g., "From the Dark" in one issue of *Home Brew* (given the other issues) might be regarded as a fragment of "Herbert West—Reanimator." Yet they are fragments in some philosophically more mysterious way.

We may attempt to approach the question in another manner. If we cannot postulate a definite text of which "Azathoth" is a fragment, we may suggest that it is a fragmentary aspect of a field of texts which, typically enough, weave together to form intertext. S. T. Joshi has pointed out that the piece in question thematically foreshadows at least one other text: "The fragment 'Azathoth' (1922) tells little about the entity, and seems—in its depiction of a man's quest to escape tawdry modernity by dream-voyagings—an adumbration of *The Dream-Quest of Unknown Kadath*" (*Reader's Guide* 42). But we may point out other such connections, not necessary time-relational in the same way. The imagery, in "Azathoth," of "strange dolphins and sea-nymphs" certainly interweaves with similar imagery in "The Strange High House in the Mist" (1926)—"Trident-beating Neptune was there, and sportive tritons and fantastic nereids, and upon dolphins' backs was balanced a vast crenulate shell" (*CF* 2.94)—a tale from which we recall a protagonist-quest not unlike that of the novel-fragment's nameless dreamer—and in "Azathoth" we may trace, as well, thematic similarities to such other subsequent texts as "The Silver Key" (1926), in terms of the notion of escaping from the ennui of life.

But "Azathoth" points backward in time too; it is hard to miss its thematic and narrative similarity to "Celephaïs," in which we find Kuranes seeking his desired city in lands of dream, and finding it one night only to leave behind "the body of a tramp" to be tossed by the tides, just as in "Azathoth" we read that the unnamed protagonist has departed for his journey into dream worlds leaving behind "the body that leaned stiffly from the lonely window" (*CF* 1.338). (One is even reminded, here, of the ending of "The Haunter of the Dark," *mutatis mutandis*.) Clearly, these accounts leave us well capable of asking: what then? Where further does the text lead? If "Azathoth" is a fragment, then "Celephaïs" is fragmentarily open-ended in a very similar manner. I venture to coin a term here, *fragmeme:* a textual unit of incompleteness that interrelates with other such units in a mutually defining way; i.e., a fragmeme is a linguistic sign or field of signs underscoring incompleteness as a mutually enabling condition of signs. The ending of "Azathoth"—"And in the course of many cycles they [the tides of far spheres] tenderly left him sleeping on a green sunrise shore; a green shore fragrant with lotus-blossoms and starred by red camalotes" (*CF* 1.338)—is a passage-level fragmeme pointing away not only to other identifiable texts of similar thematic concern but also to an unlimited and undefinable universe of possible contiguity in terms of which the fragmeme reflects upon its own further text-generating incompleteness. (The same may be said for the ending of "Celephaïs," where Kuranes, in Ooth-Nargai, still reigns and will reign forever; this suggestion, far from pinning down the future, leaves it more open to speculation than ever—if Kuranes is always to reign in Ooth-Nargai, then an eventful future lies before us, if a future can lie "before," and we ask: what things will happen, what things will be said and thought and felt, while Kuranes reigns?)

The text "Azathoth," itself an extended fragmeme, points in many directions away from itself to a larger field of text (certainly to include "XXII. Azathoth" of *Fungi from Yuggoth*), a differential web of textuality (pointing back to the novel-fragment "Azathoth") in which "Azathoth" defines itself by its incompleteness and in which each text is a 'fragment' definable only, and at best, in terms of its relation to other texts: a relation by which each text imbues each other text. and is imbued by each other text, with a necessary incompleteness without which a text could not function as it does. We shall not be able to identify "insides" or "outsides" to these texts, the very binary opposition of inside/outside being self-deconstructing; *Dream-Quest* and "Celephaïs" and "The Silver Key" and other texts are as much "inside" the fragment "Azathoth" as "outside" it—"Azathoth" is a sprawling relational network of text that is most "fragmentary" by simply *being* a text: borderless, insideless, outsideless, edgeless, subtly woven into a scintillating field of moving textuality. (De Camp's Lovecraft biography indexes, under the fragment *Azathoth,* a number of references merely to Azathoth the "daemon-sultan," thus unwittingly suggesting that the text "Azathoth" enjoys a relation of mutual containment with other texts that treat of the "god" Azathoth.) The text that we call "Azathoth" is at once a fragmeme, a web of fragmemes pointing to each other, and a field of relations relating them to each other by their mutual implications of incompleteness. It is an eternally incomplete self-commentary upon incompleteness; i.e., it is a text highlighting its fragmentary nature and the fragmentary nature of other texts. And as a text, it naturally evokes multiple and problematized readings, "disturbing itself," as someone has defined textual deconstruction, "along its own fault-lines," fault-lines which run ever out into the very fabric of language.

Looking at the "Azathoth" text itself ('itself' being, as has been suggested, a thorny notion), we may observe that in a fashion typical of literary texts, it works covertly to subvert its own supposedly central or stable features. In particular, the text purports to position the unnamed dreamer as a central consciousness about which everything will pivot, but (as one might especially expect anyway in a canon of work wherein the notion of anthropocentrism is continually eroded) this centrality is subtly but observably dismantled.

The protagonist is brought on stage in the opening paragraph as if expected to be central in importance: when the world had grown stale and ugly and bereft of the beauty of dreams, "there was a man who travelled out of life on a quest into the spaces whither the world's dreams had fled" (*CF* 1.337). Yet the text loses no time in subverting this apparent centrality. The dreamer is described as coming home to a dismal room where his one window opened only onto a grimy city scene "where other windows stared in dull despair" (*CF* 1.337). We may regard the staring of windows (common with Lovecraft: the window/eye metaphor) either as a rhetorical anthropomorphism, in which case nonhuman things have displaced the human capacity for reflection, or as a sort of metonymy by which the windows have been made to substitute for those persons who might live behind them and look out through them, in which case, again, attention has been drawn away from the supposedly center-stage dreamer. The text goes on to say: "From that casement one might see only walls and windows, except sometimes when one leaned far out and peered aloft" (*CF* 1.337), and it is interesting that the impersonal pronoun *one* has replaced the dreamer; the text could have said, but does not, that *he* might see only walls and windows, and that he leaned out. It would seem that the dreamer, here, is relegated to the status of a sort of synecdoche, a part representing the whole, in which he stands for a vague but larger group of people who might have lived in the room and might have looked out the same window. In any case, the centrality of the dreamer is covertly assailed, early on.

The text continues in this inclination to spotlight yet efface the dreamer, in its handling of narrative point of view. We read that the dreamer, looking at a small patch of sky above the dreary city, watched the stars and called them by name, and was inclined "to follow them in fancy when they glided regretfully out of sight" (*CF* 1.338); and we notice something curious: if the point of view were pivoted in a central-intelligence way about the dreamer, "regrettably" would have been a more appropriate word than "regretfully." ("Regretfully," if the point of view is to remain with the dreamer, functions like the misplaced "hopefully" in "The mail will hopefully arrive.") It is the stars that are gliding "regretfully," and the effect is to move the center of consciousness to them, and away from the dreamer. What we have here is no mere infelicity of diction, but rather a striking example of texts' capacity to subvert their own seemingly stable workings. The machination of decentering the dreamer finds further expression when we read, in the passage immediately following, that one night "the dream-haunted skies swelled down to the lonely watcher's window" (*CF* 1.338) so that the skies assumed the initiative that the dreamer, who might in dream have moved to the skies rather than vice-versa, should supposedly have enjoyed. (Notice, also, that the skies in being "dream-haunted" are anthopomorphized.) The dreamer here, and passim, is passive rather than active; he is only acted upon, in this matter at least, and even when he acts, as in "toiling all day among shadow and turmoil" (*CF* 1.337), we see this action as being largely effaced in terms of narrative significance.

It is even curious that the dreamer is characterized as a dreamer at all, for in the opening paragraph we read of "tall towers grim and ugly, in whose shadow none might dream" (*CF* 1.337); this use of "none" seems to place the dreamer in a class of people containing no one, and thus to question his very existence. True, he enters the realm of dream only when the skies swell down to his room and bear him away from the grim city, but he does watch the stars out of sight and follow them "in fancy," and that, after all, is a species of dreaming. He is, ineluctably, a dreamer in a place where there are no dreamers.

The point of view of the text encounters more self-displacement in the final sentence, when the dreamer is left "sleeping on a green sunrise shore . . . fragrant with lotus-blossoms and starred by red camalotes" (*CF* 1.338). "Fragrant," in its sensory suggestions, indicates a point of view occupied by the dreamer—but the dreamer is sleeping, and has yet to "awake," as it were, to a capacity to find the shore "fragrant." Clearly the point of view here has shifted outward from the dreamer's consciousness to a sort of omniscience, and again the effect is to deny centrality to that very figure that the text pretends to make central.

"Azathoth," as we have seen, weaves together with other canonical texts, and indeed with such extracanonical texts as those of Dunsany, so that in hoping to sound its depths we find ourselves standing on the brink of an abyss. We comment in conclusion here only that even a "fragment" may constitute a far-ranging world of shifting and enigmatic text. It is significant that Lovecraft, in one of the letters cited, refers to beginning "work—or play" with the text, admitting a playful aspect to its formation, because of course all texts have their ludic qualities, such as the capacity here of "Azathoth" to sport with its own structure. Lovecraft said, "Probably I'll never finish it. . . ." Neither will we.

Aporia and Paradox in "The Outsider"

H. P. Lovecraft's "The Outsider" (*CF* 1.265–72) carries as its central thematic content the notion of self-awareness, the mythic heroic quest for self-understanding. Whether viewed as an allegorical figure making the eternally iterated journey through the Jungian psyche to find wholeness (see Mosig) or as the embodiment of some other critical precept, the narrator, the Outsider herself,[1] clearly quests for self-knowledge in her perilous climb up the "black ruined tower," her sojourn across open countryside to the "venerable ivied castle," and her apocalyptic moment at the mirror. But in terms of a deconstructionist reading of the logic of the tale, she opens, in discovering her nature, a Pandora's box of interwoven paradox.

Superficially, the text draws a strong contrast between the Outsider and the revelers in the castle. The "merry company" consists of normal, living people whose contrast with the carrion horror that the Outsider finds in the mirror could scarcely be more pronounced. Yet it is a common circumstance in the self-deconstructing function of texts that such apparently simple bipolar differences must become dismantled by

1. Mollie Burleson provides a strong argument to the effect that the Outsider, though theretofore generally assumed male, is probably a woman. I find the argument compelling and will employ the feminine pronoun. Interestingly, in the original appearance of this article in *CoC* No. 49 (1987), while I was, like everyone else, still calling the Outsider "he," I did unwittingly make that reference to the Outsider's opening a Pandora's box, and this image of course makes more sense when the Outsider is understood to be a woman. This is an example of the manner in which texts "read" other texts; the later Mollie Burleson text was needed, from the outset, as a "reading head" (as Jacques Derrida would say) for my article. In any event, the question of gender in HPL's fiction is one that, I predict, will loom ever larger as time goes on, and Mollie's original insight into the-Outsider-as-woman is destined to be regarded as an essential turning-point in the reading of HPL.

other, more subtle, less dismantlable differences, differences not between the two sides of the bipolarity, but ways in which each supposedly distinct side of the binary opposition differs problematically with itself; indeed, in any such analysis, superficial differences can continue to appear to be real only by suppression of those more internal differences by whose uncovering they are dismantled. Such is the case with the Outsider and her "merry company."

A primary source of contrast resides in the very question of self-discovery. The Outsider, upon touching the mirror, comes to an understanding of her own nature; it is significant that she is the only figure present to find such understanding—no doubt every person in the hall has looked in the mirror and known the face staring back to be his or her own, yet the revelers, by this act, learn nothing of importance about themselves. They have not climbed the frightful stone tower into the moonlight; they have not *earned* self-knowledge. The Outsider's experience is one of learning; the revelers, who become "a herd of delirious fugitives," have no mental experience at all except primal reactions out of fear. And yet we may ask whether each of these characterizations is not alloyed with elements antithetical to "itself."

The Outsider, though reaching a new self-awareness, a "single and fleeting avalanche of soul-annihilating memory," does so only to lose it in the next moment: "I forgot what had horrified me, and the burst of black memory vanished in a chaos of echoing images." She is still sufficiently in possession of her former mentality to return to her trapdoor and try to open it, to try to return to her customary life, and it is only upon finding this return impossible that she adopts her "new wildness and freedom." In her actions subsequent to the revelation at the mirror, the text self-subverts its theme of the Outsider's acquisition of self-understanding, and proceeds to self-subvert even the self-subversion in portraying the Outsider's adoption of her new life, albeit under duress. The partygoers, on the other hand, who learn nothing from the mirror, perhaps do learn something from the experience on another level; they must have seen in the Outsider what she has seen in herself: an "abhorrent travesty on the human shape"—and at least at some unconscious level they must know that the Outsider is what they themselves will become in the dissolution of the grave; they thus find a species of self-knowing to which they can respond only by fleeing,

fleeing in effect from themselves. Thus one finds ambiguities on each side that complement ambiguities on the other. To the extent that the Outsider learns less of herself than might be supposed and the revelers lack self-discovery, the Outsider resembles the revelers; to the extent that the Outsider does, after a fashion, find self-understanding while at least some implied self-understanding must filter through to the revelers, the Outsider again resembles the revelers. The difference between the two is imbued with complexities arising from the way in which the Outsider differs from herself, and the way in which the revelers differ from themselves, in mutually complementing heterogeneity.

But further questions arise in terms of whether the Outsider *is,* or whether she remains, an outsider. On a level too symbolically significant to be dismissed as merely the level of word-play, it is striking that after the Outsider's appearance in the great hall, it is she who remains inside and the revelers who are outside. To the extent that the Outsider has, in a way, achieved self-awareness, the suggestion is that she has become an "insider," as it were; and to the extent that the "merry company" has failed to achieve any new self-awareness, they have become outsiders, still unfamiliar with the selves they might have come to know, separated from themselves, banished from the lighted arena of knowledge. Again, the text has essentially subverted itself in this spatial symbolism, suggesting a reversal of roles or characterizations. Yet these ambiguities interweave with those previously mentioned, in that there is still a question as to whether either the Outsider or the partygoers do attain self-knowledge.

In considering these matters, one finds one's discernments drawn into aporia, or irresolvable alternation—the heterogeneities of reading oscillate against one another in logical loops of vibration that are set ringing by the touching finger at the mirror. But it is important to realize that such paradoxical content, far from detracting from the "value" of the text, stands as *necessary* to its functioning. The dénouement of "The Outsider" would be a wholly different textual matter, one not so rich in interpretative potential, without the inwoven fabric of paradox. The reader is as embroiled in paradox as is the Outsider herself; indeed, in a sense, the reader becomes the Outsider by reading the tale. The whole content of the Outsider's experience at the mirror is no more or less uncertain than is the question of our knowing ourselves with any completeness. It is the nature of indwelling paradox that whole knowledge and certainty are not to be. One suspects that, like the synecdochic Outsider, we all oscillate continually between self-knowledge and darkness—and that at some points of this oscillation, darkness and self-knowledge are one and the same.

Is Lovecraft's "Ph'nglui mglw'nafh . . ." a Cryptogram?

Around 1956 when, at the age of fourteen or so, I first read Lovecraft's "The Call of Cthulhu," I had already been interested in cryptography for some time, and seeing the utterance

Ph'nglui mglw'nafh Cthulhu R'lyeh wgah'nagl fhtagn

immediately set me to wondering if it might be a cryptogram of some kind, concealing some veiled text presumably known only to Lovecraft. Some portions of the ciphertext or cryptotext (as I will call it for convenience, whether it really is one or not) are just barely pronounceable—I once caused a scene at a Lovecraft conference at which I was speaking in France in 1995, by (upon request, actually) bellowing out the whole sentence in, I would like to think, flawless R'lyehian—but such 'words' as *mglw'nafh* give the impression, despite the occasional presence of a vowel, of being just the sort of scarcely euphonious letter-jumble that one sees in a cryptogram. Note that Lovecraft himself refers to the phrase *Cthulhu fhtagn* as an "almost unpronounceable jumble of letters" (*CF* 2.26).

The intriguing thing about this cryptotext is that its textual length, 41 letters, exactly matches the length of the sentence given, in the story, as the supposed translation:

In his house at R'lyeh dead Cthulhu waits dreaming.

One may establish that this 'translation' is not in fact a cryptographic solution, at least not with regard to any simple one-to-one substitution scheme, or even a simple substitution combined with columnar transposition (of necessity not a complete rectangular transposition tableau since the text is length 41, a prime number—unless there are one or more 'null' characters), by pointing out that the symbol frequency distributions are non-isomorphic, i.e. structurally different:

CIPHERTEXT: ($\sum f = 41$)

A	B	C	D	E	F	G	H	I	J	K	L	M	N	O	P	Q	R	S	T	U	V	W	X	Y	Z
4		1		1	2	5	7	1			5	1	4		1		1		2	3		2		1	

PLAINTEXT: ($\sum f = 41$)

A	B	C	D	E	F	G	H	I	J	K	L	M	N	O	P	Q	R	S	T	U	V	W	X	Y	Z
4		1	3	4		1	5	4			2	1	2	1			2	3	3	3		1		1	

where for example in the ciphertext distribution there is a symbol occurring 7 times but no such parallel occurrence in the other distribution. The incidence counts are not even the same: one distribution contains sixteen different symbols, the other seventeen. (The ciphertext frequency distribution, though—a few higher frequency characters and a number of lower frequency—is not unlike a typical cryptographic pattern with regard to one-to-one substitution from plaintext.)

In any case it would of course be problematical for the ciphertext to contain the strings CTHULHU and R'LYEH when the plaintext (translation) contains them too; usually the two have no character strings of significant length in common. The plaintext names would be enciphered.

But of course this only means that if *Ph'nglui mglw'nafh* . . . is a cryptogram, the given 'translation' ("In his house . . .") is not likely to be the solution—scarcely surprising, as Lovecraft could well have had something else in mind altogether if he was really out to perpetrate a sort of textual in-joke. That is, the strange passage in question may still be a cryptotext with some other solution. The only thing to do is attempt to solve it.

One tries the obvious approaches first. Perhaps the cryptotext might have been a "Caesar cipher" produced by linear alphabetical shift; i.e., with every letter shifted a fixed number of steps forward or back. But alas, the possible Caesar shifts produce nothing coherent:

PH'NGLUI MGLW'NAFH CTHULHU R'LYEH WGAH'NAGL FHTAGN
QI'OHMVJ NHMX'OBGI DUIVMIV S'MZFI XHBI'OBHM GIUBHO
RJ'PINWK OINY'PCHJ EVJWNJW T'NAGJ YICJ'PCIN HJVCIP
SK'QJOXL PJOZ'QDIK FWKXOKX U'OBHK ZJDK'QDJO IKWDJQ
TL'RKPYM QKPA'REJL GXLYPLY V'PCIL AKEL'REKP JLXEKR
UM'SLQZN RLQB'SFKM HYMZQMZ W'QDJM BLFM'SFLQ KMYFLS
VN'TMRAO SMRC'TGLN IZNARNA X'REKN CMGN'TGMR LNZGMT
WO'UNSBP TNSD'UHMO JAOBSOB Y'SFLO DNHO'UHNS MOAHNU
XP'VOTCQ UOTE'VINP KBPCTPC Z'TGMP EOIP'VIOT NPBIOV
YQ'WPUDR VPUF'WJOQ LCQDUQD A'UHNQ FPJQ'WJPU OQCJPW
ZR'XQVES WQVG'XKPR MDREVRE B'VIOR GQKR'XKQV PRDKQX
AS'YRWFT XRWH'YLQS NESFWSF C'WJPS HRLS'YLRW QSELRY
BT'ZSXGU YXXI'ZMRT OFTGXTG D'XKQT ISMT'ZMSX RTFMSZ
CU'ATYHV ZTYJ'ANSU PGUHYUH E'YLRU JTNU'ANTY SUGNTA
DV'BUZIW AUZK'BOTV QHVIZVI F'ZMSV KUOV'BOUZ TVHOUB
EW'CVAJX BVAL'CPUW RIWJAWJ G'ANTW LVPW'CPVA UWIPVC
FX'DWBKY CWBM'DQVX SJXKBXK H'BOUX MWQX'DQWB VXJQWD
GY'EXCLZ DXCN'ERWY TKYLCYL I'CPVY NXRY'ERXC WYKRXE
HZ'FYDMA EYDO"FSXZ ULZMDZM J'DQWZ OYSZ'FSYD XZLSYF
IA'GZENB FZEP'GTYA VMANEAN K'ERXA PZTA'GTZE YAMTZG
JB'HAFOC GAFQ'HUZB WNBOFBO L'FSYB QAUB'HUAF ZBNUAH
KC'IBGPD HBGR'IVAC XOCPGCP M'GTZC RBVC'IVBG ACOVBI
LD'JCHQE ICHS'JWBD YPDQHDQ N'HUAD SCWD'JWCH BDPWCJ
ME'KDIRF JDIT'KXCE ZQERIER O'IVBE TDXE'KXDI CEQXDK
NF'LEJSG KEJU'LYDF ARFSJFS P'JWCF UEYF'LYEJ DFRYEL
OG'MFKTH LFKV'MZEG BSGTKGT Q'KXDG VFZG'MZFK EGSZFM

(One further shift brings the text cyclically back to the original form.)

The possibility of a "staggered" shift remains—e.g., one symbol shifted one place, the next shifted two places, etc., but then some portion of a solution should appear along some diagonal in the above tableau, and to date I have found none.

The question of some other simple substitution scheme remains open, e.g. a keyed-alphabet substitution not directly accessible by shift-tableau solution even reading the diagonals. My own attempts to find such a solution, on the basis of letter frequency and word morphology, are ongoing, with full awareness on my part of course that there may *be* no solution.

Beyond the expedient of simple substitution, many other possibilities exist. As I pointed out in "Lovecraft and the World as Cryptogram," Lovecraft in "The Dunwich Horror" evinced at least a superficial, quite possibly more than superficial, interest in cryptanalysis when he referenced all sorts of cryptological authorities in the text of the story, with regard to attempts to decipher Wilbur Whateley's diary—rather embarrassingly, Lovecraft clearly lifted much of this out of the ninth edition of the *Encyclopaedia Britannica,* though this is not to deny that he had some genuine interest, if not a lot of expertise, in the subject—providing, in any event, some hints as to the cryptographic systems that had caught his attention, in particular the Vigénère-type systems that Lovecraft actually described in "The Dunwich Horror": "those subtlest and most ingenious of cryptograms, in which many separate lists of corresponding letters are arranged like the multiplication table, and the message built up with arbitrary key-words known only to the initiated" (*CF* 2.449).

Actually the Vigénère tableau to which this refers is more like an addition table, having the "successive shift" structure (shown here in abbreviated form)

(Key→) A B C D . . . Z

(Plain↓) A A B C D . . . Z (Cipher letters
B B C D E . . . A inside the table)
C C D E F . . . B
D D E F G . . . C
. . . . . .
. . . . . .
Z Z A B C . . . Y

where from a mathematician's point of view the 26 letters in numerical form are treated as an additive Abelian group with A = 0, B = 1, C = 2, . . ., Z = 25 and with "addition modulo-26" as the binary operation. For example, for a key-letter L (L = 11) and a plaintext letter T (T = 19) the resulting ciphertext letter is E (L + T = 30 which reduces modulo-26 to the value 4 = E), as an alternative to actually using the Vigénère tableau. I should perhaps remark that if Lovecraft was tinkering around with these things, he would have been much more likely to use a tableau than to do the modulo-26 additions and subtractions, given that he expressly detested mathematics (and given that at that point little or nothing had been written, in the accessible press anyway, about the mathematical aspects of cryptanalysis).

Let us denote any key letter as K, any plaintext letter as P, and any ciphertext letter as C. Aside from mixed-alphabet variations (usually called "quagmire ciphers," something Lovecraft almost surely would have known nothing about), there are three distinct straight-but-linearly-shifted Vigénère-type polyalphabetic encipherment systems: the classic Vigénère cipher (in which, using the notation mentioned, C = K + P, K = C - P, P = C - K, all operations modulo-26), the Beaufort cipher system (in which C = K - P, K = C + P, P = K - C), and the so-called Variant cipher (in which C = P - K, K = P - C, P = C + K).

Doing some trial-and-error encipherments with these, I found some years ago that with the Beaufort system, the name CTHULHU appears (well, almost appears) as ciphertext when one starts enciphering the word THEOSOPHIST(S) or THEOSOPHY—like a sly hint, the word *theosophists* appears as the first word in the second paragraph of "The Call of Cthulhu"—a phenomenon I noticed merely because I was wondering if the plaintext message (if any) might begin with the definite article *the*, and saw that when one does a Beaufort back-formation to produce part of the key, the result for cipher = CTH and plaintext = THE is key = VAL. Trying a cyclically repeating keyword VALID (admittedly a hypothetical key-word of unclear motivation, not that there must necessarily be a 'reason' for choosing a key-word), I found the configuration to be:

K] V A L I D V A L I D V A
P] T H E O S O P H I S T S
C] C T H U L H L E A L C I

(similarly, THEOSOPHY encrypts as CTHULHLEK), where one sees that the pattern veers off past the sixth letter. (The seventh ciphertext letter L is not so strange when one recalls R. H. Barlow's claim that

Lovecraft originally meant to have an extra L at the end of the name.) Interestingly, Lovecraft once referred (*SL* 5.11) to "my rather careful devising of this name," and if he devised it cryptographically, the process would indeed have been easy to characterize as "careful."

This cryptographic turn of events could all be a coincidence, of course, but if it is, it's a truly remarkable one, since—even if we credit only the first six letters—the chance appearance of the exact sequence CTHULH has a random probability of $(1/26)^6 = 1/308915776 = 0.000000003237128$, or about three chances in one billion.

The trouble, however, with regard to the whole cryptotext, is that the implied keyword VALID, when cyclically placed such as to (almost) produce the name CTHULHU, does not imply any intelligible plaintext globally, even though when one 'backs it up' it starts in the right position:

K] VALIDVA LIDVALID VALIDVA LIDVA LIDVALID VALIDV
P] GTYCSBS ZCSZNLDW THEOSOG UXFRT PCDONLCS QTSIXI
C] PHNGLUI MGLWNAFH CTHULHU RLYEH WGAHNAGL FHTAGN

Of course the slightest alteration in any of this changes just about everything, in a key-driven polyalphabetic encipherment; e.g., if one does add an L to the name CTHULHU, the whole configuration beyond that point changes because of the altered placement of the key-word. (The possibility exists, too, of *errors* in encipherment, in which case analysis is all the more difficult.)

A further difficulty is that when one indeed supposes that there may be irregularities in placing the key-word, the various positional possibilities still do not produce, e.g., the 'word' *fhtagn* (which Lovecraft references separately: *Cthulhu fhtagn*) from any coherent plaintext:

K] VALIDVA DVALID IDVALI LIDVAL ALIDVA
P] QTSIXI YOHLCQ DWCAFV GBKVUY VEPDPN
C] FHTAGN FHTAGN FHTAGN FHTAGN FHTAGN

and similarly for (e.g.) *R'lyeh* and *Ph'nglui*, neither of which, under variously cycled placements of the key-word, proceeds from any recognizable back-formed plaintext.

Besides the fact that obviously countless other key-words are possible, and other hypothetical plaintexts, there are many other encipherment systems besides the ones mentioned here, but the more esoteric they get, the less likely it is that Lovecraft would have used them, even though, like Poe (from whom I suspect he derived his interest in the subject, as did I), he was evidently fascinated with crypto-writing. At this point I would have to say that the question of whether *"Ph'nglui mglw'nafh . . ."* really is a cryptogram remains unsettled, but my intuition still suggests to me that it probably is. Whether we will ever solve it, if so, is another open question.

The Dream-Quest of Unknown Kadath

When H. P. Lovecraft wrote *The Dream-Quest of Unknown Kadath* (1926–27), he demonstrated—at least for later generations; he never tried to get the work published—that his work cannot be thoroughly categorized without risk of oversimplification. Some critics have yielded to the temptation to divide Lovecraft's works exclusively into such categories as Dunsanian fantasy (after the fashion of Lord Dunsany: such works as "Celephaïs," 1920); dream narratives ("The Statement of Randolph Carter," 1919); New England horror tales ("The Colour out of Space," 1927); and Lovecraft Mythos tales ("The Dunwich Horror," 1928), as if these categories were independent. It is tempting, also, to think of Lovecraft as having passed through distinct periods of influence, particularly a "Poe period" and a "Dunsany period." *The Dream-Quest of Unknown Kadath* puts the lie to such reductionist approaches to the Lovecraft canon. It is clearly a work heavily influenced by Lord Dunsany, with its lofty and sonorous language and its compelling treatment of man's relation to primordial gods, but it is a Dunsanian fantasy written several years after the period of Lovecraft's major experimentation with Dunsanian themes and style, in a period in which Lovecraft is primarily thought of as producing such non-Dunsanian Lovecraft Mythos works as "The Call of Cthulhu" (1926). The novel is much more than a late-arriving Dunsanian effort, however; by this time, Lovecraft, far from merely copying Lord Dunsany, had deeply assimilated what he had found of value in that author, transmuting his style to suit the purpose of expressing ideas and visions uniquely Lovecraftian.

The novel cuts across categories, for it is redolent also of the Lovecraft Mythos conception in that it deals with man's soul-chilling relationship with such ancient godlike entities as Nyarlathotep and Azathoth. It is obviously a dream narrative and, in a somewhat less obvious way, a New England tale as well—such quaint dreamland cities as

Ulthar and Celephaïs are Lovecraftian responses to favorite New England places, including Providence, Salem, and Marblehead. It is as if Lovecraft sought to express all his major emotionalities—his admiration for Dunsany, his vicarious liking of bold adventure, his love of New England, his fondness for cats, his fascination with dreams, his sense of brooding horror, and his preoccupation with the Mythos notion of man's precarious position in the cosmos—in one work, a work not even divided into chapters but rather allowed to run as a free confluence of his fondest thoughts and feelings. Perhaps more than any other single Lovecraft work, *The Dream-Quest of Unknown Kadath* is a charming and prismatic self-portrait.

The novel nevertheless stands on its own merits apart from biographical considerations and is a deeply interpretable work. The setting alone places it apart from other such fantasy-adventure creations. Randolph Carter, a scarcely veiled Lovecraft persona "old in the land of dream" (*CF* 2.101), has glimpsed in his dreams a marvelous sunset city, and he yearns for it desperately; but further glimpses of it are not forthcoming, and Carter feels "the bondage of dream's tyrannous gods" (*CF* 2.99) who have denied him the vision. He descends into dreamland to carry on an epic quest for his beloved city. This realm of dream is portrayed as an actual domain accessible to deep dreamers. The domain of dream lies in part "not far from the gates of the waking world" (*CF* 2.99) but contains depths remote from the familiar haunts of humans and falls under the dominion of immemorial gods known as the Great Ones, who dwell in an onyx castle in Kadath in the Cold Waste. By setting this weirdly picaresque adventure in such a postulated dream world, rather than merely in a distant age or far spacial realm of the familiar waking universe, Lovecraft sets his protagonist upon a journey that literally has characteristics enjoyed only symbolically by similar protagonists elsewhere in literature. Carter, by sojourning in dreamland, literally indulges in a quest through the depths of the psyche. It is common in literature for some journey to be a symbolic quest through the psyche—Marlow in Joseph Conrad's *Heart of Darkness* (1902) journeys symbolically into the deep unconscious when he sails up the Congo River into the darkness of the jungle—but it is far from common for the psychic journey to be literal, as in the case of Randolph Carter.

The novel, in fact, lends itself well to Jungian interpretation, for at its heart lies the notion of dream, and dreams in Jungian theory obtrude upon the personal unconscious as a result of the activity of archetypes, those mysterious patternings that operate in the collective unconscious of the deep psyche. By journeying deep within the realm of dream, Carter traverses an inner cosmos; the novel is replete with symbolism to reinforce this view.

For example, when Carter descends the seven hundred steps to the Gate of Deeper Slumber and passes into the Enchanted Wood, the home of the piquant Zoogs, he finds "a circle of great mossy stones" left by "older and more terrible dwellers long forgotten" (*CF* 2.102), and one readily sees this circle in Jungian symbolic terms as the circle of individuation, the eternal mandala. To achieve psychic wholeness, the questing hero must plunge into the very depths of his psyche, confront his Shadow or counter-ego, come to terms with it, and return with an integrated, whole psychic identity, thus completing the circle and achieving the whole Self. The circle of stones in the novel signals that this is the nature of what lies ahead for Carter to accomplish. The fact of the stones being mossy and being left by old dwellers "long forgotten" nicely parallels the notion that the structure of the psyche is immemorially ancient and too deep, in part, to be consciously known—the mandala itself is an archetypal pattern implanted far down in the collective unconscious and often encountered as a symbol in dreams. Also, the Lovecraftian suggestion that his dreamland is a genuinely existing realm that is "down there" for people in general closely parallels Carl Jung's notion of the collectively or commonality of the unconscious mind's deepest patternings—the notion that there is a profound archetypal depth of being that humans all share, and that dreams symbolically illuminate its nature.

The necessity of Carter's confronting his counter-ego, the other and darker side of himself, is symbolized as well by the matter of the great carven face on Mount Ngranek in the land of dreams. Besides reflecting a probable Nathaniel Hawthorne influence (see Hawthorne's "The Great Stone Face"), this carven visage has much symbolic significance. Carter must look upon the stone face on the remote side of the mountain in order to learn to recognize the facial lineaments of the Great Ones, because these lineaments will be reflected in mortal faces near unknown Kadath—the gods often consort with humans. (The great carven face has long-lobed ears reminiscent of the carven faces on Easter Island, by which Lovecraft is known to have been fascinated.) The stone face lies on the mountainside facing away from the accessible world of humans, just as the ego and counter-ego "face" in opposite directions by being opposed forces in the psyche, but forces, nevertheless, which must be integrated. In the dreamland quest, Carter and the dreaded gods of Kadath must come to terms if he is to achieve wholeness, and the gods, symbolized by the stone face, operate as his counter-ego. Ultimately, the counter-ego or Shadow is oneself, and since the Great Ones hold court in the deep realm of dreams, they constitute an archetypal facet of Carter's own psyche. Jung identifies the "god archetype"—the pattern in the collective unconscious by which man formulates notions of gods—with the ego archetype, and by this pattern of identification, one comes around to the idea that the ego and counter-ego are opposite faces of the same coin, just as the opposite sides of Mount Ngranek represent bipolarities of one psychic reality.

Carter's adventures in dreamland are reminiscent of those of many a hero figure in literature. He is the mythic questing hero, whose quest in this case is not merely symbolically but literally a quest for the Self—he must satisfy his deepest need, the craving to find again the elusive sunset city. It is significant that although his quest is an exceedingly prideful one (in that he presumes to sway the gods), his motives are entirely aesthetic rather than being informed by greed, desire for adventure, or other such impulses. His beloved city is "a fever of the gods, a fanfare of supernal trumpets and a clash of immortal cymbals" (*CF* 2.206)—that is, an archetypally profound cornerstone of his very original being—and he yearns with the heart of a poet for the city's "walls, temples, colonnades and arched bridges of veined marble, silver-basined fountains of prismatic spray in broad squares and perfumed gardens, and wide streets marching between delicate trees and blossom-laden urns and ivory statues in gleaming rows" (*CF* 2.98). Clearly Lovecraft is reflecting here both his own love of New England beauty and his fascination with the delicacies of Greco-Roman antiquity.

Randolph Carter is an oneiric Ulysses, voyaging from peril to peril, doing battle with gugs, ghasts, and moon-beasts as he perseveres in his single-minded quest of the marvelous city. He experiences moments of exquisite horror, as when the galley in which he sails passes through the Basalt Pillars of the West into an abyss and he glimpses as black, amorphous stirrings "the nameless larvae of the Other Gods" (*CF* 2.133). He forms an alliance with Pickman—an artist who vanishes in Lovecraft's slightly earlier tale "Pickman's Model" (1926)—with Pickman's fellow ghouls, and even with the dreaded night-gaunts. These creatures are flying horrors which were derived from Lovecraft's own childhood dreams. Clearly, *The Dream-Quest of Unknown Kadath* is a highly personal work, connecting with Lovecraft's earlier stories and expressing his various predilections.

The novel's conclusion, foreshadowed philosophically in Lovecraft's early Dunsanian tale "Celephaïs" (1920), comes when Carter, finally wafted into the onyx castle of the Great Ones atop Kadath, meets Nyarlathotep, the Crawling Chaos, who discloses to him the truth about the marvelous sunset city: that it is "only the sum of what you have seen and loved in youth" (*CF* 2.206), the remembered and accumulated charm of New England byways. Nyarlathotep nicely reinforces the Jungian interpretability of the novel by saying of the memory sources of Carter's sunset city: "These, Randolph Carter, are your city; for they are yourself" (*CF* 2.207). Carter returns to the waking world with the same sort of enlightenment as that imparted by a Zen master to a monk who had asked him how to seek one's original Buddha-nature; the master replied that to do so is like going off on an ox in search of the ox. This revelation goes a long way toward illuminating the beauty-charmed, reminiscing mind and heart of H. P. Lovecraft.

The Mythic Hero Archetype in "The Dunwich Horror"

Lovecraft's "The Dunwich Horror" presents rich opportunity for mythic interpretation, and this critical approach reveals a great deal about the nature of the work. A casual reading of the story suggests simply that Henry Armitage, facing alien forces for which the reader is to feel repulsion, acts heroically in vanquishing the horror. The story appears to have a kind of "good versus evil" flavor, recalling August Derleth's peculiar notion that the Lovecraft Mythos parallels the Christian Mythos ("H. P. Lovecraft and His Work" xiii); such is one's impression if what one sees in "The Dunwich Horror" is a drama wherein the "good guys" rush in at the end to rout the "bad guys." A more thoughtful reading casts some doubt on the real significance of Armitage's victory. But, more importantly, a reading with attention to mythic or archetypal detail skews that in terms of the hero archetype, Lovecraft—consciously or otherwise—has in "The Dunwich Horror" fictionally underscored his personal view of man's insect-like position in the cosmos by presenting a mythic inversion of what a more casual, sub-mythic reading would suggest. Not only does Armitage fall decidedly short of the characteristics of the archetypal hero—these characteristics, indeed, one discerns only in Armitage's alien adversaries, Wilbur Whateley and his twin brother.

On the face of it, the story presents Armitage as a kind of hero in the popular sense; by his own quick and ingenious action and at great peril to himself, he meets the horror and puts it down by counter-sorcery. But there is textual evidence that his "victory" is a decidedly hollow one. Wilbur Whateley and his nameless brother are spawns of Yog-Sothoth, the old Wizard Whateley presumably having arranged a May-Eve mating with his half-wit daughter Lavinia. (Note that in Roman legend a Lavinia is given in marriage, by her father Latinus, to a hero: the Trojan Aeneas.) There is no reason to suppose that the occurrence is, or will be, unique. The passage selected by Wilbur from the Latin *Necronomicon* says of the Old Ones: "By Their smell can men sometimes know Them near, but of Their semblance can no man know, *saving only in the features of those They have begotten on mankind,* and of those there are many sorts" (*CF* 2.434), suggesting that such begetting has occurred, or will occur, repeatedly; there will be other Lavinias, and other wizards like old Whateley to arrange such monstrous procreations. Armitage, in the end, tells the Dunwich farmers, "We have no business calling in such things from outside, and only very wicked people and very wicked cults ever try to" (*CF* 2.466), suggesting that (as in "The Call of Cthulhu") there are cults devoted to alliance with the Old Ones. The *Necronomicon* sonorously prophesies their eventual success: "Man rules now where They ruled once; They shall soon rule where man rules now. After summer is winter, and after winter summer. They wait patient and potent, for here shall They reign again" (*CF* 2.434). Thus Armitage has merely put down a local manifestation of a horror that can be repeated elsewhere, at other times, with more effect.

Indeed, if one is to look even for a temporary savior of mankind in the Dunwich affair, the savior would have to be the dog in the Miskatonic library, for this beast dispatches Wilbur before he and his brother can proceed with the grand design. (So much for the messianic vision in Lovecraft's world.) On his deathbed old Wizard Whateley has reminded Wilbur that "ef it busts quarters or gits aout afore ye opens to Yog-Sothoth, it's all over an' no use" (*CF* 2.431), and it is Wilbur's failure to return that allows the brother's premature and thus relatively inconsequential release.

Armitage, further, does not bear any of the archetypal tags of the mythic hero. He merely enters the story, late in his life, at a point where his erudition is needed, acting to quell the Dunwich disturbance, and he represents the "hero" only in the sub-mythic sense; his brief quest, though courageous, is certainly not one of mythic proportions. There are plentiful signs of the true hero archetype in "The Dunwich Horror," but by a curious irony they belong wholly to Armitage's monstrous adversaries, who bear a remarkable number of the necessary traits.

These horrific entities may perhaps be seen as exemplifying what has been called the Twin Cycle of the hero myth, one of four myth cycles or categories to be found in the realm of hero mythology (see Henderson, "Ancient Myths").[1] In the Twin hero myth, the twins operate as invincible heroes at first, but eventually succumb to an overreaching hybris and the resulting excesses of their own power. Clearly Wilbur and his brother find their end because of dreadfully ambitious plans, which obliquely at least may be seen as a kind of pridefulness—obliquely, because in the Lovecraft oeuvre it is in general doubtful practice to ascribe human emotions to such beings, though here the creatures are partly human and expressly have motives that from a purely human viewpoint could be seen as a species of hybris. In the Twin myth it is generally necessary, but difficult, to reunite the twins once they are separated; the narrative flow of "The Dunwich Horror" bears this out, in that Wilbur and his brother, separated by the quest for the *Necronomicon* and its vital formulae, must be—but are not—reunited by Wilbur's return from Arkham to Dunwich in time to prevent the brother's premature emergence so that they may carry on the planned sorcery in proper fashion.

But in the Twin Cycle the twins may be thought of *as a single entity,* and it is from this point of view that one may readily discern in Wilbur and his brother the main features of the mythic hero as given by what is called the "monomyth" underlying all hero mythology. The monomyth has eight stages: miraculous conception, initiation, withdrawal, quest, death, descent to the underworld, rebirth, and ascension (Leeming, passim). It will be shown that the Dunwich twins fit all eight stages remarkably well.

The first stage of the monomyth concerns miraculous conception (as in the virgin birth of Quetzalcoatl or Jesus, or the immaculate conception of Buddha, Lao-Tzu, or Horus); and the Dunwich story provides a classic example of this myth. Traditionally, a disguised god sires the hero; Yog-Sothoth, in May-Eve rites on Sentinel Hill, has sired the twins, though whether the father was disguised we do not know. Tra-

---

1. The other categories are termed the Trickster Cycle, the Hare Cycle, and the Red Horn Cycle, as characterized by Dr. Paul Radin from the example of Winnebago Indian myth.

ditionally, the infant is threatened (as Dionysos by the Titans, Jesus by Herod) and must be hidden; Wilbur is shunned by villagers and threatened by dogs (with the recurrent mention of menacing dogs foreshadowing his demise), and while he "hides" by covering his partly monstrous body strategically with clothing, the brother is literally hidden in the Whateley farmhouse, a second womb that grows as he grows, and in which he is nurtured and allowed to attain enormous size.

The second stage of the monomyth concerns the childhood and initiation of the hero. In "The Dunwich Horror" Wilbur takes part, with his mother and grandfather, in unseen rites at May-Eve and All Hallows Eve on Sentinel Hill, and thus is initiated, as it were, into the cult of Yog-Sothoth, though the reader is told little of these rites. In fact, as Lord Raglan points out, we are typically told little or nothing of the mythic hero's childhood (179–80), and in "The Dunwich Horror" after Wilbur's fourth year, the narration skips to his tenth year (*CF* 2.427), and this skip must be assumed to involve a good deal of development in Wilbur. But we do see the extraordinary development during his first few years. In the childhood and initiation myth pattern, it is common for the hero to show uncanny wisdom as a child—see Buddha and Jesus, for examples—and Wilbur's development is rapid not only physically, to parallel his brother's on a smaller scale, but mentally. He begins to talk at the age of eleven months, as clearly as a child of three or four years, and by nineteen months he is "a fluent and incredibly intelligent talker." By the age of four, Wilbur reads fluently and avidly, and has learned to "chant in bizarre rhythms which [chill] the listener with a sense of unexplainable terror" (*CF* 2.427).

The hero monomyth's third stage has to do with the hero's preparation, meditation, and withdrawal. Typically, the hero withdraws to some secluded place, as Buddha to the Bodhi tree, Moses to his mountain, Jesus to the wilderness, Mohammed to his cave. Here again "The Dunwich Horror" fits the pattern. Wilbur's grandfather puts in order a room in the old farmhouse for him, with the rare and ancient books that have lain about the house in disarray—"for they're goin' to be all of his larnin'"—and Wilbur pores over them and undergoes catechism "through long, hushed afternoons" in preparation for his quest (*CF* 2.426). The grandfather, in fact, clearly acts as the sort of "tutelary figure" often present in this type of hero myth, a guardian or mentor who offsets the hero's early inability to perform alone (Henderson 101). (Wilbur has, after all, learned to read even the Latin *Necronomicon* by the time he visits Arkham.) The grandfather also acts as a guardian to Wilbur's monstrous brother, hidden upstairs, who cannot thrive without the prodigious supply of cattle that the old man provides.

The fourth stage of the monomyth concerns trial and quest; the hero always embarks on some quest, as for example the quest of Gilgamesh for the plant of life, or Sir Gawain for the chapel of the Green Knight, or Percival for the Holy Grail. In "The Dunwich Horror" Wilbur, after his preparatory period of withdrawal with the grandfather and his books, sets out in an effort to obtain the complete Latin texts with which he can pursue his sorcery on behalf of Yog-Sothoth. This "little quest" for the *Necronomicon* in the face of difficult obstacles (Henry Armitage, the guard dog, general enmity) is embedded in the grander quest, that of "opening the gates" to Yog-Sothoth and loosing unthinkable horrors upon the world. In such hero myths, the hero typically seeks some sort of life renewal, and Wilbur's diary, deciphered by Armitage, shows a concern of this sort. Writing of his brother, he says, "The other face"—the human face with Lavinia's features, monstrously enlarged—"may wear off some." Extending this concern to himself, he continues, "I wonder how I shall look when the earth is cleared off and there are no earth beings on it. He that came with the Aklo Sabaoth said I may be transfigured, there being much of outside to work on" (*CF* 2.451). Some of the sardonic comment of Lovecraft's narration shows through here, in that it is the human side of the twins' ancestry that Wilbur is ashamed of.

Stage five of the hero monomyth concerns the hero's death because of his quest, and Wilbur Whateley once more fits the mythic pattern. Traditionally, death often comes by dismemberment (see Osiris, Dionysos, Orpheus), and in keeping with this motif we find Wilbur, foiled in his quest for the unholy *Necronomicon,* torn to shreds by the guard dog. Traditionally in this type of myth the genitals are destroyed or lost, as with Osiris or Dionysos; in Wilbur's case they are not to be found at all, at least in terms of human anatomy: "Below the waist . . . it was the worst; for here all human resemblance left off and sheer phantasy began" (*CF* 2.439).

The sixth stage is that of descent to the underworld, and this is suggested symbolically by the descent of Wilbur's brother into Cold Spring Glen, the "great sinister ravine." The ravine is described as a hellish place and is based on an actual ravine in North New Salem, Massachusetts, deep and ominous-looking indeed, which Lovecraft visited with H. Warner Munn in 1928 shortly before writing "The Dunwich Horror." In the tale, Sally Sawyer says of the place, "I allus says Col' Spring Glen ain't no healthy nor decent place. The whip-poorwills"—psychopomps of the underworld—"an' fireflies there never did act like they was creaters o' Gawd" (*CF* 2.444), so that the symbolism of descent to the underworld is textually clear. In this sixth stage of the monomyth one traditionally also has the theme of the overcoming of the forces of death (see Heracles and Cerberus, for example), and Wilbur's death scene provides this connection, in that at Wilbur's last breath, the guard dog howls lugubriously and bolts out a window; and the psychopomp whippoorwills, gathering outside to catch Wilbur's soul (traditionally, for a journey to the underworld), "rose and raced from sight, frantic at that which they had sought for prey" (*CF* 2.440).

The seventh stage is that of resurrection and rebirth (Dionysos, Buddha, Adonis, Osiris, Jesus), and when Wilbur and his brother are considered as constituting one character, this character is symbolically reborn, for when Wilbur dies in the Miskatonic library and thus fails to return to Dunwich, the brother bursts forth from the Whateley farmhouse, his symbolic womb. In fact, the Yog-Sothoth spawn is even "reborn" in a stronger form when the brother comes forth from confinement. The notion of death and rebirth is further suggested symbolically by the brother's descent into and emergence from the ravine, much like the symbolic nature of Hamlet's leaping into and out of the grave.

The eighth and final stage of the hero monomyth is that which concerns ascension, apotheosis, and atonement. "The Dunwich Horror" fits the mythic pattern at least with regard to ascension and a kind of resolution. Wilbur's hideous brother, having left trails of destruction around the village, finally ascends Sentinel Hill with Armitage and his two colleagues in pursuit. The creature has ascended earlier, leaving a trail to and from the ravine, and in this respect perhaps he symbolically resembles Maud Bodkin's characterization of the archetypal hero, who "stands poised between height and depth" (245).[2] The brother, in keeping with Lord Raglan's description of the mythic hero, has done something like returning to his birthplace after a victory over adversaries; he has annihilated a number of the inhabitants of Dunwich, and returns to the great table-rock on Sentinel Hill, where he was not born, but conceived. Lord Raglan, in fact, also specifies that the archetypal hero often meets his end atop a hill (180). The monster's end amounts to a "tragic" (from the Yog-Sothothian point of view) failure in the grand quest, but he is returned alive to the outer realm of Yog-Sothoth, the father. And it can be pointed out again that although the quest is not successful in this instance, the *Necronomicon* clearly prophesies that such a quest will one day be completed by the Old Ones and their terrestrial avatars, as a completion of a cosmic cycle not to be denied—"They wait patient and potent, for here shall They reign again."

This cosmic cyclicity and its mythic importance are underscored continually in the story by the cyclic fashion in which Lovecraft refers to time. We see repeated reference to such cyclically recurrent points in time as May Eve and All Hallows Eve; and "the Dunwich horror itself came between Lammas and the equinox of 1928" (*CF* 2.437). The horror is thus linked to cosmic cycles of time that transcend, in their significance, mere calendar dates of human reckoning.

Similarly, "The Dunwich Horror" contains various other motifs and images suggesting the high appropriateness of a mythic interpretation, the interpretation that best shows what Lovecraft is doing with heroism in the story. The epigraph from Charles Lamb—"the archetypes are in us, and eternal" (*CF* 2.417)—strongly suggests a mythic view; but there is internal support as well, in abundance. For example, there is the matter of the whippoorwills, psychopomps that try to capture the departing souls of the dying. Lovecraft's direct source of this motif was an actual folktale told to him by his hosts during a stay in Wilbraham, Massachusetts, just before he wrote "The Dunwich Hor-

---

2. Maud Bodkin argues eloquently for the idea that Satan is a true hero figure in *Paradise Lost.* Perhaps we are only just beginning to understand the influence of Milton on HPL, an influence of which HPL himself may well not have been conscious.

ror." But this local folklore itself parallels well the mythic tradition of the psychopomp, which was associated with the Greek god Hermes, guide of departed souls to the underworld; the traditional "herm" has often been given with a caduceus, a snake or two snakes twined around a staff, and interestingly Lovecraft gives us, in the opening descriptions of the Dunwich country, a view of the river Miskatonic (recalling the Styx?) whose line of "upper reaches has an oddly serpent-like suggestion as it winds close to the feet of the domed hills among which it rises" (*CF* 2.418). In Egyptian lore Hermes was originally known as Thoth (of which the name Yog-Sothoth may also be echoic), the bird-headed god (Henderson 154–55), so that the use of whip-poorwills as psychopomps is well in keeping with mythic tradition.

There is also the matter, again in the opening descriptions, of "queer circles of tall stone pillars" (*CF* 2.418) crowning the hills around Dunwich. This motif recalls the circle or mandala of mythic-archetypal significance, symbolizing the center or the completion of the psyche, as well as the cyclicity of cosmic events. (Jaffé 266–267) In "The Dunwich Horror" the circles of pillars are associated with the sort of sorcery by which people like Wizard Whateley invoke the horrors of the Old Ones; thus the circles have more to do with the interests of monstrous beings than with the human players on the scene, and it is not without significance, symbolically, that physically the circles stand always above man. Consistently, Lovecraft's narration suggests the preeminence of the Old Ones—their completeness, their consummation in the cosmic cycle, their ultimate prevalence—over mankind. The story's descriptive imagery continually gives this same suggestion. We are warned, for example, in our introduction to the environs of Dunwich: "Gorges and ravines of problematical depth" (the work of untrammeled nature, the ubiquity of unfathomable mystery) "intersect the way, and the crude wooden bridges" (the efforts of man to deal with the forces of nature, to come to terms with the mystery) "always seem of dubious safety" (*CF* 2.418).

Altogether, then, "The Dunwich Horror" in its mythic content presents a sardonically inverted view of the hero archetype as it traditionally applies to the interests of humankind. The character Armitage, for whom the casual reader presumably is to feel empathy, is a fictional prop whose "victory" is virtually meaningless in cosmic terms, and he is devoid of the features of the mythic hero. The monstrous twins, together, form a character for whom the casual reader is to feel loathing and antipathy, but who can be seen closely to fit the archetypal pattern of the hero in myth. To the extent that Lovecraft's Old Ones are symbolic of chaos—of the blindly indifferent forces of nature, the forces of an impersonal and purposeless cosmos—"The Dunwich Horror," by its association of the hero archetype with these forces, gives fictional articulation to a view that happens to correspond to Lovecraft's personal Weltanschauung: the view that man is but an evanescent mote in the universe of stars, a universe that neither blesses nor damns him, unless to be ignored is to be damned. It is, of course, only on the mythic level of interpretation that this sense of the story is fully evident. Seen in this way, "The Dunwich Horror" ceases to appear to be a "good versus evil" story that fits only awkwardly into the Lovecraft canon—it becomes a work centrally expressive of the vision underlying the entire Lovecraft Mythos.

Prismatic Heroes: The Colour out of Dunwich

In "The Mythic Hero Archetype in 'The Dunwich Horror,'" I demonstrated the manner in which Wilbur Whateley and his twin, in "The Dunwich Horror," closely follow the archetypal pattern of the mythic hero, an eight-stage pattern that has proved to be pervasive in strains of mythology. What I now suggest is that similar observations can be made of Lovecraft's "The Colour out of Space."[1]

In pursuing these observations, however, I shall wish to graft the two texts ("Dunwich" and "Colour") together and observe their intertextual self-commentary, and this for at least two reasons. First, since the mythic pattern of the archetypal hero has already been observed in "The Dunwich Horror," the pattern there may serve to inform the pattern in "Colour." But one may also point out that intertextual grafts or weavings-together of "different" texts are by no means unnatural, once one sees beyond the tyranny of what one might have called the "borders" of a given "single" text. In a sense, we may even say that literary texts effectively help to create each other.

Texts arise in a complex interaction between "book" and "reader," a process in which a text (once set adrift by that shadowy figure, the author, who, however brilliant, can in no way control what is going to happen as the text begins to wander through unforeseeable new signification-creating contexts) continually writes and rewrites itself by being read. And it is in this regard that texts are mutually formative—the reader brings the trace of one text into the field of another. Clearly,

1. I touched momentarily upon this arguable notion of the mythic hero archetype in "The Colour out of Space" in my *Lovecraft: Disturbing the Universe* (116) but did not pursue it there. Indeed, it is S. T. Joshi's remark in his review of that volume (*LS* Nos. 22/23 [Fall 1990]: 55)—to the effect that one might have wanted to see such a matter pursued—that has encouraged me to do so now.

our reading of Joyce's *Ulysses* is colored by our having read the *Odyssey;* but, just as clearly, our newest reading of the Homeric classic is colored by our experience with Joyce's text. These texts *impinge upon each other,* in an exchange of creative "influence" that cuts across all lines of temporality and causality.

It is thus reasonable to regard texts as interwoven, as constitutive of intertext. Some such graftings-together may be more "natural" than others (though this point is controversial)—regarding "The Colour out of Space" and "The Dunwich Horror," their commonalities would suggest that they are always already grafted upon each other, and the only question is whether we notice it or not.

It will be well here to review the mythic structure of which we will want to speak. The motif of the *hero* in mythology partakes of a "hero monomyth" structure of eight stages; they are as follows (Leeming, passim), and we briefly observe, with each stage, how it is that in "The Dunwich Horror" Wilbur and his twin (considered as one entity) satisfy the structure, so that we may then consider the same issue with reference to "The Colour out of Space":

I. *Miraculous conception or birth,* as the virgin birth of Jesus or Quetzalcoatl, or the immaculate conception of the Buddha or Lao-Tzu; a disguised god may sire the hero, as in the case of Leda and the swan (Zeus as swan). Yog-Sothoth sires the Whateley twins upon Lavinia.

II. *Initiation,* the childhood of the hero or demigod, who often shows uncanny wisdom and is often threatened and must be hidden, as in the case of the threats of Herod. The precocious Wilbur Whateley, of whose childhood we hear little otherwise, participates in Sentinel Hill rites and is threatened by dogs.

III. *Withdrawal/meditation/preparation,* as the withdrawal of the Buddha to the Bodhi tree, or Jesus to the wilderness, or Mohammed to the cave. Wilbur undergoes catechism by his grandfather (in mythic terms, a tutelary figure) in preparation for his quest.

IV. *Quest/trial,* in countless examples: the quest of Percival for the Holy Grail, of Sir Gawain for the chapel of the Green Knight. Wilbur sojourns to Miskatonic University in search of the Latin *Necronomicon* (and is of course engaged in a broader quest).

V. *Death* of the hero because of the quest, often by dismemberment as in the case of Orpheus. Wilbur meets his end in the library, ripped to shreds by the guard dog.

VI. *Descent to the underworld,* as with Jesus. Wilbur's brother (his other aspect, if we conflate the twins) symbolically descends into Cold Spring Glen.

VII. *Resurrection/rebirth,* as Dionysos, Jesus, Buddha, the Phoenix out of its ashes. Symbolically, when Wilbur dies, the brother bursts forth from its "womb," the Whateley farmhouse in which it has been nurtured.

VIII. *Ascension/return to the father,* as in the case of Jesus. The monstrous twin, in the final scene atop Sentinel Hill, is sent back to the unthinkable cosmic gulfs from which it came.

Let us see how all this is enacted once again, this time in the form of that nameless presence issuing from the meteor that falls upon the Gardner farm, but also in terms of intertext: meteor-colour-as-hero, Wilbur-as-meteor, as it were.

In "The Colour out of Space," the miraculous-birth stage of the hero monomyth clearly appears, in terms of "the great rock that fell out of the sky and bedded itself in the ground beside the well at the Nahum Gardner place" (*CF* 2.371). The meteor, a seed imparted by Father Sky, has plowed a furrow in Mother Earth; the procreative notion of Father Sky and Mother Earth is of course as old as human consciousness itself, and no clearer picture could be drawn, symbolically, of miraculous or god-driven conception. The "coloured globule" in the meteorite is a "daemon hatchling" (*CF* 2.399), and the text's reference to "the stony messenger from the stars" (*CF* 2.373)—evoking the imagery of Hermes or Mercury—works to imbue the visitor (hero, demigod) with parentage in the realm of gods. The birthplace of the entity is visited, in a manner recalling biblical parallels, by three professors from Miskatonic University—three "wise men," as it were. This would seem to make of Nahum Gardner a sort of Joseph-figure; it is he who would normally have furrowed and fertilized Mother Earth, but for the intervention of divine cuckoldry.

Indeed, Nahum even in his name is echoic of biblical connections to the text. The Douay & Rheims Bible gives, in the brief Book of Nahum (which treats of the prophecy of the retributive destruction of Nineveh): "The Lord is patient, and great in power, and will not cleanse and acquit the guilty. The Lord's ways are in a tempest, and a whirlwind, and clouds are the dust of his feet. He rebuketh the sea, and drieth it up: and bringeth all the rivers to a desert. Basan languisheth and Carmel: and the flower of Libanus fadeth away." All this talk about dust and drying up and the fading away of (metaphorical) flowers obviously puts one in mind of the effects of the meteor in Lovecraft's tale: the crumbling of vegetation, the ashen residue of the Blasted Heath. Nahum (whose Hebrew name, antithetically, means "comfort") is even said to speculate on his place in the picture of divine wrath: "It must all be a judgment of some sort; though he could not fancy what for, since he had always walked uprightly in the Lord's ways so far as he knew" (*CF* 2.384).

This rumination of Nahum's serves to remind us that we are dealing, here, with intertext, for it points up a similar passage in "The Dunwich Horror," where one of the Dunwich villagers, reflecting on the violence being meted out by the invisible monster (Wilbur's born-again brother), says: "Not but what I think it's the Lord's jedgment fer our iniquities, that no mortal kin ever set aside" (*CF* 2.458). Thus the (inter)text vacillates over the notion of culpability; Nahum has expressed the attitude that he is, so far as he knows, innocent, while the other textual passage expresses an unavoidable suggestion of guilt. Yet overall these passages serve, despite their internal difference, to underscore the notion of the meteoric arrival as a hatchling from the gods.

In the "Dunwich" aspect of this intertext, the hatchling of course consists (until we learn about his twin) of Wilbur, and he is immediately connected with *colour*, reflecting (so to speak) the "Colour" aspect of the intertext: Wilbur is "dark" in "contrast to [Lavinia's] own sickly and pink-eyed albinism" (*CF* 2.422); hence we have Wilbur-as-colour. His pigmentation is a matter of textual waffling and inconsistency; he is "swarthy" (*CF* 2.424)—brown? black?—yet later has "large-pored yellowish skin" (*CF* 2.425). With the colour from the meteor there are also problems of indeterminacy: the colour is said to produce "hectic and prismatic variants of some diseased, underlying tone" (*CF* 2.378), a description that cuts both ways, suggesting both that the colour is singularly recognizable *and* that it has "variants." The question of unity versus plurality here spills back over into the other ("Dunwich") part of the intertext, in that we are suspended between regarding Wilbur and his twin brother as *one* entity (in the manner of certain mythic traditions) or as separate beings, the term "twin" being (in typical deconstructive fashion) redolent of both suggestions: similarity/identity and doubleness/difference.

And the (inter)textual issue of the singular versus the plural (a timeless metaphysical quandary: the one and the many) is further underscored by the etymology of the word *hero* itself. The term derives from the Graeco-Latin form *heros,* which is *singular* (with plural *heroes*); the English word is a back-formation by which, in effect, the *-s* has been removed *as if* from a plural noun to render it singular—it is a little as if one said, "There are many mythos [i.e., mythoi] but only one Lovecraft *mytho.*" Thus the signifier itself partakes in, indeed adumbrates, a problematizing of singular versus plural for the hero(es) in the text: one twin-bundle or two twins, one meteoric colour or many. If one pushes farther back in the etymology of *hero,* one comes to the Indo-European root *ser-,* "to press together," "to protect," which not only adumbrates our "pressing together" of the Lovecraft hero-texts, but also gives rise to the Latin *servare,* "to keep," "to preserve," with both thematic and antithematic suggestions for our current project—in proceeding from the "Dunwich" text to the "Colour" text in quest (as it were!) of the hero, we indeed keep or preserve, or (as physicists would say of energy) conserve, a textual concern, in that we seek to keep, in "Colour," the hero-monomyth phenomenon encountered in "Dunwich"; yet "keep" suggests fixity, stability, permanence of identity, and as we are in the process of seeing, the Lovecraftian hero(es) would scarcely seem to be characterized in those reductive terms.

To continue: the second stage of the monomyth is that of initiation, and we find, in "The Colour out of Space," a veritable ritual of initiation when the professors from Miskatonic University (and here they are actually called "the wise men") perform their chemical and analytic tests on the sample from the meteor. The litany of tests performed (which the narrator coaxes out of Ammi Pierce's memory "in the usual order of use")—"Nitric acid . . . aqua regia . . . ammonia and caustic soda, alcohol and ether, nauseous carbon disulphide" (*CF* 2.373)—is strongly ritualistic in tone, especially when one realizes that this is the point in the text at which the colour-hero in another form, as Wilbur Whateley, is undergoing ritual initiation (chantings atop Sentinel Hill) as well. One begins to see the remarkable manner in which texts invade and elucidate each other. Yet the nature of the initiation of the hero here is problematical, in that while Wilbur's part in the Sentinel Hill rituals is presumably active (we do not see them and cannot be sure), the meteoric stone's part in the laboratory ritual is presumably passive: while Wilbur is probably *doing* something atop the hill, things are being done *to* the meteor fragment—yet, given the fact that the "wise men" later find their glass beakers annihilated in some unimaginable silicon-affinity reaction, we cannot be sure even of the stone's momentary passivity.

The third stage of the monomyth is that of withdrawal, and here we find a clear indication: the meteoric colour lies low for the winter. Unlike Wilbur, it would seem to have no tutelary figure to aid in its "meditations," unless it be the soon-to-be-poisoned soil itself with which the alien presence will interact. (One notices a level of intertextual self-commentary here, in that in our current interactive project, either of the texts, "Dunwich" or "Colour," is a site of meteoric invasion of the one text by the other, a hero-quest falling-upon of one text by another. Either text is a sort of "soil" with which the other can interact—not *poisonously,* we presume, though even there one is edified by Derrida's demonstration that in the *pharmakon,* poison is also cure.)

The fourth stage of the monomyth is that of the quest, the going-out of the hero, and of course the meteoric colour does go out, does spread out and seek and conquer, though in reading we do not see this quest from the point of view of the quester (it would be a bizarre exercise to imagine this tale told from *that* point of view); but then in the "Dunwich" text we see the quest only from the point of view of an editorializing narrator: "an event no less strange than Wilbur's first trip outside the Dunwich region" (*CF* 2.432). We do see the effects of the quest, of course, even early on: "April brought a kind of madness to the country folk" (*CF* 2.378), a reference recalling T. S. Eliot's "April is the cruellest month" (29). Indeed, April for these country folk leads to a waste land, eventually; in Eliot's "April . . . breeding / Lilacs out of the dead land" with an eye upon the Gardner farm we find the interesting suggestion that "breeding lilacs out" here means not their bringing-out but their elimination: the meteoric presence, after all, has produced flowers that "were such blasphemous-looking things that Nahum's oldest boy Zenas cut them down" (*CF* 2.381), so that some breeding-out (weeding out, elimination) of the healthy species would seem to have been occurring. (One sees, in this mutual encroachment involving yet another text, how uncontainable intertextuality is; as I have said before, elsewhere: one stands always at the edge of an abyss. At the very least we have the vertiginous experience of realizing that Lovecraft determines how we read Eliot.) The notion of colour-as-quester is underscored by Nahum Gardner himself, who personifies the spreading blight—"dun't know what it wants" (*CF* 2.387)—and thus highlights its relation to Wilbur Whateley, of whom, after all, Lavinia has said, "I vaow afur Gawd, I dun't know what he wants nor what he's a-tryin' to dew" (*CF* 2.432).

In the fifth stage of the monomyth we have the death of the questing hero because of the quest, and we note in this connection that by the time the narrator comes upon the scene and sees the Blasted Heath, "only a fine grey dust or ash which no wind seemed ever to blow about" (*CF* 2.369), the questing colour from the meteor has "died," as it were, or become dormant in any event, because at the Gardner farm it has eaten away all that there was to consume. In this regard it differs with its Wilbur-aspect as hero, in that while Wilbur (trying to steal the *Necronomicon* and being attacked by the guard dog) dies by failing, the meteoric colour dies by *succeeding*. We have, then, an intertextual indeterminacy between heroic success and heroic failure; it is a commonplace in the theory of myth that pre-Renaissance heroes (questing for wholeness, for Self) tend to come back whole and successful, while post-Renaissance heroes tend not to—witness, respectively, Sir Gawain and Conrad's Marlow in *The Heart of Darkness*—so that, with this intertextual Lovecraftian hero of whom no final account can be made as to success or failure, we have an eluding of such pat categorizations.

The sixth stage of the monomyth is that of descent to the underworld, and we find that the meteoric colour has gone to ground, to the roots: the trees "were twitching morbidly and spasmodically, clawing in convulsive and epileptic madness at the moonlit clouds" (*CF* 2.392) in the absence of wind. Ironically, the alien presence, while reducing everything to dead ashen residue, has given the trees an unaccustomed appearance of life.[2] Here again the intertext equivocates as to the nature of the conflated hero, in that with the root-nuzzling presence from the meteor we *see* the effects, while with Wilbur's brother descending into the "great sinister ravine" of Cold Spring Glen, the monster-hero is invisible. The two, when brought together—as if they were not always already together—create an undecidability of seeing versus not seeing, knowing versus not knowing, readability versus unreadability, as it were.

In the seventh stage, we have rebirth, and the meteoric colour shows itself reborn in a number of ways. Even during the lying-low of the winter, the colour shows itself (to echo Yeats's "The Second Coming") "slouch[ing] towards Bethlehem to be born"[3] (91) when Nahum thinks, of certain animal footprints in the snow, that there is "something not quite right about their nature and arrangement," and when the McGregor boys find a "peculiar specimen" of woodchuck (*CF* 2.376). With the coming of April (the cruelest month, provider of an undesired rebirth here as in Eliot's *The Waste Land*), "All the orchard

---

2. Steven J. Mariconda has given us a splendid exploration of the contradictory textual proclivities of this tale; see his "The Subversion of Sense in 'The Colour out of Space.'"

3. This poem has lines clearly putting one in mind of both HPL texts: "Things fall apart; the centre cannot hold; / Mere anarchy is loosed upon the world." Thus it is only with an effort at economy that we resist letting yet another wandering text come to play more substantially within our current intertext; at times, other texts crowd in so closely for attention that one has to hold them somewhat at bay. We note, here, that we have been within sight of Yeats anyway in speaking of matters that smack of "Leda and the Swan." In both instances, HPL colors the way we read Yeats, so that (in the world of reader-participatory text-creation) "influence" is not a time-linear phenomenon. That first of the great deconstructors, Friedrich Nietzsche, has of course long since deconstructed the whole temporal-priority notion of cause and effect, in *The Will to Power.* We find ever fresher reasons to know how very on-the-mark he was.

trees blossomed forth in strange colours" (*CF* 2.378), and of course the rest of the "Colour" text treats of further and ever ghastlier signs of this cruel rebirth. In the end, even when the farm has become the Blasted Heath, there is feared and suspected rebirth still in the making, in "the country notion that the blight is spreading—little by little, perhaps an inch a year" (*CF* 2.398). "Country notions" are sometimes not taken seriously, we hear: stories of frightened horses and abnormal footprints are of course "mere country talk . . . wild gossip, for superstitious rustics will say and believe anything" (*CF* 2.377). Yet in the "Dunwich" aspect of the text, there is never (for the observers) any question about taking things seriously, so that the intertext problematizes credibility and epistemological certitude.

The eighth and final stage of the monomyth is that of ascension—the return of the hero/demigod to the father—and of course we have a graphic scene in "The Colour out of Space" to fit the pattern. The alien colour-presence came from the sky, and we read, of "that riot of luminous amorphousness, that alien and undimensioned rainbow of cryptic poison from the well," that "without warning the hideous thing shot vertically up toward the sky" (*CF* 2.395–96) and that "coloured and fantastic fragments . . . followed the great morbidity that had vanished" (*CF* 2.396). (In this scene, Ammi Pierce stares through the holes in the clouds at the stars of Cygnus, and we have yet another reminder that here as in Dunwich, we are dealing with gods and heroes: Cygnus, the swan, Zeus.) Here the ascension is seen by all, unlike what happens in Dunwich, where we have only veiled and indirect description: "A single lightning-bolt shot from the purple zenith to the altar-stone, and a great tidal wave of viewless force and indescribable stench swept down" (*CF* 2.464). It is interesting that both passages employ the verb-form *shot:* in one case, "shot vertically up," in the other, "shot from the purple zenith"; i.e., shot downward, so that the text entertains mingled notions of directionality—ambiguous notions of this sort are already implicit anyway with meteors, if we can have such expressions in our language as "a meteoric rise to fame" when meteors in fact fall. But then again Lovecraft's text rises, we may say, to the occasion, with its final description of the meteoric colour's ascension, its return to the sky, to the father.

The difference, of course, between the "Dunwich" and the "Colour" accounts of this return, is that atop Sentinel Hill, the hero/demigod *is returned* to the father, with help, whereas it would appear that at the ruins of the Gardner farm, the colour-hero returns of its own volition; to the extent that one part of the intertext colors another, we may of course wonder whether this is really the case—is the meteoric colour in some sense returned to the sky/father? Did it find that the cuisine left something to be desired, that its welcome in the new soil was thus insufficiently warm to warrant staying around? We of course anthropomorphize the alien in asking these things, but even if we understand the personification to be a species of trope, we will have difficulty answering such questions. It is notable, nevertheless, that it is primarily the interfacing of the "Dunwich" text with the tale of the Gardner farm that leads us even to *pose* such questions.

There is the further problem, considering the two accounts of ascension or return to the father, that while the return would seem to be total in the case of Wilbur's brother in Dunwich, it is less than total at the Gardner farm, where, after the other observers have turned away, Ammi Pierce has turned back to see "something feebly rise, only to sink down again upon the place from which the great shapeless horror had shot into the sky" (*CF* 2.397). We learn, too, that there is apparently a lingering presence in the noisome well, and that the blight of the Blasted Heath may slowly be spreading. This possibility of not *wholly* returning to the (holy) father encourages us to ask whether the return in Dunwich has been total, and whether those well-known intimations in the *Necronomicon* (about the eventual triumph of the Old Ones) may not for new reasons be taken as suggesting that the human "victory" atop Sentinel Hill has been an evanescent one after all.

It is interesting to note, with reference to this mythic notion of return to the father—so ably parodied in "The Dunwich Horror" when Wilbur's twin bellows out his "HELP! . . . ff—ff—ff—FATHER! YOG-SOTHOTH!" (*CF* 2.464)—that in poststructuralist theories of criticism the idea of return to the father has been applied to literary texts themselves. Discussing dissemination, that phenomenon whereby texts extend themselves out beyond any controlled contexts or confines, Geoffrey Hartman characterizes Jacques Derrida's effusions on the subject as suggesting that when Derrida approaches major Western-tradition texts, they "are so separated from a direct logo-imitative intention by his deconstructive readings that they cannot be returned to the father: their author, or their author in heaven" (51). In discussing this exploration of Hartman's, G. Douglas Atkins mentions that the fact that "it is extremely difficult to bear the father's absence" is demonstrated by such texts as *Hamlet,* the *Odyssey,* and Joyce's *Ulysses,* and suggests that in textuality the inability to "return to the father," the inability of the text *simply to reduce to retrievable authorial intention,* may occasion our "trying to fill the gap by taking the father's place: in this case, posing determinacy where none otherwise exists" (Atkins 60).

In any case, such a view of the mythic notion of returning to the father, with reference to texts such as we have here considered, occasions anew a certain textual self-concern or self-commentary, and not without the sorts of self-referential paradoxes that such considerations spawn. If returning to the father amounts to interpretative certainty or hermeneutic closure by way of retrieving an intrinsic and fixed meaning in a text, then the *failure,* at the end of "The Colour out of Space," of the entirety of the meteoric colour to ascend, to return to the father, would suggest that the text is allegorizing its own lack of semantic closure, its own inability or unwillingness to submit to any finalizing, totalizing reading. Yet if a text speaks allegorically of its own unreadability, we must ask: how reliable is the language with which it does so, or seems to do so? One is led into aporia: the irresolvable oscillation inherent in saying, "I am speaking unreliably"—if indeed I am, then *am* I? That there is no escape from such a paradox is of course implicit in the nature of paradox to begin with.

But even aside from such paradoxical reelings and writhings, we have here, in the Lovecraftian hero-intertext, a most complex mythic figure—a hero-demigod who may be singular or multiple, visible or invisible, active or passive, who may die in his quest by succeeding or by failing, who may completely or incompletely return to the heavenly father. Seeing the effects of grafting text upon text—and even of having to resist the relentless siren-songs of other such possible graftings—we perhaps have only begun to imagine, in terms of textual interplay, what cryptic sorts of meteors may fall, and into what strangely fertile soils they may furrow.

Humour beneath Horror: Some Sources for "The Dunwich Horror" and "The Whisperer in Darkness"

In October 1932 H. P. Lovecraft wrote to Robert E. Howard, "I don't care for humour as an ingredient of the weird tale—in fact, I think it is a definitely diluting element" (*SL* 4.83). Clearly, Lovecraft must have referred to overt humor, humor that forms a readily discernible part of the fabric of a horror tale; for one sees in various places his fondness for in-jokes in his fiction. Some instances are rather transparent now that the fundamental facts of Lovecraft's life are known. For example, in the story "In the Walls of Eryx" (1936) when he names an annoying alien insect the "farnoth-fly," one traces the name to the fact that *Weird Tales* editor Farnsworth (to whom Lovecraft often referred as "Farnie") must at some point have rejected one too many of Lovecraft's manuscripts for further endurance. But this fondness for cryptic little references comprehensible only to a few people was not merely an outcropping at the end of Lovecraft's life; nor was it confined to the more readily traceable instances found throughout his fiction. It plays a less obvious part in two earlier stories for which Lovecraft drew heavily upon his travel impressions of the summer of 1928 in western Massachusetts and southeastern Vermont: "The Dunwich Horror" (1928) and "The Whisperer in Darkness" (1930). There is, beneath the pervasive horror of these stories, a substratum of private humor so specialized that it could have evoked a twinkle of comprehension in only a very few readers.

The summer of 1928 was a time especially replete with memorable travel experiences for Lovecraft. He accepted an invitation to visit his friend Vrest Orton at a rented summer home of Orton's in Guilford, Vermont and arrived there around 10 June, finding much fascination in the rural isolation of his environs. On 24 June he proceeded to the home of his friend W. Paul Cook in Athol, Massachusetts for a visit there, and he and Cook indulged in local rambles with their young writer friend H. Warner Munn. On 29 June Lovecraft, responding to an invitation from his amateur journalist friend Mrs. Miniter, went to the home of Mrs. Miniter and her cousin Miss Evanore Beebe in North Wilbraham, Massachusetts for yet another visit, staying until 7 July (*CE* 4.16–31). He acknowledged the probable usefulness of his impressions of this locale in a 28 July 1928 letter to revision client Zealia Bishop:

> Far to the west, across marshy meadows where at evening the fireflies dance in incredibly fantastic profusion, the benign bulk of Wilbraham Mountain rises purple and mystical. The region, being very old and remote, is full of the most extraordinary folklore; some of which will certainly find lodgment in my future stories if I ever live to write any more. (*SL* 2.246)

Although this letter does not similarly refer to any fictional intensions for his Athol impressions, both areas found lodgment in "The Dunwich Horror," written in August 1928 soon after Lovecraft's return home to Providence. (The presence of Athol sources explains the opening words, "When a traveller in north central Massachusetts . . .") And although he declines to suggest that his Vermont impressions would similarly have fictional embodiment, they indeed do, in "The Whisperer in Darkness," though oddly enough Lovecraft waited two years to write this tale.

One may break down Lovecraft's blended use of Athol and North Wilbraham impressions in "The Dunwich Horror" as follows. Much, if not all, of the physical description of landscape comes from North Wilbraham, and the character names, with two important exceptions, come from Athol town history. The descriptive portion of the quotation from Lovecraft's letter to Zealia Bishop may be compared with such descriptive passages in "The Dunwich Horror" as this:

> When the road dips again there are stretches of marshland that one instinctively dislikes, and indeed almost fears at evening when unseen whippoorwills chatter and the fireflies come out in abnormal profusion to dance to the raucous, creepily insistent rhythms of stridently piping bull-frogs. (*CF* 2.418)

Thus Lovecraft has obviously made good on his vow to use his North Wilbraham impressions—obviously as far as the physical landscape is concerned. what is not obvious is that his epistolarian reference to "most extraordinary folklore" refers specifically to the motif of the chirping whippoorwills as given in the tale:

> It is vowed that the birds are psychopomps lying in wait for the souls of the dying, and that they time their eery cries in unison with the sufferer's struggling breath. If they catch the fleeing soul when it leaves the body, they instantly flutter away chittering in daemoniac laughter; but if they fail, they subside gradually into a disappointed silence. (*CF* 2.421)

A niece of the same Evanore Beebe with whom Lovecraft stayed in North Wilbraham has verified that this whippoorwill legend, though somewhat embellished by Lovecraft, stems from an actual story told in the Beebe family.[1] Lovecraft dramatically enlarges upon his locally imbibed folklore when he tells of the reaction of the whippoorwills to the departing soul of part-human, part teratological Wilbur Whateley: "Against the moon vast clouds of feathery watchers rose and raced from sight, frantic at that which they had sought for prey" (*CF* 2.440). It is even possible that the first name of the monstrous Wilbur is an echo of the town name Wilbraham. In any event, Lovecraft is making quiet use of obscure local lore from that town, transmuted to suit his own purposes.

But the really demonstrable private humor in "The Dunwich Horror" resides in Lovecraft's use of Athol sources, which are unacknowledged in his letters. In the tale, farm families of decadent backwater Dunwich Village—whose name, by the way, is no doubt derived from the now-vanished English village of Dunwich, which over a period of several centuries was washed into the North Sea[2]—the farm families

---

1. Telephone interview with Thyra V. Calkins of Ludlow, Massachusetts, 20 March 1979. The motif of the whippoorwills as a harbinger of death occurs elsewhere in literature, e.g. in *Huckleberry Finn*. But HPL's use of it as an actual psychopomp clearly has its source in his North Wilbraham gleanings. It should be noted that HPL himself relates the whippoorwill legend in his memoir of Edith Miniter: see "Mrs. Miniter—Estimates and Recollections" (*CE* 1.378–86).

2. Algernon Charles Swinburne, "By the North Sea," in *Swinburne: Selected Poetry and Prose* 270. The editor, in a footnote, discloses that in the "Dedicatory Epistle" to his Poems, Swinburne identifies the bleak scene of "By the North Sea" as the doomed English village of Dunwich and its environs. HPL, who had not failed to read Swinburne, is quite likely to have seen this reference, and the scenic impres-

submit to the ravages of Wilbur's unthinkably monstrous twin brother, who bursts forth having been nurtured to enormous bulk in the Whateley farmhouse. The reader meets these families as the horror moves across the countryside. It devours Seth Bishop's cattle; it annihilates Elmer Frye's entire family. Earl Sawyer meets visitors to Dunwich who come to investigate; Fred Farr and Henry Wheeler are also present when outsiders come, and are among the onlookers at the end when the visitors from Miskatonic University go up Sentinel Hill to deal with the horror.

What Lovecraft apparently never publicized, even in letters to close friends, is that the names Wheeler, Farr, Sawyer, and Bishop all occur prominently in Athol town history, along with two other names to be discussed; Lovecraft must have absorbed many details of local history during his visit with Cook and Munn. The Wheeler family in Athol goes back to Zaccheus Wheeler (born 1749), one of whose granddaughters Mary (1832–1925) married Hollon Farr (Lord 663–64). There was a Sawyer Mansion at 2033 Main Street in Athol until 1948, and town history records many Sawyers (Lord 597). A George W. Bishop was appointed, in 1895, a railroad commissioner in Athol and was a longtime selectman (Lord 201). The Frye family in Athol goes back to Captain John Frye, who led a military expedition in 1758 (Lord 45); H. Warner Munn, from his youth in the Athol area, recalls knowing a Frye and going to school with a Wheeler.[3] Even Dr. Houghton, who comes to the Whateley house in the story when old Wizard Whateley (Wilbur's grandfather) is dying, is an echo of the fact that in mid-nineteenth-century Athol there was a Houghton's Block named after townsman Alvin Houghton (Lord 365).

W. Paul Cook himself remarks, in his Lovecraft memoir, that Lovecraft took the name Sentinel Hill, in "The Dunwich Horror,"

---

sions of the poem should certainly have appealed to him. Besides, Arthur Machen mentions Dunwich in his novel *The Terror*, which HPL is known to have read.

3. Letter received from H. Warner Munn, 7 February 1979. Munn says, "No, the names you mention were not of prominent families in the Athol/North New Salem area, so far as I know. I would imagine that HPL took them at random." Nevertheless, they do form a recorded part of early Athol history, and since there are too many of them, in too small a town, for coincidence, it seems certain that HPL must have learned of them.

from his Athol experience.[4] Cook does not elaborate on this borrowing, but Athol history reveals that there was, for over a century in the Moore family of Athol, a farm on West Hill, overlooking the town, called Sentinel Elm Farm after a patriarchal elm (Lord 650). Munn (in the letter cited in note 3) recalls often reposing beneath this elm in his youth, and certainly the placid beauty of the spot was as far removed from the horror of Lovecraft's fictional Sentinel Hill as anything could be. It seems likely that Sentinel Hill is a mixture of impressions, drawing its name from the Athol source but its topographical and atmospheric qualities from Lovecraft's impressions, as described in the Zealia Bishop letter, of Wilbraham Mountain.

Thus Lovecraft wrote, around the largely prosaic historical elements of a typical small New England town, a tale of cosmically grotesque horror, bringing unthinkable calamities upon characters in the tale who are, in tacit derivation, namesakes of Athol townspeople who surely would have been astonished to find themselves immersed in such horrors.

Thus it goes for the Dunwich "common folk." But the substratum of very private in-joke humor best shows itself in the derivation of the names Rice and Morgan, the protagonist Henry Armitage's colleagues who venture up Sentinel Hill finally to vanquish the Dunwich Horror. Not only do the names Rice and Morgan occur prominently in Athol town history—they occur linked in such a fashion as to leave virtually no room for coincidence. In a land transaction that must have assumed major importance locally, though it could have been of little or no interest outside Athol, a Mr. H. H. Rice sold the mill power in town to the Morgan Memorial, which used it to power a rug factory. There is, in South Athol, a Rice Hill close to the Morgan Memorial. H. H. Rice had obtained the mill from his father William Rice, who at one time had owned not only the mill but much of the surrounding country as well, so that the Morgan-Rice land transaction forms a notable

---

4. W. Paul Cook, *In Memoriam: Howard Phillips Lovecraft* (1941), in Cannon, *Lovecraft Remembered* 129. Cook says of HPL, "The only thing he carried away from the town for literary use was the name 'Sentinel Hill' . . ." This is simply not true. If Cook ever saw through some of the in-jokes in the story, he evidently had forgotten about them by the time he wrote his HPL memoir.

item of local history that Lovecraft could easily have picked up (Lord 336–37). In naming Professor Armitage's colleagues Morgan and Rice, in a story written so shortly after the Athol visit, Lovecraft was indulging in an in-joke that only Cook and Munn could reasonably have been expected to understand.

The fact that Lovecraft came away from Athol in such a literarily playful mood can also be seen in something occurring two years later when he ghostwrote "The Mound" for Zealia Bishop. In that story he named one part of his hideous subterraneous region L'thaa, which one may take as merely typical of his unearthly place-names until one notices that L'thaa is "Athol" phonetically backwards.

Lovecraft's playful attitude toward the Athol area is also notable in his reaction, as remembered half a century later by H. Warner Munn, to a local landmark to which Munn escorted him. The place was the Bear's Den in North New Salem, a deep rocky ravine with curious fissures in the sheer stone cliff at one end; topographically, Lovecraft describes the scene quite accurately in "The Dunwich Horror" when he has Sally Sawyer say, of the horror that has gone abroad and apparently slithered down into the ravine called Cold Spring Glen in the tale:

> "I calc'late [the tracks] must go into the glen itself. They would do that. I allus says Col' Spring Glen ain't no healthy nor decent place. The whippoorwills an' fireflies there never did act like they was creaters o' Gawd, an' they's them as says ye kin hear strange things a-rushin' an' a-talkin' in the air daown thar ef ye stand in the right place, atween the rock falls an' Bear's Den." (*CF* 2.444)

The rock falls and Bear's Den are indeed there in reality, and Munn recalls that when he took Lovecraft to the spot, Lovecraft examined the fissured rock mock-ominously—one large fissure runs back a few feet and pinches off, too narrow for passage, but with the suggestion of unseen recesses beyond—and remarked that what one had to fear in the ravine was not the reputed bears, but rather what might come forth from the cavernous depths to eat the bears.[5] Clearly Lovecraft was in a mood to use his Athol-area impressions in unexpected fictional ways.

---

5. Letter received from H. Warner Munn, 4 October 1977. I am indebted to Harold Munn for his kindness in giving me detailed directions by which to find the "Bear's Den" site.

Although the Dunwich farm families beset by Lovecraft's horror are drawn, in name, from Athol families, two important character names are not accounted for in this way: Armitage and Whateley, which do not occur in Athol history. Lovecraft seems to have used Athol families for the tale's "common folk" and for Rice and Morgan, setting Armitage and Whateley upon a different plane. Henry Armitage, the Miskatonic University professor, is set against Wilbur Whateley, the hybridly monstrous Dunwich denizen who confronts Armitage in an attempt to obtain the university copy of the *Necronomicon* for purposes of sorcery. Attempts to account for these two names become speculative, but given that Lovecraft demonstrably drew other names from real but obscure sources, one strongly suspects that Lovecraft had something in mind in choosing these names. One possibility—a further clear indication of wry Lovecraftian humor if it is indeed connected to his thought processes—resides in the fact that there were, historically, two bishops named Armitage and Whateley. William Edmond Armitage (1830–1873) was Bishop of the Protestant Episcopal diocese of Wisconsin and spent some seven years of his ministry in New Hampshire and Maine; he was, like Professor Armitage of the story, impressively educated ([Unsigned] "Armitage, William Edmond"). And Richard Whately (1787–1863), English logician and theologian, author of tracts on logic and rhetoric, was Archbishop of Dublin from 1831 until his death.[6] It is possible that Lovecraft saved out these two names, not derived from Athol families as were the more pedestrian figures of the tale, and named them after two prominent bishops, with the view that the two figures Henry Armitage and Wilbur Whateley stand out in the cast of characters as embattled spiritual forces, as it were—Whateley engaged in desperate efforts to admit Yog-Sothoth into the world from the outer realms by sorcery, and Armitage engaged in equally desperate efforts to prevent his doing so. Such a state of affairs would most likely have especially

6. "Whately, Richard," *Webster's Biographical Dictionary*, lst ed. (1956). Also, there is a town named Whately in the Connecticut River valley not many miles from Athol; it may have given HPL the idea, or may have suggested Archbishop Whately and, in turn, Bishop Armitage, since from the town name alone the name Armitage remains unaccounted for.

appealed to Lovecraft's sense of humor, in that he expressly had little serious use for organized religion, in letters often playfully referring to the gods of his own fictional pantheon as if he believed in them. Ultimately the question of the names Armitage and Whateley is unsettled; but it is certain that they do not share a source with the names of the more plebeian characters.

Just as Lovecraft drew heavily upon his Athol and North Wilbraham experiences to write "The Dunwich Horror," studding the tale with private derivations that amount to closely obscure in-jokes, he also drew similarly upon his Vermont visit when, two years later, he wrote "The Whisperer in Darkness." In a way somewhat more limited but no less demonstrable than that in which he proceeded in "The Dunwich Horror," he used local names and topography that could be recognized in fictional form by only his close local associates—in this case only Vrest Orton and perhaps a few other people whom he met in Guilford, Vermont.

Given that Lovecraft wrote his Vermont tale after his visit with Orton, one naturally wonders whether the besieged Akeley house in the tale has its source in a real house, and indeed the clues to Lovecraft's sources for the story begin with the Guilford house in which Orton hosted him in 1928. Orton recalled, in 1977, only that the town was Guilford (never mentioned in the story) and that the farm family living down the road from his rented summer house was named Lee.[7] This fact alone suggests real sources for story elements, for Lovecraft refers in the story to "Lee's Swamp," out of which rises Dark Mountain.[8] But the Lee clue also leads to the revelation that in back of Lovecraft's character-name Akeley lies a real Vermont family.

On Lee Road in Guilford, Grace (Mrs. Henry S.) Lee still lived in 1977, in a red brick farmhouse built in 1816 on property that was originally a land-grant by Colonial Governor Benning Wentworth (hence Henry Wentworth Akeley)—Mrs. Lee readily identified a wooden farmhouse farther down the road as that in which Orton hosted Lovecraft in 1928, and she even remembered Lovecraft walking up the road

---

7. Letter received from Vrest Orton, 21 January 1977.

8. HPL, "The Whisperer in Darkness" (*CF* 2.485). The feature in real Vermont topography corresponding to Dark Mountain is Governor Mountain.

to chat with her family.[9] The wooden house in question was built in the early 1820s by Samuel Akeley (1808–1891), who deeded it to his spinster daughter Mila (1842–1922). Samuel's father Thomas Akeley (1783–1851) built the Lee house, and in fact the Lees and the Akeleys were intermarried; Henry Lee's mother was Hattie M. Akeley (*Guilford* 267).[10] Not only does the name Akeley appear in the history of the Orton summer house—a history that Lovecraft would be very likely to investigate, with his antiquarian habits—but Mila Akeley lived as something of a recluse in "the old Akeley place," as Lovecraft calls it in the tale, and was even regarded as a witch by some area residents.[11] Thus the house had not only the sort of Colonial New England interior that would have pleased, Lovecraft, but also a dark side to its history to appeal to his sensitivity to weird lore—no doubt, to his sense of humor, because he had no belief in the supernatural precepts that are necessary to make witchcraft a meaningful notion.

Lovecraft not only borrows the character-name Akeley, he does so with a flourish that embodies yet another in-joke only comprehensible to someone familiar with the local lore of the Lee Road area in Guilford, Vermont. In "The Whisperer in Darkness" when the Winged Ones have come close to capturing Akeley and are sending fake correspondence in his name to lure Wilmarth to Vermont, they misspell the name in a telegram as *Akely* (*CF* 2.493). This playing upon the spelling of the name is an echo of the fact that the real Akeleys of southeastern Vermont entertained two spellings of the name, *Akeley* and *Akley*—not the same two spellings that Lovecraft employed, but two spellings

9. Personal interview with Mrs. Grace Lee, 29 October 1977. She described HPL as "very quiet," but said he had some long conversations with her husband Henry (hence Henry Akeley?—Mrs. Lee thought this conjecture improbable when I mentioned it to her, but I wonder) and with Henry's brother Charles. No doubt it was from them that he learned much of the local lore.

10. The name given in this work, both for Samuel and Mila, is *Akley,* but the spelling is *Akeley* on their gravestones in West Guilford Cemetery.

11. Personal interview with Robert L. Dothard of Lee Road, Guilford, Vermont, 13 August 1977. Dothard, who lived only a short walk from the Orton summer house in 1977, coincidentally was the designer of Willis Conover's book *Lovecraft at Last.* He said that his father had told him of Mila Akeley's local reputation as a witch. Dothard died in late January 1979.

nonetheless. There are both Akeley and Akley gravestones in the family burial ground near the Lee house. It can safely be assumed that Lovecraft had this double spelling in mind when he wrote his telegram episode.

Other Vermont sources are quietly present in "The Whisperer in Darkness" as well. The name Wilmarth appears to have a Guilford-area source, for it is probably not coincidental that there was a well-known Brattleboro man named Seth Wilmarth, an inventor of heavy machinery, who moved to Pawtucket, Rhode Island and became the master mechanic of the Charlestown navy yard (*Vermonters* 39). Lovecraft, in the story, also refers to "the exceedingly rare monograph of Eli Davenport" (*CF* 2.469), and there were several prominent Davenports in southern Vermont—e.g., Herbert Joseph Davenport, a well-known political economist (*Vermonters* 156), and Thomas Davenport, the inventor of the electric motor (*Vermonters* 154). In the story, Henry Akeley's son in California is named George Goodenough Akeley, and the middle name is a reflection of the fact that Lovecraft, the previous summer, had briefly visited the local poet Arthur Goodenough of West Brattleboro, and in fact went to see him again during the 1928 visit with Orton.[12] The story also contains the name Noyes, with reference to the man who, pretending to be a friend of Akeley's, meets Wilmarth at the train station when Wilmarth comes to Vermont. Noyes had long been a common name in the Brattleboro-Guilford area, and Lovecraft, in his looking into local folklore, may well have been aware that the Noyes family in the area included one "Old Mother Honeywell," reputed to be a witch and described in the autobiography of Nathan Noyes (*Guilford* 156–57). Although Lovecraft does remark, in certain amateur press writings, that the Vermont visit inspired the

---

12. HPL, "Observations on Several Parts of North America" (*CE* 4.22). The "old Akeley place" of the story seems to be a blend of impressions from the Orton summer house and the Arthur Goodenough house; certainly the fictional house is strongly connected to the Orton house through the name Akeley, but the story description of a "two-and-a-half story house of unusual size and elegance for the region, with a congeries of contiguous or arcade-linked barns, shed, and windmill behind and-to the right" (*CF* 2.512) much more closely fits the Goodenough house, the colonial interior of which must have charmed HPL at least as much as did that of the Orton house.

story, he indulges in these numerous borrowings without comment.

In fact, the dread winged ones themselves—forming a segment of the Lovecraft Mythos later revived in the novel *At the Mountains of Madness*—apparently had their genesis in Lovecraft's Vermont impressions. His narrator refers, in "The Whisperer in Darkness," to the fact that Pennacook Indian mythology was disturbingly consistent with other local folklore about the Winged Ones (*CF* 2.471). Although there is virtually no written material on Pennacook myth, the Pennacooks having been nearly obliterated in the early seventeenth century by a plague, it is known that as Western Abenakis (or Abnakis) they shared with the Eastern Abenakis a myth concerning "a dread flying creature named *bmold*" ("Western Abenaki" 159). Most likely Lovecraft picked up this motif from oral tradition, repeated to him by someone in the Guilford area, and gave it truly cosmic embellishment in the story.

Since Lovecraft stayed with Vrest Orton in Guilford, one may well ask whether Orton himself shows up in "The Whisperer in Darkness." The name Orton nowhere appears, but it has been speculated that the character Henry Wentworth Akeley, whose name is so well accounted for, is based on Orton himself. Certainly Lovecraft knew Orton to have the scholarly character described in the story for Akeley, and there is reason to believe that the two were even better acquainted, in terms of sharing their views with each other, than a superficial knowledge of their friendship would suggest. During the 1928 visit Orton wrote a long, laudatory newspaper piece on Lovecraft and his fictional theories, published under the "Pen-Drift" column in the *Brattleboro Daily Reformer*—Lovecraft nonchalantly mentions this column in the story, delivering another in-joke—and the piece shows Orton to have been quite familiar with Lovecraft's ideas and tastes (see Orton, "Weird Writer").[13] It would have been entirely in keeping with the Lovecraftian sense of humor fictionally to annihilate a close friend, patterning Henry Akeley after Orton and then having Akeley fall prey

13. I discovered this item, an unusual piece of early criticism on HPL, in the *Reformer* files, having become curious about HPL's reference, in his letter to Zealia Bishop (SL 2.245), to clipped newspaper items, one of which he called "the puff of myself" by Orton. The article calls HPL "a very great writer . . . perhaps so great that he will never be appreciated."

to the Winged Ones, who leave Akeley's surgically removed face and hands in his study chair to be found by Wilmarth in the story's closing scene. Lovecraft was later to demolish a friend fictionally in "The Haunter of the Dark" (1935), in which the protagonist Robert Blake is seized by an alien presence called forth from a (real) church tower in Providence; the character is a very thinly disguised version of Lovecraft's young correspondent Robert Bloch. The gesture of having Bloch (Blake) destroyed by the story's lurking horror was a return favor occasioned by the fact that young Bloch had recently had a character, based by permission on Lovecraft, similarly destroyed in a story of his own, "The Shambler from the Stars" (1935). Lovecraft's good friend Frank Belknap Long once had a Lovecraft-based character annihilated in a story as well, "The Space-Eaters" (1928). Thus Lovecraft belonged to a crowd of fellow literati who delighted in loosing their loathsome fictional horrors on one another, and it would not be difficult to believe that after the Orton visit and, ironically, after Orton had given Lovecraft high praise in the newspaper piece, Lovecraft would return the favor in a manner that was to grow commonplace among his acquaintances.

It is no secret to reasonably informed Lovecraft readers that Lovecraft had some fondness for in-jokes in his stories. In "The Whisperer in Darkness" itself, for example, he refers to a myth-cycle "preserved by the Atlantean high-priest Klarkash-Ton" (*CF* 2.519), and there is little difficulty in discerning that this high-priest represents Lovecraft's correspondent and fellow fantaisiste Clark Ashton Smith. Similarly, the tale is strewn with names and terms taken from his own other stories and the stories of such writers as Frank Belknap Long, Clark Ashton Smith, Lord Dunsany, Robert W. Chambers, and Robert E. Howard.

But, to the student of Lovecraftian and related writings, these are obvious. The real revelation is that Lovecraft's penchant for the in-joke in stories of profound cosmic horror does not stop at the relatively obvious. The more subtle examples, such as the "Rice and Morgan" matter, show that beneath the horrific effects of "The Dunwich Horror" and "The Whisperer in Darkness"—stories centrally important to an overview of the Lovecraft Mythos—and even beneath the level of more obvious in-jokes, Lovecraft concealed a twinkle of private humor so obscure that only considerable digging into these stories' sources brings it out. Just as in Lovecraft's tales the "horror" seen is often only a precursor to some further horror merely glimpsed or guessed at, the readily discernible in-jokes are perhaps only a hint that there are more private ones beneath the surface.

But private or not, the presence of this humorous substratum beneath the outwardly weird purport of the work reveals a complexity of artistic involvement that is far from evident in more superficial reading. It is one thing to write a realistic tale or novel around a set of travel impressions, and quite another to write around such impressions a set of horror tales with the unthinkable cosmicity of the Lovecraft Mythos. Much of the quiet humor of Lovecraft's in-jokes resides in the contrast between his commonplace travel impressions and the immensity of cosmic horror that he weaves around them. There is, here, no violation of Lovecraft's dictum that humor and horror never mix, because in these stories the hidden in-joke humor does not obtrude upon the intended weird effects. The shudders are felt by all, but the chuckles are those of private amusement—the amusement of a man to whom, after all, the universe of stars was a funny, because ultimately pointless, place.

The Thing: On the Doorstep

H. P. Lovecraft's narrator in "The Silver Key" remarks that Randolph Carter "had forgotten that all life is only a set of pictures in the brain, among which there is no difference betwixt those born of real things and those born of inward dreamings, and no cause to value the one above the other" (*CF* 2.73). It is curious that he uses the expression "real things," for—unless this is a mere infelicity of style, a phrasal redundancy like "true fact"—it suggests that one may question the reality of things, in that things that are real and things that are not may both exist and have comparable claims to "thinghood."

The passage cited comes from a context in which we read that philosophers have taught Randolph Carter to "look into the logical relation of things," and one may wonder to what extent this passage suggests that things may *be* something so rarefied as logical relations rather than objects in the traditional sense. The problem here is not with "concrete things" versus "abstract things"—in either case the problem is one of independent definability, in that we may ask in what sense there is such a "thing" as the cat on the rug, or in what sense there is such a "thing" as beauty. In any event the passage cited does threaten to weaken the barrier, if any, between "things" and "dreams," calling into question the notion that any object exists (as what Kant would call a *noumenon*, a *Ding an Sich* or "thing in itself"—henceforth referred to as a Thing, the capitalization serving to underscore the relation of this word to its German philosophical counterpart *Ding*) apart from the somewhat arbitrary constructions of consciousness, in particular apart from the self-reifying constructions of language.

Indeed Nietzsche (that first of the great deconstructors) raises the very question, in *The Will to Power,* of the Thing thought of as a well-defined, monadic, identifiable entity in the world. He argues that speakers of language have *created* the Thing as a linguistic construct to serve as a foundation for attributes which the Thing is considered to "have" (rather than to *be*). "Thingness," he says, "was first created by us" (*Will* 307 et passim). The Thing, for Nietzsche, is a categorizing fiction, a linguistic convenience brought about by the will to power in the form of the eternal human rage for order and coherence, the human habit of insisting upon imposing order and making sense of the world—we humans weave a cultural web of language around an intellectually arranged bundle of properties and point to it as a Thing, forgetting that different cultures may (and do) categorize differently, chopping the world of experience up into pieces differently—forgetting that there is thus no *absolute* reality inherent in the Thing thus postulated. Things, for Nietzsche, are edifices of talk, and the very etymology of *thing* supports this view: the Indo-European root *ten(k)-* ("to extend," "to stretch") produces not only *thing* but such surviving forms as the Danish *Folkething* (parliament), suggestive of language-wielding assemblies that determine things by talking about them, so that from the outset the Thing is fundamentally a creature of language. It is rather as if when Hamlet says that "the play's the thing," he is unwittingly characterizing the Thing as drama, deception, linguistic artifice, illusion within illusion (a play within a play)—and suggesting that in fabricating the Thing and attributing an extralinguistic existence to it, language is waxing ludic or playful.

Lovecraft's fiction (oddly, one might say—if one were concerned with matters of authorial intent—oddly for a writer proclaiming himself to be a mechanistic materialist, for whom the reality of independently existing and definable objects ought to be important, but more about this later; the matter is by no means that simple)—Lovecraft's fiction tends in numerous ways to protract this philosophical unsettling of the "thing in itself." This interrogation of the Thing is perhaps nowhere more intriguingly carried forward than in a tale whose very title announces our present concern: "The Thing on the Doorstep," the only tale in the Lovecraft canon with a title employing the word *Thing*.[1] Here, the Thing of philosophical inquiry struggles for its very existence, standing as a strangely hybrid presence upon the doorstep (the

1. HPL's fiction, however, is preceded in this regard by that of Ambrose Bierce; see my article "Bierce's 'The Damned Thing': A Nietzschean Allegory."

threshold, the border), perhaps to be allowed to pass through, perhaps not—alternatively, perhaps to pass into metaphysical acceptability, perhaps to pass beyond it.

Even a casual reading of "The Thing on the Doorstep" would convince any reader that questions of reality and identity are very much alive in the text. At various times, Asenath's mind looks out of Edward's eyes, and vice versa; one learns that Asenath, even when "herself," is (mentally) not Asenath at all but old Ephraim Waite, who has usurped his daughter's not entirely human body in an exchange of the sort that Edward Derby ultimately fears for himself. If a Thing (including a person) is supposed to have a definite being, what can one say about this corporeal/cerebral variant on the game of musical chairs? Clearly, the suggestion is that the confidently definable Thing is up for grabs: under the circumstances is Edward Derby, for instance, a Thing in the old Kantian sense?

There are problems here, to put it mildly. S. T. Joshi has pointed out (*H. P. Lovecraft: The Decline of the West* 94) that in "The Thing on the Doorstep" Lovecraft in effect thinks of the mind as defining the person, so that when Edward Derby's mind is trapped in Asenath's (Ephraim's) body, the person, properly considered, is Edward. It is indeed clear that Lovecraft himself thinks of the mind as defining the person, but one may add that the reader is not necessarily constrained to do so, at least not entirely; nor are the characters in the tale. As always, the text says more here than mere authorial intent would encompass, and it is not without significance that the narrator speaks of (e.g.) "Edward's mind" and "Edward's body," indicating that "Edward" is something *more* than just his mind alone and more than just his body alone. While certainly no one can deny that the mind plays the more primal and quintessential rôle, one may still think of the body—the outward being, that which appears before us in evidence of our senses—as helping to define the person as well (indeed if the body dies, the mind dies—even in Ephraim's case the mental presence can only hold out for a while, being, as Edward Derby says, only "half detached" [*CF* 3.356] from the body), so that there is plenty of room for a reader to consider Edward-in-Asenath's-body as a true hybrid, a being that one cannot exactly call either Edward or Asenath. In fact, such a creature is horrifying precisely *because* it raises profound questions of categoricality and identity, preserving a sense of the gulf across which one has come in meeting such an appalling instance of hybridity. The effect, for our argument here, is that if "Edward Derby" is supposed to be a Thing, a *Ding an Sich* more or less identifiable from within the narrator's memories and acquaintance—memories of his physical appearance *and* his mind—then the Thingness of this Thing is a troubled consideration when Edward's and Asenath's minds and bodies come to take on odd combinations.

To pursue our question: is (e.g.) Edward Derby, then, an objectively definable Thing in the pre-Nietzschean metaphysical sense? The question is not rhetorical, and the answer is not necessarily *simply* no, any more than simply yes. In a punning way one might say that it is significant that Asenath's unmarried name is Waite, for *waiting*[2] is what the fate of the Thing here is all about: endless self-differing (*différance*), endless deferral of the putting of any closure to our question: whether the Thing ultimately is "real" or not. What operates in the text is the Thing in the mode of perpetual deferral, the mode of unending resistance to settled thinking. In fact, even the text itself here, as *Ding an Sich,* has a shaky existence, for its supposed borders are blurred in the direction of other, impinging, texts: at the very least one needs to have read Lovecraft's "The Shadow over Innsmouth" to read "The Thing on the Doorstep." That is, even the story itself tends, by its own example *qua* text, to allegorize the questionable status of the Thing—yet without wholly turning the Thing out of doors either, else we should be unable even to refer to this text as something impinged upon by

---

2. Interestingly, *wait* comes from the Indo-European root *weg-* meaning "to be strong and lively"—the person called Asenath in the story is repeatedly described as strong, too strong for Edward's will to resist—and the same root gives us the forms *wake* (to become aware, lively) and *vegetable*: living matter, suggesting that life, the dynamic reality, is in the waiting, the deferral, the always incomplete journey itself, the non-arrival at closure. Life is a hideous (read: indeterminate, closure-resisting, unsimplistically dynamical and chaotic) Thing. By extension, for a literary text to be decided (determined single-mindedly) is textual stultification and death; to be unreadable (refusing settled or finished understanding) is to live on. In the allegorical workings of HPL's story, it is the person called Asenath Waite who most exemplifies this necessarily chaotic and indeterminate dynamism.

others. As we shall note, this double gesture (of partly denying yet provisionally affirming the *Ding an Sich*) operates throughout.

Early in the tale, the narrator Daniel Upton finds himself wondering, of his friend Edward's exchanging dependence upon his father for dependence upon his new wife Asenath: "Might not the *change* of dependence form a start toward actual *neutralisation*, leading ultimately to responsible independence?" (*CF* 3.332). Allegorically, the question is whether Edward Derby—a Thing only defined in relative terms in a dependent context, and on its way to being transferred to another such defining context—whether Derby can achieve genuine independence of definition, of absolute Thingness. The narrator's naïve logic, in supposing groundlessly that this might be the case, is undermined by all the text's subsequent events, in which the hapless Edward increasingly suffers from threatened loss of identity and definitional integrity—by this reading we take "independence" in the text as a metaphor for identity. Derby, we are told, longs to find ways of "saving his identity" (*CF* 3.334), his lost Thingness. Or the illusion of it—it has taken the protean and incomprehensible interloper Asenath to disencumber him of the notion that he *had* a fixed, inviolable self, a self whose imagined integrity she proceeds to violate.

Of Asenath "herself" (a hopelessly reductive term), the text has Edward ask the narrator, during the car ride back from northern Maine: *"Asenath . . . is there such a person?"* And he refers to her (him, it) as "that thing that calls itself Asenath" (*CF* 3.340, 341). Here we have, by conflation of these two not widely separated utterances, a textual admission that the business at hand is indeed the unsettling interrogation of the Kantian *Ding an Sich:* a "thing" calls itself Asenath (which alone would lead to difficulties enough—the Thing adopts language as its ground of being, declaring its existence by *naming* itself, yet apparently existing, anterior to this action, as an agential reality to be able to do so), yet we hear Edward ask if there is any such (objective, definable, monadic) person. Later when the narrator, recalling Edward's transformation in the car, says, "I caught myself again and again trying to account for the thing" (*CF* 3.344), we need only to read "Thing" for "thing" to see the text declaring its own covert thematicism, its own agenda of trying to "account for" the flickering half-reality of the metaphysically elusive Thing.

For half-reality is what one finds: an undetermined, paradoxical trace-state in which the Thing dwells, independently real *and* not real. The text plays out the drama of this indeterminacy in all its accounts of "personality exchange"—Asenath's and Edward's minds inhabiting each other's body, Asenath's outward form concealing the presence of Ephraim's mind, Edward's consciousness entombed in Asenath's rotting corpse at the end. Clearly each of these bizarre displacements represents a challenge to the integrity of Thingness, an unsettling of the comfortable notion that what looks like Edward is "really" Edward, or even the notion that what seems like Asenath possessing Edward's body is "really" Asenath. But the other side of the coin here is that the text not only challenges the monadic Thing with each of these displacements but also *reinscribes* Thingness in a larger and more troubled web of context: for each of these displacements works effectively in the text only insofar as we retain a notion of what the proper circumstances *should* be, a notion, however simplistic, of what is "normal." For example, it is to no effect that we read of Asenath's frenzied eyes staring out of Edward's sockets unless we retain a sense of the unnerving distance across which we have been catapulted to entertain the spectacle of this abnormality—a sense of what is *wrong:* a notion of the Edward (understood more or less in terms of not unduly variable Thingness) whose eyes should be looking out of their own sockets. To appreciate displacement, we must have some idea of what has been displaced: some understanding of the impropriety of differences.

Thus a Thing-displaced is both the less-than-comprehensible residue of an identity-destroying transformation *and* the still-comprehensible subject of precisely that transformation. The text slyly allegorizes this double nature of the endangered but not wholly vanquished *Ding an Sich* when the terrified Edward Derby tells the narrator of what he has seen in the woods of Maine: "The Hooded Thing bleated 'Kamog! Kamog!'" (*CF* 3.338). Here, "Thing" is even capitalized (like its German cognate *Ding*), and the gesture of *hooding* is a tellingly double one: to hood something is to cover it, eclipse it, remove it from sight—but to hood something is also to draw attention to it, to choose it *for* hooding, even (in academic circles) to honor it—hooding something pretends to cover or remove it but really allows it to remain beneath the hood *sous rature,* under (incomplete) erasure as it were. This is the text's ultimate treatment of the (hooded) Thing: it is shadowed, problematized, driven to the brink—but not quite *over* the brink.

In fact, the text's very title suggests this marginal status, the state of being "on the doorstep." We see the door in the story as a potential entranceway: the frightful lich that shows up on Upton's doorstep seems to threaten to come in, and needless to say, doors are commonly enough regarded as means of ingress. Yet etymologically the notion of a door is more properly a matter of *egress*. The Indo-European root is *dhwer-*, from which derives the Latin *foras*, "toward the outside," "out through the doors," as well as the English *foreign*. The narrator's beleaguered door is at once a possible means of letting something in or a means of keeping it out. Edward Derby, in Asenath's putrefying corpse—the very embodiment, literally, of lost integrity, compromised Thingness—lurks on the doorstep both physically and figurally, and we both do and do not admit this identity-questioning wraith to the comfort of our parlor. The story itself is an allegory of the fate of the Thing: to be forever on the doorstep, on the threshold, at the boundary (headed in? headed out? which is which?)—the wavery boundary standing in deconstructive uncertainty between the Thing of Kantian metaphysics and the Thing of Nietzschean nihilism.

"Kill that thing," Derby writes—*"kill it"* (*CF* 3.356). We may indeed, with Nietzsche, kill the Thing. But to kill it is to admit, in a confluence of affirmation and denial, that there is something to kill; and to admit the killability of the Thing is to reinscribe it in a place where we threaten to kill it anew, in perpetuity. The Thing, which stands forever on the doorstep, both is and is not.

And even to the extent that we see the Nietzschean side of the opposition in ascendancy, Lovecraft philosophically stands to gain something. While it may seem strange, at first, to conflate the position of mechanistic materialism with the notion that the Thing has no objective reality beyond its existence as a convenience of language, one may alternatively argue that this very negation only affirms a worldview common throughout Lovecraft's work: the view that humankind, insignificant in the cosmos, becomes outright comic when it imposes its insectile image upon the universe, anthropomorphizing, creating gods in its own image. And what could be more characteristic of this projective and anthropomorphic practice than the human habit of assuming that the whole universe in some absolute sense is carved up into "things" along the contours of one's own particular linguistic or cultural preference?

If Nietzsche is right in saying that it is we humans in our lust for order who have created the Thing, then in so doing we have once again played the fool on the mysterious cosmic stage that is Lovecraft's world.

Lovecraft's Poetry

Lovecraft's "The Unknown": A Sort of Runic Rhyme

The reappearance and reascription[1] of an obscure Lovecraft poem is a matter of considerable interest, even when Lovecraft himself, in the 30 July 1923 letter to Clark Ashton Smith in which he gives the text of the poem and dates its composition to 1916, diffidently disparages the piece as a "futile fragment." While this particular poem may indeed on first glance seem to offer relatively little of interest, a closer reading reveals a rich field of potential in the text. Here is the poem:

> A seething sky—
>   A mottled moon—
> Waves surging high—
>   Storm's raving rune;
>
> Wild clouds a-reel—
>   Wild winds a-shout—
> Black vapours steal
>   In ghastly rout.
>
> Thro' rift is shot
>   The moon's wan grace—
> But *God! That blot*
>   *Upon its face!* (*AT* 38)

---

1. S. T. Joshi pointed out to me that the poem had actually appeared in the *Conservative* (October 1916), oddly enough under Winifred Jackson's pseudonym Elizabeth Berkeley. Curiously, when looking up this appearance of the text I found that in this version the line which HPL's holograph gives as "Wild winds a-shout" appears as "Wild sounds a-shout." The change to "winds" is a clear improvement.

In terms of traditional structure, simplicity seems to reign here; the meter is basically iambic dimeter, with a syllable-count maintained nearly to a fault. The *abab* rhyme scheme is unexceptional. Indeed, in terms of prosodic practice, the poem affects a mechanical simplicity that would call its value as poetry into question—one expects a little more looseness of structure, a little more freedom, a little more engagement with complexity—were it not for other considerations that show the poem's apparent simplicity to be illusory. As we shall see, "The Unknown"—a poem hidden away in an obscure journal and ascribed to someone else, thus a poem appropriately titled, with a titular whiff of self-reference that will not by any means be the only such whiff—deals with the unstable bipolarity revelation/concealment in a manner deeply problematical and paradoxical.

The poem opens stark and scenic, with strikingly succinct descriptions ("seething sky," "mottled moon") that are simply thrown before our eyes without syntactic connection with predicate structures—the "seething sky" (where "seething" is adjectival) and the "mottled moon" are not said to do anything—the sky does not, e.g., shroud the night, the moon does not float—rather, these images, as nominal syntactic structures, are just projected as graphic pictures to behold. This scenic setting-up of images suggests, without delay (but without promise of freedom from contrary complications either), a *revelatory* complexion for the poem: images will open up, are opening up, before us—we will be shown. Further imagery seems to underscore this notion, as when the "black vapours" are routed to make a "rift" through which we see the "moon's wan grace." It is as if a curtain is lifted for us to see what has lain concealed.

But then the text moves to unsettle what it seems to have been laboring to establish, for what is revealed is a blot upon the face of the newly unhidden moon, a stain obscuring the moon's face anew (blotting part of it out). The lunar surface is unveiled only to be veiled again, so that what is unveiled is the condition of veiling. Here the blot works on multiple levels to obscure, since the power of the poem is precisely that we do not learn what it is that so horrifically stains the lunar face: the blot conceals, withholds, its own significance as capably as it conceals what it literally covers—indeed, more capably, because we know what the face of the moon looks like, but we do not know the significance of the ominous blot. Yet the presence of such a blot is also a revelation, a disclosure of what the fugitive "vapours" have been concealing; the text threatens, or promises, to collapse the binary opposition of revelation/concealment deconstructively in showing that concealment is revelation—*a concealment is revealed, and the meaning of the revelation is concealed*—that neither concealment nor revelation functions here without an enabling trace of the other. What is at stake here is the indeterminate possibility of knowledge, a thematic concern which the poem's title adumbrates.

It is not only in the imagery of the blot that the text moves with such contrary gestures beneath and against itself, with regard to the problem of revelation and concealment. The poem opens with a reference to the sky, and we make two observations on this point.

First, one tends to associate the sky with openness and revelation (the sky lies open and limitless above us, revealing a panorama of stars)—but, oddly enough, the word sky derives from an Indo-European root *(s)keu* meaning" to cover," "to conceal" (suggesting the sky as a "cover" for the earth), so that even here we encounter the revelation/concealment problem. (The sky, although it is a "see-thing" sky promising some horrific sight, may also, with its "wild clouds," obscure the view it promises.) For the second point, we must observe that there is a certain iconography in the poem. The line about the sky occurs, like the sky itself from an earthbound observer's perspective, topmost, with the "mottled moon" foregrounded at the next level down, below which we have "waves surging high," "clouds a-reel," and "winds a-shout." Below these, we have the presumably sea-level or ground-level perceptions of the observer: "Thro' rift is shot / The moon's wan grace," so that through the rift one comes to see ("shot" down towards one's viewpoint) that which was above the "vapours." "Rift" here is *graphically* a break in a long string of nature- or storm-related words— "sky," "moon," "waves," "storm," "clouds," "winds," "vapours"—suggesting that these terms too may be textually self-descriptive, indicating a stormy field of reading.

These iconographic features—the text as *mise en abyme,* carrying a picture of itself, and thus a picture of itself carrying a picture of itself, etc. in infinite regression—would strongly suggest self-reference generally, and it is in this regard that we can see the text's most problematized engagement with the revelation/concealment bipolarity.

With this prospect in mind, we examine what is perhaps the poem's most striking line: "Storm's raving rune." This line comes to us with a sort of ludic parody, a pseudoparallelism; the real parallelism of the first two lines rather leads us to expect the same in passing from "Waves surging high" to "Storm's raving rune," but "Storm's" is of course a genitive form, not a plural, and in general the syntax of the fourth line falls away from that of the third in spite of the similarity in sound and rhythm: "surging high," "raving rune."

A *rune* is a number of things: as an early Norse graphic symbol, an alphabetic grapheme, it is obviously redolent of writing and textuality as such—but a rune is also a *cryptic* symbol, a puzzle, a concealer of meanings. As in the case of *sky,* but with broader implications this time, we have here a signifier whose propensity for linguistic play encompasses both revelation and concealment—as a grapheme or part of a graphemic system, a rune both points (as signifiers customarily do) to other signifiers (across networks of which "meanings" may be distributed) and conceals or obfuscates the very gesture of significational pointing. To the extent, then, that the text deals in self-reference—where the storm is the storm of textuality itself—the poem is its own "raving" (wild, like the winds) "rune," its own double gesture of self-revelation and self-concealment. Like Poe's bells, it is "a sort of Runic rhyme."[2]

But is it "keeping time, time, time"? *Moon* imagery seems to suggest as much; *moon* derives from the root *me-*, "measure," "the marking of time," whence also *month, menses,* and even *meter.* But the moon is "mottled," partly blotted out, inconstant. In any case, what about metric time here? We have already remarked that the poem's meter maintains a perfect syllable count. However, the integrity of the iambic dimeter is unsettled (and so much the better—prosodic literariness resides in such unsettlement) by the fact that the pattern of stresses is not so unadorned as it would appear.

---

2. In "Storm's raving rune" there occurs of course another echo of Poe, in that" raving," given the connection already noted via "rune," tends to put one in mind of "raven." This is a notable example of irrational yet irresistibly interesting word-play of the sort that enriches intertextual reading whether we admit it out loud or not.

In the scansion of "Waves surging high— / Storm's raving rune" (as well as in the first three lines of the second stanza) we see not quite the simple "short-long" rhythm of iambic dimeter but rather a modification, in each of these lines, of the first iamb, so that each line actually scans as "*long*-long short-long." The effect, besides being splendidly mimetic (the metric slowing-down of "Waves" conjures up a ponderous slow-motion picture of the turbulent sea), raises questions of centrality and marginality, in that compared to the leading iambs of the lines "A seething sky" and "A mottled moon," the modified poetic feet containing "Waves" and "Storm's" carry these two terms precisely where the unaccented indefinite articles have gone before, suggesting a parallel effacement or marginalizing of the very terms whose meter, in the modified scansion, has been slowed down to centralize. The text both dwells on the stormy imagery of the surging waves and threatens it with an obscuring displacement, as if the text itself, in self-mimesis, *were* the storm, well equipped with "clouds" and "vapours" with which to promulgate obscurity and concealment, yet parting itself (in rifts) for our partial, tentative viewing of what is hidden.

And here, of course, lies the delectable paradox. If we interpret the text as characterizing itself as *runic*—waxing cryptically sly, hiding something of itself in its own ever-shifting "vapours"—then we aspire to a reading, a decipherment, of the runes, a penetration of their puzzle. But to the extent that we have claimed to read the runes, we will have denied something of the runic nature that we have found in them, although (and because) the reading has been that they were runic. Reading the text implies that the text is unreadable, and thus calls into question the very reading that calls into question that the reading calls into question that—etc.: veritable waves of paradox.

Little wonder the dominant imagery of the text is that of a storm, where the "moon's wan grace" —the light of reading, if it purports even momentarily to dispel the darkness of textual turmoil—is wan indeed.

On Lovecraft's "Nemesis"

H. P. Lovecraft's early but powerful "Nemesis" (*AT* 46–48), by any prosodic standard arguably one of his best poems, offers us the brooding utterances of a sort of dream-presence, a persona appearing to be an undying embodiment of the collective unconscious, or a timeless dreamer who seems doomed to eternal memory by some primordial sin of the spirit. The poem, unendingly interpretable, presents a variety of problems, not the least of which is the question of who or what its persona, its "I," may be: a single memory-haunted dreamer?—a figure seemingly singular but really synecdochically representative of us all?—the text itself, dwelling self-referentially upon its own linguistic machinations?—the reader, whose critical perusal the text anticipates? There can be, of course, no final or single-minded settlement of such questions; but we may nevertheless take a close look at "Nemesis" to see something of the nature of its difficulties. As can scarcely be surprising, it will be seen that, like any richly figural literary text, the poem presents a wealth of indeterminacy and piquant self-subversion denying the possibility of settled reading.

The work opens (and, cyclically, closes): "Through the ghoul-guarded gateways of slumber, / Past the wan-mooned abysses of night, / I have lived o'er my lives without number, / I have sounded all things with my sight; / And I struggle and shriek ere the daybreak, bring driven to madness with fright." Right away, aside from the ongoing and unsolvable problem of identity of the persona, one is struck with the poem's metaphors, which posit a number of problematical notions, e.g., the confounding of time with space. Night, for the persona, is characterized not by qualities of time but by "abysses," spacial lacunae that seem to stand agape in the dreamer's world. Slumber, no mere temporal condition of the mind, has spacially suggestive "gateways" that are "ghoul-guarded"—one wonders: to keep someone out, or to keep someone or something in? Gateways, in any case, are of course as bidirectional as the double faces of Janus (appropriately, for an opening stanza that is also a closing stanza), in that they are both ways in and ways out, and (more paradoxically) are both conduits of passage and blockages of passage. It is intriguing that the poem's persona speaks of being past (rather than in or into) "the wan-mooned abysses of night"—past night, into what further region or condition? The suggestion is one of open-ended and indeterminate horror; yet the text subverts this very suggestion, in having the persona exclaim, "I have lived o'er my lives without number" and "I have sounded all things with my sight"—oddly totalizing claims that appear to place the persona in the position of having, already, experienced all there is to experience, without further possibilities; this suggestion finds iteration in the text's continuing use of the present perfect tense, in an anaphoric series that we will have occasion here to examine.

Yet again, in the end, the text subverts this very subversion by suggesting that the persona's curse of memory and perception has not ended and will never do so: "Nor can respite be found in the tomb: / Down the infinite aeons come beating the wings of unmerciful gloom." Here again we find spacial and temporal imagery confounded, with stretches of time spoken of as if they were corridors in space. In a conflation of time and space, a persona extended in time may be extended in space as well, and thus multiple; we shall further examine this question of non-self-identity.

Subsequent to the opening stanza, the text offers the device of anaphora to keep the pace moving, in its repetition (in the first lines of the successive stanzas) of the phrase "I have" with the past participles of various verbs: "I have whirled," "I have drifted," "I have plunged," "I have stumbled," "I have scanned," "I have peered," "I have haunted." The superficial effect is to grant continuance of identity to the persona, suggesting a single, wearily haunted, long-enduring "I" who has done all these things in the caverns (or time-gulfs) of dream. Yet the very nature of the sequence is such that the text subverts this notion of continuous self-identity; the very fact that the "I" is repeated through a sequence of contexts is a textual postulation of change, of shifting, of non-self-identity: for to repeat is to change—to repeat a signifier is to embed it in new contexts, and thus to change it, since the signifier is "defined," as it were, only by its contexts, which shift. The "I" changes by reappearance; otherwise, a subsequent occurrence would be merely the initial occurrence. There is no single "I," but rather a flux-driven spectrum of "I"s, no one of which has any privileged existence without reference to all the others with which it contrasts itself. (*Nemesis* derives from the same Indo-European root *nem-* that is responsible for *nomad;* the poem's "I" is not so much a fixed individual as a wandering legion of beings.) The text postures between claims of fixity of identity on the one hand, and, on the other, claims of the unthinkability of such fixity. Yet each pole of this opposition turns out to be the enabling condition of the other. It is impossible to reflect on the refusal of the persona to be a monadic, fixed entity without considering that, by one way of looking at the text, it might have been so; one cannot meaningfully contemplate the notion that something apparently singular is not really so, without thinking that it was, after all, apparently singular. Conversely, it is meaningless to dwell upon the supposedly unchanging character of the persona without reflecting that "unchanging" ineluctably puts one in mind of change at the outset. As so often happens in literary texts, the poles of the binary opposition collapse together against any ideological or categorical species of wishful thinking that they might have remained apart.

But the anaphora of the stanzas' opening lines presents further complexities. One notices that the verbs thus employed reveal a continuous narrowing of imagery and action. In "I have whirled with the earth at the dawning," "whirled" suggests an action that must be, like the primordial motions of newly formed planets, protracted over countless aeons and over immeasurable stretches of space. In "I have drifted o'er seas without ending," "drifted," contextually describing a drifting over seas, is likewise suggestive of a protracted motion, though on a lesser scale than whirled. In "I have plunged like a deer through the arches," "plunged" creates imagery of somewhat protracted but this time more limited motion, motion directed toward a spacial destination or (at least) a place of stopping. In "I have stumbled by cave riddled mountains," "stumbled" portrays a yet more limited motion, and a slower one, an earthbound motion rather than a motion of the air. In "I have scanned the vast ivy-clad palace," "scanned" has reduced the motion to a movement of the eyes only, while in "I have peered from the casements in wonder," "peered" describes activity in which even the eyes do not need to move. And in "I have haunted the tombs of the ages," "haunted" suggests an activity that, far from containing any necessary motion, does not even presuppose (in contrast with eyes that peer) any physical presence, in that one pictures, for a "presence" that haunts, a ghostly entity at most, a mere consciousness without substance. The imagery steadily narrows in scope of action. Yet the text, in the process of presenting this imagery, interrupts itself with displacements of direction, displacements given by lines within the stanzas. Between whirled and drifted, we have "I have seen the dark universe yawning," where seen is a verb more sequentially belonging in the vicinity of the later scanned and peered. Similarly, between scanned and peered we find "I have trod its untenanted hall," with trod describing an action more sequentially suitable to a placement in the vicinity of the earlier plunged and stumbled. The text disturbs its own continuity, as if to say that any too facile a reading, any too hopeful a view of settled structure, is simplistic.

Even if one regards the narrowing of action-imagery as reasonably stable structure, the text presents further problems with it, in that the narrowing that takes place is a narrowing in the realms of dream: realms eternal, realms archetypal and cosmic, realms redolent not of narrowness but of unbounded breadth. The text has thus insisted upon collapsing yet another binary opposition: the bipolarity of narrowness versus breadth. The sequencing of verbs, though self-disturbed, describes a narrowing that takes place in a field of infinite breadth; and, conversely, the very range of effect in these verbs (from planetary whirling down to peering and haunting) suggests a breadth in the process of narrowing, a broad and extensive amount of narrowing. In-dwelling (as a matter of textual necessity) with each pole of the opposition as its enabling condition, is a trace of the other, supposedly contrasted, pole—if the text's broad dream-realms did not contain narrowing, the text would have no focus, and if the process of narrowing were not broad in extent, the text would have no scope. One sees here an example of how literary texts not only do subvert their own structures, but must do so.

We return to the problem of who, or what, the persona is. If one momentarily takes the "I" of the poem to be the text itself, or to be the textually anticipated critical reader (an effect brought about simply by reading the poem aloud oneself), one finds high irony in the strange claim "I have sounded all things with my sight," since the very energies of the poem are spent in describing (and textually demonstrating) the impossibility of "sounding all things," or nailing down all interpretative possibilities, or getting, ever, to the bottom of things. It is even possible that the text (allegorizing its own self-oppositions) speaks in an assortment of contending or competing voices. Where we have "I have lived o'er my lives without number" and "I have sounded all things with my sight"—a voice denying the possibility of further or new developments—the text follows with "And I struggle and shriek ere the daybreak, being driven to madness with fright": as if to say, "And on the other hand I (unlike you who have just spoken) still anticipate further struggles." Perhaps it is then the experience-exhausted "I" who returns with his "I have whirled," "I have drifted," etc. Yet as we have seen, this "I," scarcely a singular presence, breaks down into a medley of (non-)identities. Even if one rather reductively regards the poem's "I" as a memory-haunted dreamer (or as metonymy for ourselves, a race of dreamers), one encounters all the difficulties of non-self-identity through textual iteration as already described.

No matter who or what the "I" may be, or whether the poem is or is not (and we know that it both is and is not) an anticipatory allegory of its own reading, the supposedly present structures of the text work hard both at appearing to be stable and at subverting such appearances. In closing with the "same" stanza as that with which it opens—though the closing stanza only appears to be the same: it is really different both by virtue of being repeated, and by virtue of the experience of reading by the time one reaches the end—the text suggests both closure and cyclicity, both a folding-in and a cosmic unfolding-out. (One notes that the verbal narrowing that occurs in the poem leads immediately, paradoxically, to a broadening out into boundless concerns: "Down infinite aeons . . .") Like its own "gateways," the poem allows no settled thinking on matters of interiority and exteriority. If we are the persona, then we are both in and out—outside of normal experience yet inside what is normal experience for the dreamer, inside the caverns of dream yet "past" them, outside any possibility of final understanding yet inside the problem of searching for it.

We may well be the persona, but the only sin of the spirit we could commit here that would call for the retributive justice of the goddess Nemesis would be the sin of pride—a prideful notion that we had ever really, totally, finally, read "Nemesis" or gotten at its "meaning" or "truth." If there is any truth, it is that reading "Nemesis" will lead us "down infinite aeons" and corridors of language in which indeed we will see "the dark universe yawning," and in which we will find interpretative "abysses" where readings yet unborn will, like the "black planets" of the text, "roll in their horror unheeded, without knowledge or lustre or name." That is, without privilege-granting "heeding," without any possible claim to final knowledge, without the specious "lustre" of any imagined mastery over interpretation, and without even the apparent fixity of names. In this respect, the text allegorizes the readings it provokes in its own bottomless pits of night.

On Lovecraft's "The Ancient Track"

"There was no hand to hold me back / That night I found the ancient track"—so begins (and ends) H. P. Lovecraft's forty-four-line poem "The Ancient Track" (*AT* 79–80), if it can be said to have a beginning or an end. The poem's first-person narrator describes a sort of memory-quest in which she follows a steep path up a hill, anticipating all the while that upon reaching the top she will again see "roofs and orchards" and "distant spire and roofs" in a moonlit valley landscape long familiar to her. At the crest, however, she sees a "valley of the lost and dead" in which a "malignant moon" casts its cold radiance upon what she describes as "ruined walls I never knew." Contemplating this "mad scene," she comes to reflect "that my loved past had never been," and to realize that she is no longer on a trail "descending to that long dead vale"; rather—"Around was fog—ahead, the spray / Of star-streams in the Milky Way." As we shall see, the experience of this poem is a far stranger journey even than one might think.

Even on a casual reading it is evident that much of the poem's energies expend themselves on a tantalizing indeterminacy over the reality or illusoriness of the narrator's memories. These (perhaps) remembered images appear so real that the narrator, thinking of them as she ascends the hill, seems actually to see them: "This tree, that wall—I knew them well." She reflects that the expected "roofs and orchards fell / Familiarly upon my mind / As from a past not far behind." Here the word *as* equivocates on the very point of the memories' reality, since it not only means "as if" (suggesting that the memories may be illusory: only *as if* truly remembered) but also "as" in the sense of the context "as indeed being from a past not far behind" (suggesting that the memories are real). What is at issue here is fact versus illusion, memory versus pseudomemory, perception versus imagination, presence versus absence—affirmation versus negation.

Contrasting sharply with the narrator's verisimilar memories, the scene over the hill turns out to be a real but unremembered place of the "lost and dead" where "weeds and vines" grow on "ruined walls," and where the narrator quickly comes to feel that the fog's "curling talons mocked the thought / That I had ever known this spot." But even this drastic turn becomes outdone by the further twist, a dream-like *volte-face* that finds the narrator in effect staring into the abyss of space, to see only "star-streams in the Milky Way." Seemingly, the narrator's sense of memory has been shattered; her recollections have been proven false, her present perceptions (of a "long dead vale" into which she should be, but apparently is not, descending) have been shown untrustworthy.

Yet the effect of reading the text is that her memories are not *simply* false, any more than simply true. Such exclusive binary logic will not suffice here. For textual effect, both the reality and the illusoriness of the narrator's memories are necessary, as incompatible but simultaneously vital readings. If indeed her memories are simply accurate, and if the further revelations (the dead valley, the pathway into the starry abyss) are oneiric or hallucinatory, then the poem is no more than an account of a memory-quest turned sour by a nightmare; conversely, if the narrator's memories are simply imagined, and if the dead valley and starry abyss are what is real, then as final stark realities they suffer by being uncontrasted with mundane and expected memory-scenes that *should* have been there as a real scenario which the final nightmare vision has replaced. If the narrator is simply enveloped in real horror and is deluded as to what she thinks is memory, then the narrative is too common to be of much interest; if her memories are real and the dead valley and the starry abyss are not, then the events again lack interest. Ultimately the account is truly captivating only if the narrator's memories both are and are *not* real, and if the dead valley and the vista of the Milky Way both are and are not real, suspended in an indeterminacy of plural reading.

Again, what is at hand in the poem is an unstable bipolarity between affirmation and negation, and the text unwittingly finds a number of ways to allegorize the nature of this strangest journey of all, the journey into the tenebrous logic between yes and no, a journey in which the experience is in the going rather than in the arriving—in the "ancient track" itself rather than in any specification of a destination to which it leads. Etymologically, *track* stems from the Indo-European root *tragh-*, "to draw," "to pull," and it is significant here that this same root is responsible not only for the word *trek*—underscoring the tendency of the path and the journey to coincide: as Yeats asks, "How can we know the dancer from the dance?"—but also for the word *trace*, with all its applications to close reading. Here, in each pole of the opposition memory/pseudomemory, there resides a covert trace of the opposite pole, in that memory is "pseudomemory" vindicated, while pseudomemory is "memory" disproven. Pseudomemory is pseudomemory only if in its content it conceivably could have been true memory, and true memory (in the poem's context) is appreciable as true memory—of a scene somehow vanquished—only with the suggestion that it may have been pseudomemory after all. In saying that "my loved past had never been," the poem's persona may of course be an unreliable narrator, but the point is that she is neither simply reliable nor unreliable; the *trace* operates everywhere to insert an element of indeterminacy between the binary poles of affirmation and negation.

But aside from the linguistic provenance of *track*, *trek*, and *trace*—in which we note the connectedness of the path, the journey, and the mutual containment of opposites—the text of the poem offers far other etymological connections. The narrator suggests that she expects to see the familiar scene of her memories "with ten more upward paces gone," and much hangs upon the word *paces*, which, as "paces gone," confounds past (to which it is in fact etymologically related) and future—in that if the ten upward paces are "gone" they may be gone in retrospect or may be expected to become gone; the narrator, after all, reliving her memories or pseudomemories, thinks she has climbed this path before, and there is no simple linearity of time reference here, with regard to her paces. *Pace* derives from the Indo-European root *pet-*, "to open out," "to spread," which is responsible not only for *past* (a past participial form of the Middle English *passen*, to pass—to trek, to go along a track!) but also for the French *pas*. And here the intrigue really begins.

Pas in French of course means "step," as in *faux pas;* in this sense it is cognate with (e.g.) the English *pace* and the Spanish *paseo*. But *pas* when used with the negative *ne* also means "not," as in *"je ne sais pas,"* and it is a curious fact that these two words *pas* ("step") and *pas* (which has by itself come to mean "not," as in *pas mal*) enjoy parallel derivation, both from the Latin *passus*.[1] Since the primary signification seems to be "step," the usage as "not" seems strange at first glance. Larousse explains *pas* ("not") by saying that it expresses *"l'idée d'une toute petite mesure."* That is, in *"il ne travaille pas,"* for example, one is saying that "he doesn't work even a little bit." This usage is easier to understand in connection with the use of the more emphatic French negative *point* ("bit," "speck," "point"): *"il ne travaille point,"* "he doesn't work at all." *Pas* as (only, even) "a little step" is used similarly in such structures of negation. Yet a certain paradox indwells this usage, since even when it is glossed as "not," *pas* means "a little bit," an existing modicum.

The point (*point; pas,* a further step into the text) here is that the word *pace* covertly raises anew the whole issue of negation versus affirmation. It is ineluctable here that the pace, the step, binds itself up with the bipolarity of the affirmative and the negative. A pace is both positive and negative, a double gesture: it is a step *away* from one position while it is a step *to* another; it is an admission of the openness of a gap between the positions, while simultaneously it is a closing of the same gap. One who paces becomes at once absent and present, becomes removed from one place and becomes newly arrived at another. This duplicity of the step (this *pas de deux!*) thus invades the domain of the negative *pas*, which is both "a little bit" and "not at all." Etymologically, this connection allegorizes the whole poem's concern with negation, its very pacing, its concern with not-being. (Even the term *ancient,* in the title, derives from the root *ant-* meaning "before" or "against,"

---

1. With regard to the double duty of the French word *pas* as "not" and "step," one may note an astonishing parallel that has no logical or etymological reason to exist, yet does exist. In Chinese, the word *bu* means "not," and a graphologically different but phonologically identical word *bu* means "step." (The Chinese characters are different, but the pronunciations are the same, even the same tone.) One could scarcely hope for a more delectable example of the uncontainably playful nature of language in the global sense: language as writing, language as quantum field of signfication, language as weaver of sometimes irrational yet uncannily persistent patterns. (In this regard, one may note that there is also another phonologically identical Chinese word *bu* meaning "cloth"—suggestive anew of weaving, texture, textuality.)

whence the negative prefixes *an-* and *un-*. This theme of negation and reversal runs beneath the text of the poem throughout.)

The text inadvertently underscores this same concern, with the persona's early reference to the "fields that teased my memory." *Field* derives from the Indo-European *pela-*, "flat and broad," whence also the Latin *planus* and the English *palm,* the flat of the hand, so that this line unwittingly connects with those three lines in the poem in which the persona says, "There was no hand to hold me back": so that "no hand" etymologically suggests "no field(s)," raising anew the issue of the existence or nonexistence of those supposed memories over which the poem has already in so many ways equivocated. This same root *pela-* is responsible also for the English *plat,* meaning a small piece of ground—a *plot.* Hence the text comes around to the theme of its own reading—plot, textuality, semantic *fields.* And here we may return (via the provenance of the titular ancient *track*) to the matter of the *trace,* and to the thematics of tracks as marks, as writing in the most primordial sense: the ancient track, the always already anterior condition of writing as differentiation, spacing, marking. In this case, as we have seen, the tracking or marking or writing is an incursion into deeply problematic fields, those twilit realms between affirmation and negation, between presence and absence.

The track of the poem is thus in this larger thematic sense the track *of* the poem, the self-referential story of writing and reading. The poem's narrative voice pursues a remembered reading, as "from a past not far behind," a reading to which she tries to return along the track, the mark, the very path of the writing that she thinks she recalls reading, as it were. But her attempt to retrieve this reading grows ever more problematized; first her frustrated quest turns up only a "valley of the lost and dead"—the site of the irretrievable reading, the lost memory—and then becomes more perturbed still, in leading only to an abyss, "star-streams in the Milky Way," via her reflection that "my loved past had never been." It is as if the text comments on its own undecidability, its own ludic refusal to allow an unproblematized following of the track, a path to unambiguous reading and retrievable origins.

The text even questions its own self-reference, its tendency to comment on reading-per-se in parallel to its own reading; for, in certain respects, the poem stands opposed to its own manner of reading.

One notes that the couplet "There was no hand to hold me back / That night I found the ancient track" occurs three times: once at the beginning, once in the middle, and once at the close of the poem. These are not really the *same* couplet of course, because iteration is change; something repeated is not originary, simply because the repetition *is* a repetition, a citation, an echo, and not an original utterance; repeated utterances are different in that they are colored by what has gone before. And the contextual circumstances of this iterated couplet are varied in an interesting way as well.

In the first instance, the couplet occurs with full enjambment; i.e., with run-on to the following line "Over the hill . . ." In the second instance the couplet ends with a comma and a pause, with no run-on to the following line. And of course in the final instance the couplet ends with a period, and no line follows. The complexion of the couplet thus changes continuously from more connected (through enjambement) to less connected (first with a pause, then with a full stop). But in a way this progression opposes itself to the imagery of the poem. In the opening instance, the couplet is maximally connected to what follows, yet what follows is, in terms of the poem's thematics, minimal: the persona's memories, which, even if real, are mundane. In the closing instance, the couplet is minimally connected to what follows, yet in terms of imagery and reading, what the couplet should lead on to is maximal: readerly speculations on that deepest mystery of all, the starry abyss, the "star-streams in the Milky Way," the most fecund field of all, the milk-fed plenitude of the cosmos, the ga-*lactic* universe of stars. Thus while devoting itself symbolically to tracking, marking, writing, and reading, the poem doubles back on itself to reverse its own self-reflections.

In all these respects, the text invites readings of untrammeled imagination, invites following the primordial track, the trek, the trace. There is, after all, no hand to hold us back.

Scansion Problems in Lovecraft's "Mirage"

Sonnet XXIII in Lovecraft's *Fungi from Yuggoth* (*AT* 89) presents a certain curious problem in scansion, one that allegorizes another, larger problem dealing in what we may also call "scansion," by analogical extension, on another level and from another direction, in the poem. What is at stake here is integrity of systems—whether of literary praxis, or of reading, or of metaphysical belief—and the question of preservation or subversion of systems.

The text is as follows:

1] I do not know if ever it existed—
2] That lost world floating dimly on Time's stream—
3] And yet I see it often, violet-misted,
4] And shimmering at the back of some vague dream.
5] There were strange towers and curious lapping rivers,
6] Labyrinths of wonder, and low vaults of light,
7] And bough-crossed skies of flame, like that which quivers
8] Wistfully just before a winter's night.

9] Great moors led off to sedgy shores unpeopled,
10] Where vast birds wheeled, while on a windswept hill
11] There was a village, ancient and white-steepled,
12] With evening chimes for which I listen still.
13] I do not know what land it is—or dare
14] Ask when or why I was, or will be, there.

With regard to the form of the sonnet, there would appear to be little here to view as metrically irregular, other than the occurrence, in odd-numbered lines, of "weak" endings; i.e., unaccented terminal syllables in excess of the basis syllable count. There are minor elisions required to maintain a strict scanning of iambic pentameter: reading "shimmering" as disyllabic in line 4, "towers" as monosyllabic and "curious" as disyllabic in line 5, "evening" as disyllabic in line 12. There is nothing remarkable here; in fact, the sites of such potential elisions mark the prosody as possessing a certain looseness, a certain maturity, as it were, in not succumbing to such Procrustean devices as writing "tow'rs" or "shimm'ring," or to the temptation to eschew these words altogether in favor of alternatives preserving a perfectly mechanical scansion. While the sonnet form theoretically requires precise iambic pentameter, it is well known that a certain (really, uncertain, for how can we describe it precisely?) deviation from this rigid norm has the effect of enlivening the language of verse within the preserved metrical form, though deviation of another sort or degree might prove ill-suited to the purpose; the balance, of course, is a delicate one.

The sonnet "Mirage" presents us, in line 6, with a scansion problem not so readily settled as, say, the question of whether to think of "evening" (in line 12) as disyllabic (if we wish to adhere slavishly to the form) or trisyllabic (if we wish to be a bit more comfortably free)—line 12 is (loose, breathing) iambic pentameter even if we do retain the three syllables of "evening." But the situation of line 6 is such that variations in scanning may materially alter the metrical nature of the line. Like the poem's persona, who reflects that there have been "evening chimes, for which I listen still," we too, in scanning line 6, listen for "evening" (even-ing, smoothing, regularizing, analyzing) "chimes" (countings of time); we may hear an extra toll of the bells, but with textual winds blowing we cannot be sure.

In "Labyrinths of wonder, and low vaults of light," when we regard "labyrinths" as fully trisyllabic, the line acquires an extra foot—actually, an extra but defective iamb lacking the unaccented syllable (or at best stealing its effect from the final unaccented syllable of the previous line)—and becomes an alexandrine, with a clear count of six distinct accents, producing the anomaly of a sonnet containing a line of iambic hexameter.

But there is some uncertainty as to this result; is line 6 really an alexandrine? Conceivably, "labyrinths" may be read disyllabically (with elision: "LAB'rinths"), whereupon the line reverts to iambic pentameter; the scansion then actually gives the first foot as a trochee in place of an iamb—a not uncommon metrical variation, as occurring, for example, in line 8 of this poem ("Wistfully . . ."). Whether one would be justified in such an elision of the syllable *-y-* in labyrinth is an open question; in such parallel forms as the French *labyrinthe* or the Spanish *laberinto,* the corresponding elision would be markedly discouraged, though English-language lexicographers give the syllable *-y-* only as a "schwa," not inconceivable as an elision. It is clear, in any case, that the line is of problematical scansion, and it turns out to be strangely appropriate that the site of the difficulty is the word labyrinth, since the further problems we may raise, pursuing the matter, do indeed tend to become labyrinthine. (One thinks, in connection with labyrinths, of Daedalus, and ineluctably of Joyce's Stephen Daedalus, and one senses the ever-close yawning of an abyss.)

What is scansion, anyway? In its usual context of prosodic analysis, it is the attempt to determine the metrical and rhythmic qualities of verse by marking accented and unaccented syllables, counting metrical feet (iambs, trochees, dactyls, anapaests, amphibrachs, or whatever), and searching out patterns that thus "make sense." Which is to say: it is the attempt to see poetic language as fitting one preconceived mold or another. In reading, for example, a sonnet, we expect to count a line out as iambic pentameter, and regard a slight (notable but essentially form-preserving) swerve from this expected pattern as a departure from a norm, though perhaps a tolerable or even a happy departure if the effect is to loosen the rhythm from its strict mechanics while keeping the metrical norm within sight. In any event, scansion amounts to an attempt at control (a Nietzschean will to power?), an attempt to read reliable structure into what one perhaps fears will not behave unless taken in hand.

In that regard, we find another sort of "scansion" going on in the poem itself: the attempt of the persona (as a construct of the necessity of "reading" the world: a scan-scion) to "scan" his universe; i.e., to determine its parameters and limits—has his "lost world floating dimly on Time's stream" been a real memory or merely a dream, and if real, does it still exist? And to what effect for him? (The very expression "Time's stream" echoes the notion of scansion: beating out time in a progression. But his scansion problem is far more metaphysical.)

In the final couplet the persona says, "I do not know what land it is—or dare / Ask when or *why* I was, or will be, there" (emphasis added). These lines, as we shall see, lead to a great deal of difficulty. We first observe, though, the interrogative word why in line 14; just as the question of the *-y-* poses problems in line 6—do we elide or retain the *-y-*, do we impose the preconceived order on the textual line or do we admit that the text recalcitrantly rejects this rage for order?—just as the question of the *-y-* poses this problem, the question of the why, for the persona, poses a problem allegorically adumbrated by our own original difficulty with scansion: does the persona omit or retain the "why"? (Historically, the letter Y is related to the letters U and V, hence to W, the signpost of interrogative words; and *-y-* here does unendingly pose questions, interrogating and embarrassing the metrical form.)

One may wonder if there is really any doubt whether the persona retains the "why"; i.e., whether he asks or does not ask why he "was, or will be, there" in that perhaps real, perhaps oneiric "lost world." The answer is: yes, there is a great deal of doubt, because of the ultimately self-referential and paradoxical language of the final couplet. When one says, I do not dare ask when or why I was, or will be, there, then has one in fact asked that question or not? One has said: I do not dare ask it—yet the form of the utterance strongly hints of the very asking that it denies. Although one may read this statement as saying, in effect, "There is a question about why I was or will be there in that lost world, but I have not specifically gone so far as to pose it to myself, because I'm afraid to do so," nonetheless the articulation of what the poem's persona supposedly dares not ask himself has a perverse way of posing, or seeming to pose, the question anyway, operating much as do such statements as "I'm not going to mention the time you came home drunk"—the rhetorical device known as *praeteritio*. Yet again, we might read the persona's statement as saying something like "I do ask myself why I was or will be there, but I dare not contemplate the answer."

The problem, in any case, is that the statement of the couplet is paradoxical in form; rather than tending toward some sort of resolution, as couplets in English sonnets traditionally do, this couplet only problematizes. When the persona makes his statement about not daring to ask, can he be believed? Perhaps he is a Jamesian unreliable narrator, in which case all bets are off, as to his utterances. But if we do credit his statements, we still encounter curious problems. His remark in the couplet is somewhat like saying, "I do not venture to make this statement." If the statement is true, then it cannot have been made (at least not by the "I"), but how can an unmade statement be "true"? The dialectics of binary logic would appear to break down rather quickly for an utterance like this.

The retention or occlusion of the persona's "why"—his problem of "scanning" his universe, of trying to reconcile his irregular vision of the "lost world floating dimly on Time's stream" with a regular world that credits such visions only as deviations or dreams—seems to parallel our own problems of scansion, of retention or elision of the *-y-*, of trying to reconcile the irregular possibility of an alexandrine with a regular schema: the well-regulated matrix of the sonnet form that credits only iambic pentameter as metrically sound. If in scanning line 6 we retain the *-y-* (admitting into the sonnet's metrical world the anomaly of an alexandrine), the parallel development for the persona would be to retain the "why"—to ask, outright, why he "was, or will be, there," and thus to admit into his otherwise ordinary world the anomaly of a dream-vision turned real. If, on the other hand, we elide the *-y-* (forcing the metrical form to be "regular" by refusing to countenance that the *-y-* might have demanded inclusion, might have obtruded upon the system), the parallel development for the persona would be to suppress the "why"—to decline to ask why he "was, or will be, there," presumably out of fear of asking, not daring to ask, because asking would again imply belief in perturbations of the normal system, admission of unthinkable anomaly into an otherwise well-ordered world. (It is curious to reflect here that maintaining normality or reality requires suppressing something; what does this say about "reality"?)

Thus the image, through this allegorical mapping, of the indeterminate scansion of "labyrinth," is the eternally uncertain oscillation, for the persona, between admitting the reality of the dream-vision and refusing to do so. Yet again, with regard to this allegory of the *-y-* and the "why," it is not even clear that the two undecidable oscillations are "in phase," so to speak. In the case of retaining the *-y-* (admitting abnormal scansion) and retaining the asking of "why," it may be that if the persona does ask why he was or will be there in the "lost world," he may be implying not belief in that world but unbelief: he perhaps does not "dare" ask why he was there because to do so would make it as if he believed in the reality of that world when he does not—i.e., perhaps he does not want unnecessarily to perturb the normal order of things. And in the case of suppressing the *-y-* (insisting on normality of scansion) and suppressing the asking of "why," perhaps in not asking why he was or will be there in the "lost world" he may be implying that he does believe in the potential obtrusion of the abnormal—the source, then, of his not daring to ask. If it is thus, then the "why" oscillation operates out of phase with the *-y-* uncertainty, though still connected with it in an uncanny way.

It is remarkable enough that a question of mechanical scansion may be read as prefiguring a larger question of Weltanschauung, of reading the whole fabric of one's universe—since, obviously, to admit the visitable reality of a dreamscape would be to change one's world radically and forever. But the intriguing thing about this allegorical mapping of mechanical scansion onto metaphysical "scansion" is that if the question of the alexandrine remains, as it must, unresolved, then the mapped image of this irresolvability is the persona's irresolvable question of world-view—in keeping with the title, his "mirage": etymologically, his "seeing," his troubled vision of his world.

Lovecraft's Cheshire Cat

On 24 September 1934 Lovecraft wrote a letter to James F. Morton (*SL* 5.36) in which he lamented, in verse, the recent death of a favorite neighborhood cat whom he called Samuel Perkins. The poem, which is untitled in the letter but which was later called "Little Sam Perkins" in printed collections of his works, reads as follows:

> The antient garden seems tonight
> A deeper gloom to bear,
> As if some silent shadow's blight
> Were hov'ring in the air.
>
> With hidden griefs the grasses sway,
> Unable quite to word them—
> Remembering from yesterday
> The little paws that stirr'd them. (*AT* 439)[37]

To anyone biographically familiar with Lovecraft and aware of the fondness he felt toward cats, this piece stands out as a tender reminiscence whose very simplicity makes it moving—remarkably so, one might say, for one whose pen gave us horrors ranging from the crassly graphic hideousness of "Herbert West—Reanimator" to the more subtle terrors of "The Shadow out of Time."

But quite beyond this tender simplicity, there are curious things about this text. In its seemingly unremitting gloom, there lurk not "hidden griefs" only, but also hidden smiles, strange and piquant.

For anyone intimately familiar with Lovecraft and his world, it is

37. In other printed versions of this poem, e.g., the Arkham House *Collected Poems,* "tonight" has been changed to "at night," with a couple of minor alterations besides. We shall not pursue the difference here between these textual states, though the implications could be shown to be profound.

difficult to stand back and maintain the distance—willfully forgetting for the moment, as it were, much that one knows about the circumstances of this poem's composition—but necessary to see what else the poem, as freestanding text, has to say. It says a great deal; but perhaps its most striking features reside in what it does not say outright.

It is a little startling to notice that the poem never once refers specifically to a cat; only in the final line do we read anything even indirectly referring to a lost animal-friend, and even there we see only a metonymic reference to "little paws," a synecdoche representing the lamented pet but not identifying it as a cat. Let us pretend to be textual visitors from far, far outside, knowing nothing of Lovecraft. From such a viewpoint, we could establish that the animal in question is a cat only by expanding our text out into realms where it weaves itself into intertext, joining the Lovecraft letters and other biographical matters. Even in the letter to James F. Morton in which Lovecraft introduces the poem, there is no direct mention of cats; Lovecraft here says only that "Little Sam Perkins, the tiny ball of black fur whom you saw in August, is no more!" (In this letter, we as sleuths from faraway lands would have to draw our inferences from the reference to Kappa Alpha Tau, and it is curious that we find a linkage between cats and letters of the alphabet; we shall return to this point.) To find any specific, direct identification of this "ball of black fur" as a cat, one must run one's fingers farther out into the web of intertext, consulting other Lovecraft letters in which the animal is specified as a member of a litter of kittens in a neighborhood boarding house.

In the poem itself, it is difficult to say whether we would ever readily identify the departed animal as a cat. (And, assuming ignorance of biographical and historical matters, is the animal necessarily dead? Perhaps it has merely been taken away, though the reference to "griefs" and "gloom" may suggest the darker possibility.) Could not "little paws" that "stirr'd" the grasses belong to another sort of animal? Without our accustomed biographical lens through which to view the text, it is probably not possible strictly to prove that the lamented creature is a cat. Nevertheless, there is a certain suggestion (or suggestiveness) within the text to that effect, however unprovable from the viewpoint of the outsider; one may perhaps infer the likelihood that the poem's persona refers to a departed creature once loved, probably a domestic pet (see the localizing reference to the "antient garden" with its "grasses") —and a guess that the pet, then, was a cat (as cats are given to playing in such places) might not be unreasonable.

In any case, the text presents an oscillating enigma of presence and absence, to the extent that we (outsiders for whom Lovecraft's letters, reminiscent of similar matters in "The Shadow out of Time," have been imperfectly expunged) even speculate that what is being spoken of here is a cat. (The importance of its species will be seen.) The cat—let us provisionally and momentarily credit this speculation for the purpose of commentary—is absent, or sometimes absent, in at least three ways: he may or may not even be a cat (but we have agreed to suppose for the moment that he is); he is not specifically mentioned in the text beyond the synecdochic "little paws"; and whatever he is or was, he is either physically removed or (perhaps more likely) has died. Yet in a sense he is "present," too, with the effect of the text. Presence and absence here, as a doomed opposition, depend on each other. Were the cat not absent (departed), there of course would be no such text, since the poem is evidently an elegy; and in this case we could not have the cat presented to us as a kind of memory-presence; i.e., presence, or even the illusion of it, depends upon absence. Yet, conversely, without any semblance of presence at all, i.e., without textual portrayal of the cat, we could not know, even vaguely, what was so lamentably absent, so that absence (if it is to be the absence of something) depends upon a kind of presence; the cat is known to be absent due to its "presence" in discourse, just as it is textually "present" to us, at all, only by motivation of its absence. (By a slightly different formulation, where we think of the salient opposition as being former presence/present-time absence, we have a similar result: the former presence of the cat is not poetically poignant without the cat's present-time absence, and its present-time absence is of course trivialized unless it was formerly present. We speak here of presence or absence from the viewpoint of the poem's persona.) It is characteristic of elegiac writing that the bipolarity presence/absence is self-deconstructing, in that neither of its poles can ultimately be privileged altogether, though we draw much of the energy of reading from absence, which smacks of departure and probable death, hence the gloomy tone of the text. Here, the cat propagates this tone by being absent.

Much to the point, one critic has said that "it can impose an atmosphere without being present" (351). The critic was William Empson; his remark, however, occurs in the context of a discussion of Lewis Carroll's *Alice in Wonderland,* and refers to the Cheshire Cat, that wonderful repository of uncertainty, paradox, and linguistic playfulness. As is well known, Carroll's (Charles Dodgson's) Cheshire Cat appears and disappears at will, scintillating with an eternal indeterminacy as to presence or absence, often showing only its head, or only its enigmatic grin. (Does such a cat smile to us in similar fashion from the Lovecraft text? In a crazy sort of way, it is entirely possible that it does.)

The Cheshire Cat is caught up in the whole notion of smiling, in strange and complex ways which we cannot entirely account for by the dialectics of logic. By the time Carroll wrote *Alice in Wonderland,* the expression "grin like a Cheshire Cat" was already proverbial, and seems to have had connection with the fact that Cheshire cheeses were often made in the shape of grinning cats (47n9). Through irrational but compelling channels, we are led to recall the custom, among speakers of English, of exhorting subjects of photography to "say cheese," for the purpose of producing a smile. The fact that the English morphology of the word *cheese* produces a smile on the lips would seem to have nothing to do with the connection between the Cheshire Cat and Cheshire cheeses, yet one thing ineluctably puts one in mind of another, perhaps in a mad transgression or transcendence of binary logic not unknown to the whole spirit of Carroll's *Alice.*

The two smile-generating E's (perhaps one of Carroll's Wonderland denizens would say that smiles can be generated with E's) lead us, oddly enough, and again without the sobering effects of logic, back to the Lovecraft text, where we find, precisely, the elision of two E's: the forms "hov'ring" and "stirr'd." The latter is merely an affectation (since a modern reader would read the word monosyllabically in any event); the former is the effect of a strict adherence to meter, but, beyond this, presents a strange indecision between self-descriptive and non-self-descriptive language. If "hover" means "to float," "to linger," then in the elision of the E, the very thing the word refuses to do, at that point, is to hover; yet if "hover" means "to vacillate," then hovering is precisely what the word does do, in vacillating between having two syllables or three. One begins to suspect that there is a covert playfulness in these elided E's—letters that, like Lovecraft's cat and like the Cheshire Cat, may be regarded as (n)either present (n)or absent. (They are elided, but without a sense that they are in some sense "there," how could we perceive the elisions as elisions?)

We find these letters the most suggestive in their capital forms. (In Carroll's *Alice,* the Queen of Hearts is forever crying, "Off with their heads!" May we hear in this cry a perverse and distant echo of the enjoined elision of two capital letters? In Wonderland, anything goes.)

In the Phoenician, the prongs of the E pointed toward the left rather than the right; we find a quiet allegorization here of indeterminacy again. When the letter was absorbed into Greek, it was reoriented and ultimately was renamed *epsilon,* from *psilos,* whose Indo-European root *bhes-* is also responsible for *palimpsest.* And indeed our Lovecraft text here is many times written over (as is, of course, the *Alice* text) by the uncontainability of the contexts of reading.

The elided and ambiguously pointing E's oscillate between being absent and being somehow "present" by their absence, just as does our Lovecraftian cat, whose presence is not overtly hinted at until the poem's final line, where (being given pause) we encounter the "little paws," paws that thus (because they alone, metonymically, serve to alert us to the subject of the cat) swell to great importance. One is reminded that Shelley's literal rendering of the name Oedipus was "Swellfoot," and one is led back again (by routes cutting across all lines of logic), by way of Oedipus, to Sphinxes and cats and—to be sure—riddling. With regard to the question of binding a text to "authorial intent," upon the Oedipal impropriety of a marriage of mother (poet/maker) and son (poem); by this scheme, the text in terms of the Oedipal myth becomes blind, blind to its own machinations as indeed texts generally turn out to be.

Out of this blindness (an inability to see and thus be bound by the rigors of conventions and systems) comes, of course, the playfulness of language, and it is not without significance that when Carroll's famous Cheshire Cat vanishes, he sometimes does so from the tail up, leaving the smile for last. It is somehow always the smile, the play, the ludic quality, that remains: Alice exclaims, "Well! I've often seen a cat without a grin; but a grin without a cat! It's the most curious thing I ever saw in all my life!" (53). Yet of course it is the absence of the (rest of the) cat that inspires the grin; the Cheshire Cat, in the face of the cry of the Queen of Hearts that he be beheaded, is even beyond this threat, because, as the executioner argues, "you couldn't cut off a head unless there was a body to cut it off from," though this point is disputed by the King, who argues that "anything that had a head could be beheaded, and that you weren't to talk nonsense" (68–69). Again we are back to irresolvable questions of presence and absence, and of figural displacements and substitutions; a head synecdochically substitutes for a cat, a pair of "little paws," in Lovecraft's poem, does the same—is there, in either case, a cat? (The elision of "hov'ring" is indeed a "little pause.")

In the left-pointing and/or right-pointing prongs of the elided (but discernible) E's of Lovecraft's poem, these smile-producing E's, eternally flickering E's which may or may not be there just as the cat (if it is a cat) may or may not be there, do we discern the madly piquant visage (for Carroll's problematic cat proclaims his own madness: see 51) of a Cheshire Cat, smiling at us across unthinkable, irrational, unaccountable gulfs of text and association and history? At least do we not see, pictographically given—and perhaps in graphemes not there, well in keeping with the spirit of the thing—the whiskers of such a cat, twitching with playfulness? Perhaps it was inevitable that a chaotically disturbed and sardonic Lovecraftian universe should, sooner or later, produce the grinning specter of its own Cheshire Cat.

Lines of Verse Evoking Close Reading: Acrostic-Formulated Text

In August of 1936, in the company of Adolphe de Castro and Robert Barlow in the cemetery of St. John's off Benefit Street in Providence, H. P. Lovecraft composed an acrostic poem on the name *Edgar Allan Poe,* "In a Sequester'd Providence Churchyard Where Once Poe Walk'd" (*AT* 95–96). The first seven lines of the text are:

> Eternal brood the shadows on this ground,
> Dreaming of centuries that have gone before;
> Great elms rise solemnly by slab and mound,
> Arch'd high above a hidden world of yore.
> Round all the scene a light of memory plays,
> And dead leaves whisper of departed days,
> Longing for sights and sounds that are no more.

After a break, the final six lines are:

> Lonely and sad, a specter glides along
> Aisles where of old his living footsteps fell;
> No common glance discerns him, though his song
> Peals down through time with a mysterious spell.
> Only the few who sorcery's secret know,
> Espy amidst these tombs the shade of Poe.

The acrostic name of course appears in the initial letters of the thirteen lines.

From the outset, an acrostic text raises a number of questions and issues, not only exegetically with regard to the text itself, but more generally with implications for literary theory—in particular, for post-structuralist views of language as plural, problematical, nonlinear.

The initial letters of the lines spell out a name that is also mentioned, in part, in the body of the poem. One commonly understands basic graphemes (in this case, individual letters) to lie beneath the level at which written signs can convey meaning; "bat," for example, depending on the greatly variegated contexts in which it may be embedded, means many things, but (one supposes) "b-," aside from naming a letter of the alphabet, does not mean anything: it is in a sense "semiotic" (i.e., it is a graphic sign) but sub-semantic. However, this supposition of sub-semanticism is open to doubt for a number of reasons.

Clearly, a grapheme like "b-" approaches semantic status, the capacity to convey meaning, only in context—only insofar as it finds itself in the position of being adjoined to other graphemes. (One notices that there are certain expectations on this score when we express the grapheme as "b-" instead of, say, "-b" or "-b-" as we might have done.) But so far as dependency on context is concerned, the same is true for larger graphic elements: whole words, phrases, sentences.

And what of *multiple* embeddings of linguistic elements in their contexts? Consider the word "bat" in this (at least) double context:

That
Jones will bat better this season.
is
a
vampire.

(This is a two-dimensional intersection; one could of course have intersections of higher order.) Here, "bat" is a verb in one context and a noun in the other, and even if the horizontal context had read (say) "This baseball bat is broken," the two resulting nouns would have pointed in vastly different directions. This phenomenon of multiple embeddings, of course, only adds to linguistic complexities present from the beginning, for one already finds plurisignification in *each* context. "Jones will bat better this season," rather than having anything to do with baseball, could be a sly metaphorical reference to someone's probable erotic "scoring" with a new sexual partner, while "That bat is a vampire," rather than being a simple statement about certain fauna, could be a wealthy retired man's unkind remark about a lady acquaintance he thinks is out to get his money: "That old bat is the sort that would drain you dry." In any case, without the surroundment of meaning-generative contexts, we would not have any idea what to make of "bat" at all; it might almost as well be a single letter, and indeed the chief difference is that a single letter would be capable of leading us on into more numerous contexts. (An intriguing question is this: does such a wealth of contexts make a linguistic sign more or less "meaningful"? It produces more possibilities of meaning, but problematizes the specificity with which we can assign particular meaning.)

The interesting thing about an acrostic like Lovecraft's is that in it we find essentially the same sort of cross-contextualization occurring on the graphemic level, with individual letters. Linguistic signifiers have the quality of pointing away from themselves, pointing to other signifiers, and simple graphemes (though not really so simple after all) do precisely that. The "P-" initializing the eleventh line, for example, with the multiple context

Peals
O. . . .
E. . . .

raises the same sorts of questions we have observed before.

Horizontally, "P-" embeds itself in a context in which it points to further graphemes that lead on to "Peals" only because of juxtaposition (like electrons and other subatomic particles, neither "P-" nor "-e-," etc. can really be defined except in terms of their relational field), and since "Peals" is after all a sememe, carrying meaning, the graphemic constituent "P-" in this manner takes on a quasi-semantic quality that is plural to the extent that "Peals" is semantically plural. ("Peals" can literally mean something like "rings," or, as one may more readily suppose, can metaphorically mean something like "resounds" in the sense of reverberations in literary history—with, of course, an echo of Poe's "The Bells" in either case.)

Vertically, "P-" takes on a quasi-semantic quality in forming a field with its juxtaposed—but in this case not on first glance so obviously juxtaposed—fellow graphemes to lead on to "Poe," which is itself plural of potential: "Poe" may point to a man who was once editor of the

Southern Literary Messenger, or may metonymically suggest a certain corpus of literary texts, as when one speaks of "reading Poe." That "P-" in "Peals" and "P-" in "Poe" are essentially different things is implicit in the fact that they *are* in different contexts, but also in their possessing dissimilar relational properties: they are not only adjoined to different things ("-e-" and "-o-"), but to different *kinds* of things, because in "Peals," the adjoined "-e-" has narrative connectivity only in the horizontal context, while in "Poe," the adjoined "-o-" has narrative connectivity in both the horizontal and vertical contexts, since it initializes "Only" in line 12.

As in the example of "bat," the embedding of a linguistic element in contexts that stretch away both horizontally and vertically is only a simplified way of showing that any such graphic element can find itself embedded in *many* different contexts at once. And if we see "P-" as being enmeshed in graphic fields that themselves may produce pluralities of meaning, in either the horizontal or vertical (or potentially other) directions, then we find that even a simple grapheme may partake of the protean qualities more commonly associated with larger linguistic elements; it would seem that no element on the scene, be it proton or molecule or cell, is too humble to have its share in the mystery.

But perhaps the most striking fascination in this acrostic poem resides in its capacity to allegorize or reflect, self-referentially, the very qualities of textuality that make such literary texts possible to begin with, while interrogating its own structure.

The whole question of structure comes readily into play when one realizes that the poem appears to be a sonnet but technically is not; strictly speaking, a sonnet should have fourteen lines which one commonly divides into an initial octave and a final sestet, though some sonnets (the Miltonic) omit the break and may even have enjambement between the eighth and ninth lines. Although the name *Edgar Allan Poe* does not have enough letters to support a true sonnet, Lovecraft's acrostic poem rather deftly *imitates* a sonnet, with an initial septet instead of an octave, then a break, then a sestet that even ends, English-sonnet-fashion, with a rhymed couplet. (Overall the truncated rhyme scheme is ABABCCB/DEDEFF. The *sound* of the -CCB part of the septet, returning to the B-rhyme in an asymmetric way, is remarkably Poesque, so that the text reflects Poe in yet another way.) This imitation of form is so compelling that the poem actually once appeared in the magazine *Weird Tales* (May 1938) with the title "Where Once Poe Walked: An Acrostic Sonnet." But the interesting thing about all this is really that the imitation has the effect of unsettling simple binary oppositions; in terms of classic binary logic with its law of the "excluded middle," one would have supposed that a poem either was a sonnet or was not, but such oppositions have a habit of collapsing. In this case, what one notices is that in observing that Lovecraft's acrostic poem is not a sonnet, one is entangled in the whole tradition of characteristics that sonnets typically possess; the poem's not being a regular sonnet is remarkable only in its *closeness* to being one (we would not, for example, say anything particularly noteworthy in remarking that Lovecraft's eleven-stanza poem "Nemesis" is not a sonnet, because it does not even remotely resemble one)—so that in the "non-sonnet" side of the bipolarity "sonnet/non-sonnet" there covertly dwells the trace of the true sonnet. Conversely, of course, a true sonnet only defines itself in terms of those alternative forms that it is not: it is not, for example, a fourteen-line octave/sestet poem in any trochaic meter, or in iambic tetrameter, or in anapaestic pentameter. In its specificity, it implies a rich field of things that it *almost* is.

Here, if an exhumed Lovecraft were to "rectify" his poem by adding a line, say, between the fifth and sixth lines with a rhyme matching "more" (for the pattern ABABCBCB/DEDEFF), the very gesture would show that in the (then) true sonnet there would reside a covert trace of the non-sonnet: whatever the new line's initial letter, one would see that the acrostic message EDGAR ALLAN POE had been perturbed, in terms of what *should* have been an acrostic only possible in a non-sonnet that was a *near*-sonnet. Even if, say, the interpolated line (between lines 5 and 6) were to read, "Recalling a faint past it would restore," so that the acrostic message reflected the perhaps minimally mutilated cryptotext EDGARR ALLAN POE, the change would only underscore the distance of the true sonnet from the cryptotextually truer near-sonnet.

It is in fact remarkable that the actual acrostic message is EDGARAL / LANPOE (a "mysterious spell," as line 11 says), where the poem has made so extreme an effort to deconstruct or unsettle the distinction between sonnet and non-sonnet as to preserve the octave/sestet break by dividing the name Allan in a most peculiar place (in the middle of the doubled consonant -*LL*-, strangely unphonetic when one considers that a variant on the name is *Alan,* where no such division is possible) and by *failing* to divide the name so as to have marked the space between *Allan* and *Poe.* An odd metrical feature of the poem is that in the ninth line, the leading word "Aisles" scans with an emphasis that in effect produces a trochee rather than an iamb for the initial foot of the line; the scansion is awkward, in fact, in terms of the enjambement from the word "along" of the preceding line. It is curious that this metrical irregularity occurs at precisely the point in the acrostic name *Allan* where misspelling (as *Allen*) so commonly occurs—and curious that the word *aisle* itself is, in effect, a spelling error in terms of its etymology: it derives from the Old French *aile,* "wing," and has acquired its -*s*- only through a confusion with *isle*, which is a contraction from the Latin *insula.* There is no logical reason for the traces of such "mysterious spells" to gravitate together, but in the ludic world of language, they do.

Aside from the fact that the poem obviously refers to its own workings in the fashion of *mise en abyme* (the heraldic device of a shield pictured upon a shield)—saying, e.g., "Only the few who sorcery's secret know, / Espy amidst these tombs the shade of Poe" to reflect the poem's own "mysterious spell" of Poe's *hidden* name—aside from such elementary matters of self-reference, the poem reaches beyond its supposed boundaries to allegorize readerly access to the polysemic wealth of literary texts more generally. It is the very picture of *plural reading* to see oneself reading not only the horizontal lines of the poem but also the vertical cryptotext formed by those lines' initial letters. One reads, as Jacques Derrida has remarked, with multiple "reading heads," scanning the text along many different lines of text-ure (warp and woof), affirming the existence of multitudinous lines of signification. One reads not only *along* the threads on the loom but *across* them.

Indeed, in this regard it is curious (though immediate) that the word *acrostic* has no direct etymological connection with the word *across. Acrostic* derives from two Greek sources: *acro-* ("at the pointed end," "at the top," from the Indo-European base *ak-*, "sharp," whence *acute, acid,* etc.) and *stichos* ("a line of verse," from the Indo-European base *steigh-*, "to step," "to climb," whence *stair, stile*, etc.), so that the idea, for the reader of an acrostic, would seem to be that of proceeding in steps across the tips (tiptoeing, reading carefully) of the lines, lines that are pointed, lines that point away in various directions. Interestingly, then, despite the lack of any attestable etymological link, we still do not escape the compelling notion of reading *across*, and in many directions at once.

Lovecraft's acrostic tribute to Poe, besides fulfilling what would seem to be its natural function, serves to allegorize the plural nature of reading, the ambiguity of direction among the pointings of signifiers, the troubled yet promising fecundity of texts, where we may discern, as Lovecraft's line 10 says, shades espied by "no common glance."

Works Cited

Atkins, G. Douglas. *Reading Deconstruction, Deconstructive Reading.* Lexington: University Press of Kentucky, 1983.

Bodkin, Maud. *Archetypal Patterns in Poetry.* London: Oxford University Press, 1963.

Brooke, Rupert. *The Collected Poems of Rupert Brooke.* New York: John Lane, 1915.

Burleson, Donald. "Bierce's 'The Damned Thing': A Nietzschean Allegory." *Studies in Weird Fiction* No. 13 (Summer 1993): 8–10.

———. *H. P. Lovecraft: A Critical Study.* Westport, CT: Greenwood Press, 1983.

———. *Lovecraft: Disturbing the Universe.* Lexington: University Press of Kentucky, 1990.

———. "The Lovecraft Mythos." In *Survey of Science Fiction Literature* Englewood Cliffs: Salem Press, 1979.

———. "On Lovecraft's Themes: Touching the Glass." In *An Epicure in the Terrible: A Centennial Anthology of Essays in Honor of H. P. Lovecraft,* ed. David E. Schultz and S. T. Joshi. Rutherford, NJ: Fairleigh Dickinson University Press, 1991. New York: Hippocampus Press, 2011.

Burleson, Mollie L. "The Outsider: A Woman?" *LS* Nos. 22/23 (Fall 1990): 22–23.

Cannon, Peter, ed. *Lovecraft Remembered.* Sauk City, WI: Arkham House, 1998.

Capra, Fritjof. *The Tao of Physics: An Exploration of the Parallels between Modern Physics and Eastern Mysticism.* Berkeley, CA: Shambhala, 1975.

Carroll, Lewis. *Alice in Wonderland.* Edited by Donald J. Gray. New York: W. W. Norton (Norton Critical Edition), 1971.

Carroll, Noël. *The Philosophy of Horror; or, Paradoxes of the Heart.* New York: Routledge, 1990.

Carter, Lin. *Lovecraft: A Look Behind the Cthulhu Mythos.* New York: Ballantine, 1972.

Carter, Lin, ed. *The Spawn of Cthulhu.* New York: Ballantine, 1971.

Conklin, Groff. *Omnibus of Science Fiction.* New York: Crown, 1952.

Cook, W. Paul. *In Memoriam: Howard Phillips Lovecraft: Recollections, Appreciations, and Estimates.* North Montpelier, VT: Driftwind Press, 1941. In *Lovecraft Remembered,* ed. Peter Cannon. Sauk City, WI: Arkham House, 1998. 106–56.

Davis, Sonia H. *The Private Life of H. P. Lovecraft.* Ed. S. T. Joshi. West Warwick, RI: Necronomicon Press, 1985.

de Camp, L. Sprague. *Lovecraft: A Biography.* Garden City, NY: Doubleday, 1975.

Derleth, August. "H. P. Lovecraft and His Work." In H. P. Lovecraft. *The Dunwich Horror and Others.* Sauk City, WI: Arkham House, 1963. ix–xx.

Derrida, Jacques. *Éperons: Les Styles de Nietzsche.* Paris: Flammarion, 1978.

Douglas, Mary. *Purity and Danger.* London: Routledge & Kegan Paul, 1966.

Eliot, T. S. *The Waste Land and Other Poems.* New York: Harvest/HBJ, 1962.

Empson, William. "The Child as Swain." In Lewis Carroll, *Alice in Wonderland.* Ed. Donald J. Gray. New York: W. W. Norton (Norton Critical Edition), 1971.

Fadiman, Clifton. "Ambrose Bierce: Portrait of a Misanthrope." In *The Collected Writings of Ambrose Bierce.* Secaucus, NJ: Citadel Press, 1946.

Gaines, Helen Fouche. *Cryptanalysis: A Study of Ciphers and Their Solution.* New York: Dover, 1956.

Hartman, Geoffrey H. *Saving the Text: Literature/Derrida/Philosophy.* Baltimore: Johns Hopkins University Press, 1981.

Hawthorne, Nathaniel. *The Complete Novels and Selected Tales of Nathaniel Hawthorne.* Ed. Norman Holmes Pearson. New York: Modern Library, 1937.

———. *Passages from the American Notebooks.* Boston: Houghton Mifflin, 1887.

Hayles, N. Katherine. *Chaos Bound: Orderly Disorder in Contemporary Literature and Science.* Ithaca, NY: Cornell University Press, 1990.

Henderson, Joseph L. "Ancient Myths and Modern Man." In *Man and His Symbols,* ed. Carl G. Jung. Garden City, NY: Doubleday, 1964. 101–07.

Homer. *The Odyssey.* Tr. E. V. Rieu. London: Penguin, 1991.

Jaffé, Aniela. "Symbolism in the Visual Arts." In *Man and His Symbols,* ed. Carl G. Jung. Garden City, NY: Doubleday, 1964. 230–69.

Johnson, Barbara. "Allegory's Strip-Tease: *The White Waterlily.*" In *The Critical Difference.* Baltimore: Johns Hopkins University Press, 1985.

Johnson, Samuel. "Preface to the Plays of William Shakespeare." In *Dr Johnson on Shakespeare.* Ed. W. K. Wimsatt. Harmondsworth, UK: Penguin, 1969.

Joshi, S. T. *H. P. Lovecraft: A Comprehensive Bibliography.* Tampa, FL: University of Tampa Press, 2009.

———. *H. P. Lovecraft: The Decline of the West.* Mercer Island, WA: Starmont House, 1990.

———. *H. P. Lovecraft.* Starmont Reader's Guide 13. Mercer Island, WA: Starmont House, 1982.

Joshi, S. T., ed. *H. P. Lovecraft: Four Decades of Criticism.* Athens: Ohio University Press, 1980.

Krutch, Joseph Wood. *The Modern Temper.* New York: Harcourt, Brace, 1929.

Lao Tsu (Lao Tzu). *Tao Te Ching.* Tr. Gia-Fu Feng and Jane English. New York: Vintage, 1972.

Leeming, Joseph Adams. *Mythology: The Voyage of the Hero.* Philadelphia: J. B. Lippincott, 1973.

Long, Frank Belknap. *Howard Phillips Lovecraft: Dreamer on the Nightside.* Sauk City, WI: Arkham House, 1975.

Lord, William G. *History of Athol, Massachusetts.* Athol, MA: W. G. Lord, 1953.

Lovecraft, H. P. *The Ancient Track: The Complete Poetical Works of H. P. Lovecraft.* Ed. S. T. Joshi. 2nd ed. New York: Hippocampus Press, 2013.

———. *The Annotated Supernatural Horror in Literature.* Ed. S. T. Joshi. 2nd ed. New York: Hippocampus Press, 2012.

———. *Collected Essays.* Ed. S. T. Joshi. New York: Hippocampus Press, 2004–06. 5 vols.

———. *Collected Fiction: A Variorum Edition.* Ed. S. T. Joshi. New York: Hippocampus Press, 2015–16. 4 vols.

———. *Collected Poems.* Sauk City, WI: Arkham House, 1963.

———. *Cry Horror!* New York: Avon, 1958?.

———. *The Dunwich Horror and Others.* Sauk City, WI: Arkham House, 1963.

———. *Fungi from Yuggoth: and Other Poems.* New York: Ballantine Books, 1971.

———. *O Fortunate Floridian: H. P. Lovecraft's Letters to R. H. Barlow.* Ed. S. T. Joshi and David E. Schultz. Tampa, FL: University of Tampa Press, 2007.

———. *Selected Letters.* Ed. August Derleth, Donald Wandrei, and James Turner. Sauk City, WI: Arkham House, 1965–76. 5 vols.

Lovecraft, H. P., and August Derleth. *Essential Solitude: The Letters of H. P. Lovecraft and August Derleth.* Ed. David E. Schultz and S. T. Joshi. New York: Hippocampus Press, 2008. 2 vols.

Lovecraft, H. P., and Willis Conover. *Lovecraft at Last.* Arlington, VA: Carrollton-Clark, 1975. New York: Cooper Square Press, 2002.

Mariconda, Steven J. "The Subversion of Sense in 'The Colour out of Space.'" *LS* Nos. 19/20 (Fall 1989): 20–22. In Mariconda's *H. P. Lovecraft: Art, Artifact, and Reality.* New York: Hippocampus Press, 2013. 184–89.

Melville, Herman. *Billy Budd.* In Melville's *Complete Works.* Vol. 13. London: Constable, 1924.

———. "The Piazza." In *Billy Budd and Other Tales.* New York: New American Library, 1961. 89–102.

Mosig, Dirk. "The Four Faces of the Outsider." In *Essays Lovecraftian,* ed. Darrell Schweitzer. Baltimore: T-K Graphics, 1976. 17–34.

Neilson, William Allan. "Whately, Richard." In *Webster's Biographical Dictionary: A Dictionary of Names of Noteworthy Persons with Pronunciations and Concise Biographies.* Springfield, MA: G. & C. Merriam Co., 1956.

Nietzsche, Friedrich. *Beyond Good and Evil.* Tr. R. J. Hollingdale. Harmondsworth, UK: Penguin, 1988.

———. *The Will to Power.* Tr. Walter Kaufmann and R. J. Hollingdale. New York: Vintage, 1968.

Orton, Vrest. "A Weird Writer Is in Our Midst." *Brattleboro Daily Reformer* (16 June 1928): 2. Rpt. in *A Weird Writer in Our Midst: Early Criticism of H. P. Lovecraft,* ed. S. T. Joshi. New York: Hippocampus Press, 2010. 51–54.

Raglan, Lord. *The Hero: A Study in Tradition, Myth, and Drama.* New York: Oxford University Press, 1937.

Shipley, Joseph T. *The Origins of English Words: A Discursive Dictionary of Indo-European Roots.* Baltimore: Johns Hopkins University Press, 1984.

Shreffler, Philip A. *The H. P. Lovecraft Companion.* Westport, CT: Greenwood Press, 1977.

Suzuki, D. T. *An Introduction to Zen Buddhism.* New York: Grove Press, 1964.

Swinburne, Algernon Charles. *Swinburne: Selected Poetry and Prose.* Ed. John D. Rosenberg. New York: Modern Library, 1968.

[Unsigned.] "Armitage, William Edmond." In *National Cyclopaedia of American Biography.* New York: J. T. White, 1909. 11:58.

———. *Official History of Guilford, Vermont, 1678–1961.* Guilford, VT: Broad Brook Grange, 1961. [Abbreviated in the text as *Guilford.*]

———. *Vermonters.* Montpelier: Vermont Historical Society, 1937.

———. "Western Abenaki." In *Handbook of North American Indians,* gen. ed. William C. Sturtevant. Washington: Smithsonian Institution, 1978. 15:159.

Watts, Alan. *Beyond Theology: The Art of Godmanship.* New York: Pantheon, 1964.

———. *The Book (On the Taboo against Knowing Who You Are).* New York: Pantheon, 1966.

———. *In My Own Way: An Autobiography, 1915–1965.* New York : Pantheon, 1972.

———. *The Way of Zen.* New York : Pantheon, 1957.

Watts, Alan, and Al Chung-liang Huang. *Tao: The Watercourse Way.* New York: Pantheon, 1975.

Wittgenstein, Ludwig. *Tractatus Logico-Philosophicus.* London: Routledge & Kegan Paul, 1929.

Yeats, William Butler. *Selected Poems and Two Plays of William Butler Yeats.* New York: Collier, 1966.

Works about Lovecraft by Donald R. Burleson

Books

Begging to Differ: Deconstructionist Readings. Bristol, RI: Hobgoblin Press, 1992.

H. P. Lovecraft: A Critical Study. Westport, CT: Greenwood Press, 1983.

Lovecraft: Disturbing the Universe. Lexington: University Press of Kentucky, 1990.

Articles

"Ambrose Bierce and H. P. Lovecraft." In Ambrose Bierce. *21 Letters of Ambrose Bierce.* West Warwick, RI: Necronomicon Press, 1991. 5–8.

"Aporia and Paradox in 'The Outsider.'" *CoC* 49 (Lammas 1987): 41–42. In *Begging to Differ* (q.v.).

"*At the Mountains of Madness.*" In *Survey of Science Fiction Literature,* ed. Frank Magill. Englewood Cliffs, NJ: Salem Press, 1979. 1.97–101.

"*The Case of Charles Dexter Ward.*" In *Survey of Modern Fantasy Literature,* ed. Frank Magill. Englewood Cliffs, NJ: Salem Press, 1983. 1.203–6.

"Darkness and Light: Lovecraft's Impact on My Life." Original to this collection.

"*The Dream-Quest of Unknown Kadath.*" In *Survey of Modern Fantasy Literature,* ed. Frank Magill. Englewood Cliffs, NJ: Salem Press, 1983. 1.431–35.

"The Fictive World of H. P. Lovecraft." *Mage* 5 (Spring 1986): 36–39.

"Fra Mosigius." *CoC* No. 33 (Lammas 1985): 37–38.

"H. P. Lovecraft." In *Supernatural Fiction Writers,* ed. E. F. Bleiler. New York: Scribner's, 1985. 853–59.

"H. P. Lovecraft: The Hawthorne Influence." *Extrapolation* 22, No. 3 (Fall 1981): 262–69.

"Humour beneath Horror: Some Sources for 'The Dunwich Horror' and 'The Whisperer in Darkness.'" *LS* No. 2 (Spring 1980): 5–15. In *The Fantastic Worlds of H. P. Lovecraft,* ed. James Van Hise. Yucca Valley, CA: James Van Hise, 1999. 60–70. In *Works of H. P. Lovecraft,* ed. Sadao Miyakabe and Shiro Nachi. Tokyo: Kokusho-Kankohkai, 1985. Vol. 9.

"Iranon & Kuranes: An Intertextual Gloss." *CoC* No. 53 (Candlemas 1988): 31–33.

"Is Lovecraft's 'Ph'nglui mglw'nafh . . .' a Cryptogram?" Original to this collection.

"L?vecr?ft: What's in a Name?" *CoC* No. 82 (Hallowmas 1992): 17–20.

"Lines of Verse Evoking Close Reading: Acrostic-Formulated Text." *CoC* No. 85 (Hallowmas 1993): 9–12.

"Lovecraft: An American Allegory." *CoC* No. 78 (St. John's Eve 1991): 16–19. In *Begging to Differ* (q.v.).

"Lovecraft and Adjectivitis: A Deconstructionist View." *LS* No. 31 (Fall 1994): 22–24.

"Lovecraft and Chaos." *CoC* No. 89 (Eastertide 1995): 8–10.

"Lovecraft and Chiasmus / Chiasmus and Lovecraft." *LS* No. 13 (Fall 1986): 72–75, 80.

"Lovecraft and Gender." *LS* No. 27 (Fall 1992): 21–25.

"Lovecraft and Interstitiality." *LS* No. 37 (Fall 1997): 25–34.

"Lovecraft and Mystery Hill." *NEARA* [New England Antiquities Research Association] *Journal* 14, No. 4 (Spring 1980): 84–86.

"Lovecraft and Romanticism." *LS* Nos. 19/20 (Fall 1989): 28–31.

"Lovecraft and the Death of Tragedy." *CoC* No. 66 (Lammas 1989): 11–14.

"Lovecraft and the World as Cryptogram." *LS* No. 16 (Spring 1988): 14–18.

"Lovecraft: Dreams and Reality." In *The H. P. Lovecraft Centennial Conference: Proceedings,* ed. S. T. Joshi. West Warwick, RI: Necronomicon Press, 1990. 73–75. *Books at Brown* 28/29 (1991–92): 7–12 (revised).

"Lovecraft, H. P." In *Encyclopedia Americana.* Danbury, CT: Grolier, 1986. 17.808–9.

"Lovecraft, précurseur de la théorie de la déconstruction." In *H. P. Lovecraft: Fantastique, mythe et modernité.* Colloque de Cerisy. Paris: Editions Dervy, 2002. 35–48.

"Lovecraft: Textual Keys." *LS* No. 32 (Spring 1995): 27–30.
"The Lovecraft Mythos." In *Survey of Science Fiction Literature*, ed. Frank Magill. Englewood Cliffs, NJ: Salem Press, 1979. 3.1284–88.
"Lovecraft's Cheshire Cat." *CoC* No. 76 (Hallowmas 1990): 19–22.
"Lovecraft's 'The Colour out of Space.'" *Explicator* 52, No. 1 (Fall 1993): 48–50. *CoC* No. 93 (Lammas 1996): 19–20 (as "H. P. Lovecraft's 'The Colour out of Space'").
"Lovecraft's Humankind: Orphans in the Cosmos." *Providence Sunday Journal Magazine* (8 August 1990): 9–10 (abridged as "A cosmos utterly indifferent . . ."). *LS* Nos. 22/23 (Fall 1990): 43–44 (as part of "Six Views of Lovecraft").
"Lovecraft's 'The Unknown': A Sort of Runic Rhyme." *LS* No. 26 (Spring 1992): 19–21.
"Lovecraftian Branches in Rimel's 'Tree.'" *CoC* No. 17 (Hallowmas 1983): 3–4. As part of "A Symposium on 'The Tree on the Hill.'"
"'The Music of Erich Zann' as Fugue." *LS* No. 6 (Spring 1982): 14–17.
"The Mythic Hero Archetype in 'The Dunwich Horror.'" *LS* No. 4 (Spring 1981): 3–9. In *A Century Less a Dream: Selected Criticism on H. P. Lovecraft*, ed. Scott Connors. Holicong, PA: Wildside Press, 2002. 206–13.
"A Note on 'The Book.'" *LS* Nos. 42/43 (Autumn 2001): 52–54.
"A Note on Lovecraft and Rupert Brooke." *LS* No. 11 (Fall 1985): 51–53.
"A Note on Lovecraft, Mathematics and the Outer Spheres." *CoC* No. 4 (Eastertide 1982): 23–24.
"A Note on Metaphor vs. Metonymy in 'The Dunwich Horror.'" *LS* No. 38 (Spring 1998): 16–17.
"Notes on Lovecraft's 'The Bells': A Carillon." *LS* No. 17 (Fall 1988): 34–35. In *Begging to Differ* (q.v.).
"On Lovecraft's Fragment 'Azathoth.'" *LS* Nos. 22/23 (Fall 1990): 10–12, 23.
"On Lovecraft's 'Harbour Whistles.'" *CoC* No. 74 (Lammas 1990): 12–13.
"On Lovecraft's 'Nemesis.'" *LS* No. 21 (Spring 1990): 40–41.
"On Lovecraft's 'The Ancient Track.'" *LS* No. 28 (Spring 1993): 17–20.
"On Lovecraft's 'The Messenger.'" *CoC* No. 57 (St. John's Eve 1988): 15–18. In *Begging to Differ* (q.v.).

"On Lovecraft's 'The Wood.'" *CoC* No. 57 (St. John's Eve 1988): 30–32. In *Begging to Differ* (q.v.).

"On Lovecraft's Themes: Touching the Glass." In *An Epicure in the Terrible: A Centennial Anthology of Essays in Honor of H. P. Lovecraft,* ed. David E. Schultz and S. T. Joshi. Rutherford, NJ: Fairleigh Dickinson University Press, 1991. 135–47. New York: Hippocampus Press, 2011. 139–52.

"Open to Criticism." *CoC* No. 98 (Eastertide 1998): 7–10.

"Prismatic Heroes: The Colour out of Dunwich." *LS* No. 25 (Fall 1991): 13–18. In *Begging to Differ* (q.v.). In *A Century Less a Dream: Selected Criticism on H. P. Lovecraft,* ed. Scott Connors. Holicong, PA: Wildside Press, 2002. 214–23.

"Providence and Lovecraft's Fiction." In *The H. P. Lovecraft Centennial Conference: Proceedings,* ed. S. T. Joshi. West Warwick, RI: Necronomicon Press, 1990. 10–12.

"Scansion Problems in Lovecraft's 'Mirage.'" *LS* No. 24 (Spring 1991): 18–19, 21.

"The Short Fiction of H. P. Lovecraft." In *Survey of Science Fiction Literature,* ed. Frank Magill. Englewood Cliffs, NJ: Salem Press, 1979. Vol. 4, 1973–77.

"The Short Fiction of Lovecraft." In *Survey of Modern Fantasy Literature,* ed. Frank Magill. Englewood Cliffs, NJ: Salem Press, 1983. Vol. 4, 1621–28.

"Some Comments on the Dunsany–Lovecraft Influence." *CoC* No. 15 (Lammas 1983): 3, 29.

"Strange High Houses: Lovecraft & Melville." *CoC* No. 80 (Eastertide 1992): 25–26, 29.

"Swan Songs: Lovecraft and Yeats." *LS* No. 18 (Spring 1989): 14–17. In *Begging to Differ* (q.v.).

"A Textual Oddity in 'The Quest of Iranon.'" *LS* No. 34 (Spring 1996): 24–26.

"'The Terrible Old Man': A Deconstruction." *LS* No. 15 (Fall 1987): 65–68. In *Begging to Differ* (q.v.): 42–45.

"The Thing: On the Doorstep." *LS* No. 33 (Fall 1995): 14–18.

[Tribute to Dirk W. Mosig.] In Dirk W. Mosig. *Mosig at Last: A Psychologist Looks at H. P. Lovecraft.* West Warwick, RI: Necronomicon Press, 1997. 121–23.

"Why (Not) Deconstruct Lovecraft?" *CoC* No. 66 (Lammas 1989): 44–47.
"Zen and the Art of Lovecraft." *LS* No. 10 (Spring 1985): 31–35. In *Works of H. P. Lovecraft,* ed. Sadao Miyakabe and Shiro Nachi. Tokyo: Kokusho-Kankohkai, 1985. Vol. 8.

Reviews

Review of Henry L. P. Beckwith, Jr., *Lovecraft's Providence and Adjacent Parts. LS* No. 2 (Spring 1980): 34–36.
Review of Peter Cannon, *H. P. Lovecraft. LS* No. 18 (Spring 1989): 22.
Review of John Taylor Gatto, *The Major Works of H. P. Lovecraft: A Critical Commentary. Eldritch Tales* 1, No. 4 (October 1978): 75–77.
Review of S. T. Joshi, *A Dreamer and a Visionary: H. P. Lovecraft in his Time. LS* No. 44 (2004): 119–20.
Review of S. T. Joshi, *H. P. Lovecraft. LS* No. 7 (Fall 1982): 36–39.
Review of S. T. Joshi, *H. P. Lovecraft: The Decline of the West. LS* Nos. 22/23 (Fall 1990): 57–59.
Review of S. T. Joshi, *H. P. Lovecraft: Four Decades of Criticism. LS* No. 3 (Fall 1980): 28–34.
Review of H. P. Lovecraft, *Uncollected Prose and Poetry. LS* No. 1 (Fall 1979): 40–46.
Review of Barton Levi St. Armand, *The Roots of Horror in the Fiction of H. P. Lovecraft. Eldritch Tales* 1, No. 4 (October 1978): 69–74.
Review of Barton Levi St. Armand, *The Roots of Horror in the Fiction of H. P. Lovecraft. Gothic* 1, No. 1 (June 1979): 29–31 (as "Two Views of St. Armand's Lovecraft"; with John L. McInnis).
Review of J. Vernon Shea, *In Search of Lovecraft. LS* No. 25 (Fall 1991): 34–35.

Index

www.ingramcontent.com/pod-product-compliance
Lightning Source LLC
Chambersburg PA
CBHW071330190426
43193CB00041B/1048
9781614981381